NOMAD CODES

ALSO BY ERIK DAVIS

TechGnosis: Myth, Magic, and Mysticism in the Age of Information

Led Zeppelin IV

The Visionary State: A Journey through California's Spiritual Landscape
(WITH PHOTOGRAPHS BY MICHAEL RAUNER)

Nomad Codes

Adventures in Modern Esoterica

Erik Davis

Illustrations by SUSAN WILLMARTH

yeti / Verse Chorus Press

YETI books are published by Verse Chorus Press in association with YETI.
PO Box 14806, Portland OR 97293. yetipublishing.com. versechorus.com

Cover painting by Fred Tomaselli
Book design by Steve Connell / Transgraphic (transgraphic.net)

Printed in China by C&C Offset Printing Co., Ltd.

FIRST EDITION

Library of Congress Cataloging-in-Publication Data

Davis, Erik.
Nomad codes : adventures in modern esoterica / Erik Davis ; illustrations by Susan Willmarth. – 1st ed.
p. cm.
ISBN 978-1-891241-54-3 (pbk.)
1. Occultism. I. Title.
BF1411.D385 2010
130–dc22

2010025060

CONTENTS

INNER SPACE

MAD SCIENCE

KALIFORNIKA

CODA

ERIK'S TRIP

By Marcus Boon

My first memory of Erik Davis is of playing the Japanese game of Go with him in an apartment in Brooklyn in the dark days of the early 1990s, while the plagues of AIDS, the New World Order, and our own young male testosterone-addled consciousnesses swirled around us. Dinosaur Jr. or the first Sun City Girls record was on the stereo as antidote, and there were stacks of comix, used pulp sci-fi novels and other pop arcana all around, glowing with totemic intensity. We played Go because we were both high on Deleuze and Guattari's recently translated theory bible, *A Thousand Plateaus,* which approved of Go as a rhizomatic, non-hierarchical game. It all felt like something out of a back issue of *Doctor Strange,* the two of us seated cross-legged on some abstract gaming board, calling forth whatever powers we could. We were both interested in materialist magic, some kind of key that would unlock and transform the universe around us, and one of the places we sought it was in writing.

Erik has been one of the chief chroniclers of some of the madness of our times, publishing his work in magazines that make up a catalogue of the US hipster avant-garde post-1980s: the *Village Voice, Details, Mondo 2000, Wired,* the *Wire, Salon, Gnosis, Yeti, 21C, Feed, Strange*

Attractor, Reality Sandwich, Arthur. Sometimes one of these magazines morphs into the mainstream and an actual paycheck, sometimes one of them sinks without a trace. Either way, except for the web-based *Feed* and *Reality Sandwich,* these are some of the last vital gasps of the Gutenberg galaxy, the universe of the printed word whose outer limits Erik has explored, without any security or guarantees.

Erik is known for his writing about gnosis, subject of his acclaimed first book, *Techgnosis: Myth, Magic and Mysticism in the Age of Information.* But what is the gnostic situation? A basic definition: you are in a trap and you need to escape! Many of us have lived our whole lives in this strange trap that's variously given the names of late capitalism, postmodernity, or simply Babylon. What happens to writing and writers in this situation? Greil Marcus wrote that to understand Lester Bangs, you'd have to recognize that the greatest American writer of the 1970s might write nothing but record reviews. To understand Erik and his fascination with weirdness and esoterica of many kinds, you'd have to recognize that just writing record reviews would be way too conservative an approach to actually describing our world today.

Erik has been one of the most enthusiastic advocates of Philip K. Dick's writing and vision of the future, and like that great master of late-twentieth-century fiction, Erik has made his way on his own, without academic backing, through the deserts of the real and all the strange encampments lurking there, whether in Nevada, New York, San Francisco, or London. Like Dick, Erik is a native Californian, and a passage from a letter from Dick to Polish sci-fi writer Stanislaw Lem illuminates something of the method and environment that they share. Lem had previously praised Dick as the only great sci-fi writer around (besides himself, presumably!), but sniffed that it was unfortunate that Dick appeared to be so obsessed with such tawdry, disreputable subject matter. Dick responded:

> But you see, Mr. Lem, there is no culture here in California, only trash. And we who grew up here and live here and write here have nothing else to include as elements in our work; you can see this

> in *On the Road*. I mean it. The West Coast has no tradition, no dignity, no ethics—this is where that monster Richard Nixon grew up. How can one create novels based on this reality which do not contain trash, because the alternative is to go into dreadful fantasies of what it ought to be like; one must work with the trash, pit it against itself, as you so aptly put it in your article. Hence the elements in such books of mine as *Ubik*. If God manifested Himself to us here He would do so in the form of a spray can advertised on TV.

Dick died in 1982, but the trash has continued to pile up sky-high. Using the word "trash" sounds condescending—but the point is that in our society, anything of value is thrown out, devalued, abandoned and forgotten. Take Erik's second book, a magisterial reading of Led Zeppelin's fourth LP that appeared in the 33⅓ series of books (OK, I lied, Erik does write about records too). *Zoso* is a mass-cultural artifact, and the object of a million banalities. What Erik does is draw out a whole esoteric history that informs the record, both in its production and reception, tracking the way that revolutionary energies are both displaced onto and secretly resting in an object of everyday life. What distinguishes Erik's work from the mass of pop-cultural meditations and academic cultural studies that have blossomed since the 1980s is his affirmation of religious or spiritual energies as valid aspects of this everyday world. But it's a critical spirituality that Erik affirms, equally skeptical of postmodern irony, dogmatic materialism, and born-again fervor, even as it remains open to the world as he finds it.

There is a tradition here that Erik is a part of, a tradition of religious dissent—independent, non-conformist, often hedonistic in orientation. Its most recent form is the great revelations of the 1960s, whose echoes and ripples were still everywhere in Erik's 1970s SoCal childhood. From there, we go back to the older, weirder America, the DIY transcendentalists and Great Awakeners who persist in the margins and rooming-houses of the imagination, back to the vast history of vanquished seekers, the Ranters and other heretics of the English Revolution who crossed the Atlantic, the Albigensians and Anabaptists and other dissenters from Christian orthodoxy who haunt European history, right back to the Gnostic sects of the Biblical era, trying to square Jesus with Epicurus and the Upanishads, and beyond that to the murky characters lurking at the very beginning of what is called history, who refused to get down with the priests of the Rig Veda or the founders of the state of Uruk. And that's just in the Western lineage, which is only one small part of the history of what has gone on on this planet. A lot of unfinished business . . . which is why it persists and returns today.

Second definition of the gnostic situation: a flash of illumination that allows you to escape. But how do you do that? Erik's interests are a catalog of the spaces and practices by which contemporary people have tried to trigger the flash that allows escape. They include: yoga, Buddhism, Taoism, and other Asian religious traditions; hermeticism, Neopaganism, and other Western esoteric traditions; psychedelics, of both the old (LSD, shrooms) and new (DMT and MDMA) diaspora; theory, notably of the Deleuze and Guattari lineage, but including skirmishes with Žižek and anarcho-mystic Hakim Bey; pop- and subcultural artifacts including zines, comix, fandoms; festival/party/pilgrimage scenes such as the Rainbow Gathering, the global outlaw rave scene that originated in Goa, and Burning Man, of which Erik is the most celebrated chronicler; the personal computer and the Internet, and the proliferation of cultural forms around them, including MUDs and MOOs; most of the interesting music scenes of the last twenty years, from the Mekons' post-punk through the '90s alt diaspora, psy-trance and other electronic sounds to the freak folk scene and enduring tricksters such as the Sun City Girls.

Did anybody actually escape through any of these means and forms? That's a secret—you have to find out for yourself! But what makes Erik a writer in the heroic sense of the word is his ability to get on the bus and take the ride without a whole lot of delusions or Romanticism about achieved utopias. The problem of "failed transcendence" is not high on Erik's list of priorities, and he can put up with all manner of goofy shtick if the result is a generous and progressive social situation—as in the case of Burning Man, for example. There's a whole vocabulary of enjoyment that comes with this: "fun" of course, but also the "juicy," the "tasty" and the "yummy"—moments where righteous vision is attained, usually through some kind of protocol or practice.

Erik's work has an ambiguous relationship to the world of academia. A graduate of Yale during the heyday of literary theory, he gravitated instead towards a tai chi teacher he would visit after his Hegel and Nietzsche seminar who said to him: "PhDs don't impress me. People who've confronted the void impress me!" The category of "the impressive" is a puzzling one to me—after all, there is no one to impress but the gods in the zones where anything that really matters happens—but it's an important one in Erik's lexicon, both in terms of what he's attracted to and his own stance. I take it to refer to the importance of the gift economy to him, the generosity of attainment which serves as a vehicle of friendship, prestige, and community. It recognizes the authority of practice over theory, event over system, action over word—with the twist that, as with all great writers, he still is drawn to write about this stuff!

Erik moved back to California in 1995 and has become a cultural archeologist of the region, uncovering scenes and characters including the alternative film and visual arts worlds of LA and San Francisco, figures like Wallace Berman and Jordan Belson, and the locations and histories described in his third book, *The Visionary State: A Journey through California's Spiritual Landscape*. Perhaps Erik's solution to the gnostic dilemma—which, as scholars such as Hans Jonas have noted, is one of existential homelessness—is to explore the groundless ground of what is called home, which for him means the state of California, and the various attempts to found intentional communities there, and to attain realization.

The title of this foreword is taken from a song on Sonic Youth's remarkable record *Daydream Nation*, which came out around the time that I first met Erik. This record, which both of us love or have loved, is always associated in my mind with him. The sense on that record of urgency struggling to make itself known in the face of an overwhelmingly deep, sluggish trance, a trance which the band is all too familiar with, reminds me of Erik's work, as do the enormous surges of euphoric clarity, which *do* break through that trance, again and again.

PREFACE

Two insights lay in wait for me when Yeti graciously asked me to compile this collection. As I began combing through twenty years of reviews, essays, articles, fantasies, and profiles, I realized, first off, that reading most of that stuff makes me woozy. *This will not do* was a constant refrain. So I cherry-picked shorter and snappier pieces whose prose crackled and sang regardless of the topic, which was, as often as not, the (semi-) popular music of the day. When Marcus Boon took a look at my initial selection, he complained bluntly that a lot of the pieces seemed dated and slight. He argued that it was my more substantial if sometimes less razzle-dazzle essays that were most worthy of being preserved in cellulose. He was right.

Once I returned to the sifting process with this in mind, the second realization came to me: that a single concern threaded its way through the bulk of my eclectic scribblings, or rather that a single terrain kept appearing between the lines of whatever subjects and genres I was exploring. Call it occulture, or, as I have here, modern esoterica. It's a hazy no-man's-land located somewhere between anthropology and mystical pulp, between the zendo and the metal club, between cultural criticism and extraordinary experience, whether psychedelic, or yogic, or technological. It is dodgy terrain to explore; I like to think that it calls for the intrepid adventurer to shed any territorial claims and go nomad.

Of course, even nomads come from somewhere. My desire to write about and engage with spiritual culture, both my own and that of others, was sparked during my Southern California stoner youth and shaped in particular by the zeitgeist of early- and mid-nineties America, when I lived in Brooklyn and then in San Francisco and wrote like a maniac. It was a time of bright passages and exuberant mutation, of margins colliding and thickening into skeins of novelty. The cut 'n' scratch of hip-hop gave us all permission to enact and celebrate the mix—the miscegenation of machines and memes, of highbrow and low-end, of sacred and profane. The spread of rave culture, ecstasy, and faceless electronic music also helped spur a renaissance in psychedelia, a florescence best articulated by the mushroom bard Terence McKenna. Within spiritual culture, the New Age excesses of the 1980s were outflanked by more scintillating moves, including the wonderful run of *Gnosis* magazine, the infectious viruses of a revivified American Buddhism, and the sort of ritual anarchy that marked Burning Man and other feral temporary autonomous zones. At the same time—and not coincidentally—the half-hallucinated cyberspace booted up by networked personal computers hosted a feverish eruption of experiments, debates, and virtual-reality dreams that, however naive, carved out a genuine space for the Possible. Bruce Sterling's 1991 exhortation still rings in my head, damn him: *Follow your weird.*

For weird young writing me, the mark of all this possibility was simply that I was able to get away with so much: paying the rent with Phil Dick profiles and Deleuzian analyses of children's toys, or getting flown to India on Condé Nast's dime to write about dancing freaks. As the dot-com bubble grew to obscene proportions in the latter part of the decade, I slaved away on the book *Techgnosis,* which I am happy to say dodged the hype and remains relevant enough to be still in print. In the new century, my career (I prefer the term *careen*) has followed a logic that remains obscure even to me—one that has moved through tech journalism, scholarly critique, memoir, blog, rock-opera libretto, and a deepening engagement with the psycho-geography of my native California.

Looking over this collection, I still wince occasionally when I come across phrases or arguments that seem forced or jejune. But I resisted the urge to crack the can of worms that real revision would have opened; I merely changed some titles and fixed the most egregious errors and tics. These are husks of time and place, then—perspectives gained from specific journeys or obsessions and then released again as the passage itself moved on.

San Francisco, June 12, 2010

ACKNOWLEDGEMENTS

I would like to thank the editors I have been fortunate to work with over the years, many of whom commissioned these pieces and helped beat them into shape (please forgive any memory slips): Doug Simmons, Joe Levy, Jeff Salamon, Scott Malcolmson, Lisa Kennedy, J. Kinney, Richard Smoley, Jon Lebkowsky, Ashley Crawford, Kevin Berger, Stephanie Syman, Jay Babcock, Mark Pilkington, Mike Jay, Alan Hunt-Badiner, Stephen Dinan, and Albert Mobilio. Also much thanks to Julian Dibbell, Robert Christgau, Mark Dery, and Peter Lamborn Wilson, wizards all. Much appreciation goes to Marcus Boon, Fred Tomaselli, and Susan Willmarth for their contributions to this book, and especially to Mike McGonigal and Steve Connell for their enthusiasm, patience, and daring. As always, I couldn't have done it without Jennifer, who has shared life with me for most of the two decades spanned by these essays and articles.

Most of these pieces have already seen the light of day; many have been trimmed and touched up and occasionally renamed herein. Many come from the *Village Voice*: "Teenage Head," "Saint Phil," "The Gone World," "The Wandering Sufi," "Calling All Gods," and "Klingon

Like Me." Another batch came from the late, great *Gnosis:* "Trickster at the Crossroads," "Calling Cthulhu," and "Snakes & Ladders." "Sampling Paradise" appeared in *Option;* "Shards of the Diamond Matrix" in *Fringeware Review;* "Dub, Scratch, and the Black Star" in *21C;* "Terence McKenna's Last Trip" in *Wired; "The Bad Shaman and the Frog"* in a British lad magazine whose name I have forgotten; "Alien Views" in *San Francisco Magazine;* "Cameo Demons" in *The Wire;* "Burmese Daze" in *Strange Attractor Journal;* "Jack Spicer's Ghosts" in *Bookforum.* A few articles came from books: "Meditating in Sensurround" from *Radical Spirit,* edited by Stephen Dinan (New World Library, 2002); "The Paisley Gate" from *Zig Zag Zen,* edited by Alan Hunt Badiner (Chronicle, 2002); and "Beyond Belief" from *AfterBurn,* edited by Lee Gilmore and Mark Van Proyen (University of New Mexico Press, 2005). Online, *Feed* published "Psychonaut" and "Remote Control," while *Salon* ran "Matrixter." "Diamond Solitaire," "Au Revoir La Contessa," "Bardo Flight," and "Aya Avatar" all first appeared on my website, www.techgnosis.com, where I regularly post.

PROLEGOMENON

TEENAGE HEAD

Confessions of a High School Stoner

I became a teenager in 1980, the year Reagan was elected president, and by the time the lizard slid into office, I was already a total stoner. I bonged skunk bud, chased JD with Coke, snorted Beauties, and had dropped my first dose of acid the previous Halloween, tripping to *Ummagumma* amidst the paisley bedsheets and pillows that lined the loft my friend Bry-Fry knocked together in his family's garage. Phasing between the reveries of a bookish childhood and the hormone-fueled angst of teendom, my mind liquefied, running through the cracks and creases of a suddenly unfolded world.

In the last couple of years, that world has seemed closer to the surface, and I don't think it's a matter of my own nostalgia. Raves, which restage the Neopagan commingling of a Woodstock I never saw in venues resembling the space stations I never will, are only the greatest and most media-friendly example of youth culture's desire to tune into trippy frequencies. There are also rappers talking hemp conspiracy theories and crafting stoned-out beats and rhymes, cyber-slackers building virtual worlds, prog rockers and jocks dancing in the dust at Lollapalooza. And it's not just the kids. If you don't see a connection between brokerage firms' increasing reliance on virtual reality representations of stock data and the *Economist's* pro-legalization cover story, you probably didn't smoke enough pot in high school.

Drugs are like sexual pleasures: experimentation is a prerequisite for judgment. For each of us, certain drugs will become allies, enemies, passing acquaintances—but first they must be encountered, knee-deep in the mud of personal history. Though the timing of my early encounters now seems a bit out-of-hand, the place was certainly more than appropriate: coastal California. As a kid, I grew up in Del Mar—the mellow, upwardly mobile surf town north of San Diego name-dropped in "Surfing, U.S.A." Just before I entered junior high, my family moved inland to Rancho Santa Fe—a wealthy and conservative realm of citrus groves, migrant Mexican workers, and geriatrics in golf carts. Stone-cold Reagan country, and me and Senzo Joe would escape into the weed, smoking out in so many lemon groves that the sharp tang of citrus peels still conjures up bud.

Pot led me into a tangible world of bubbling micro-perceptions, haunted winds, and hilarious malformations of the data-stream. But pot also gave me something that has stuck with me far longer than the urge to bake my brain: a love of slippage, founded in the realization that altering perception alters the claims reality makes on you. The various social agendas of parents, teachers, and the ghost of God could be sidestepped—not only by sullen monosyllables and the worship of unwholesome heavy-metal guitarists but by tinkering with consciousness itself. What greater rebellion than rewiring one's experience of the world?

Parents have reason for concern. At thirteen, identity is a spell woven from a bursting body, ego defenses and world views that have yet to congeal, and the prepubescent power of fantasy lurking just below the surface. That's why kids can travel so far into their headphones, role-playing games, pop star posters, and beat-up copies of *The Necronomicon*. Toss in a psychedelic—and let no one tell you that good weed cannot be a psychedelic—and the warp gets deep. Pot lets you see dragons in the clouds again.

I know, because I saw a lot of stuff, zoning out in that bedroom where every surface was covered with some numinous image: goat-gods, spaceships, mandalas, *Penthouse* pin-ups, Jesus, Jimmy Page. In that psychic house of cards, I jury-rigged my mind, teaching myself to soar off a single hit of scraped resin, the reek cloaked by blackberry incense on my hodgepodge altar crowned by a concrete Buddha. He was a birthday gift from Senzo Joe, stolen from someone's lawn, and once I swear he slyly peeled back his ponderous eyelids and stared me down.

The ominous intensity of that gaze, conjured with so little fuel, could be evidence of the dangers mind-altering drugs pose for kids. But it's difficult for big folk to make judgments about teens without projecting their own foibles and fears onto creatures who live in a completely different world—a zone that is far more complicated than a simple stage between childhood and that elusive (and highly debatable) state called maturity. The pliable subjectivities, imaginative resourcefulness, rebellious courage, cliquishness, and cultural verve that define teens also give them powerful tools and contexts for experiencing drugs, tools that most adults lack. It's no accident that many kids start taking drugs at about the same age when children in traditional societies are tossed into some terrifying rite of passage, often involving a freaked-out combination of blood, darkness, self-sufficiency, and secrets. For better or worse, acid, 'shrooms, and massive bongloads now perform this rite, leaving marks that are both scars and the deep patterns of change.

Unfortunately, dog-eared copies of Castaneda or a snide older sibling is the closest many kids come to having "a guide" for this phase shift from innocence to experience. That's where subculture steps in, offering collective identities that can shore up the threat of dissolution and excess. The public high school I attended—imagine an open-air Ridgemont High surrounded by sagebrush and rocky arroyos, with seagulls diving for your lunch meat—was a mosaic of pot-smoking cliques, their turf demarcated as succinctly as the multicolored regions in maps of the cerebral cortex: skateboarders, metal-heads, punks, goths, stoners, and the various flavors of surfer—the long-haired Zep fans, the cue balls that dug ska, and the dread-headed ones we called

Waspafarians.

Too tripped out to surf, my friends and I set ourselves somewhat apart. Our campus turf was beyond the smoking section, behind a wall, in the Gel Circle—from the verb "to gel," synonymous with "veg" and "mold," all denoting the same state of blazing slack. I suppose we were perceived as druggies rather than simply stoners, but now I'd call us heads. (Since I was issued into the world the same month as *Sgt. Pepper's*, my notion of "head" is a reading, not a recollection. For me, heads directed their radicalism toward consciousness rather than society or the defense of nature. Seizing the means of perception with techniques rather than truths, the archetypal head was neither a daisy-lover nor a bomb-thrower, but something in between, wired into cavernous headphones, devouring sci-fi paperbacks, pop physics, yogic manuals, anarchist cookbooks, all while smoking tons of pot and maintaining an account at the campus mainframe.)

It was this exploratory interiority, coupled with an ironic and parasitic relationship to the suburban circus of SoCal party culture, that defined my closest group of friends for the first few years of high school. Talking weird science, meditating, reading Hunter S. Thompson, Moebius, and *Autobiography of a Yogi*, listening to Eno, Floyd, Zappa, and, yes, Yes (with the Talking Heads our one concession to new wave), we played the hippies the punks played at killing. Yet we mixed with death-rock chicks and skinheads more than surfers, as if the extremity of our anachronism was our shock tactic.

And so much of it had to do with drugs: Thai-stick, black hash, Humboldt sens so juicy that even doubled-up in sandwich baggies and shoved into greasy blue jeans, it'd reek up Trig. There was usually speedy blotter to be had, but a beneficent wind might bring Orange Sunshine, purple microdot, four-way Windowpane. As with computers or political organization, the specific rituals this candy produced were quite self-reflexive: scrounging and pooling of petty resources, hunting down the weed man, catching rides through the tract-home maze, scoring, seeking the hidden zones, foraging for implements. We were immersed in an educational system whose ultimate goal is filling in little

round circles with No. 2 pencils, and drugs actually offered a crooked avenue to resourceful, independent problem-solving, from knocking on some housewife's door at 10 p.m. to ask for a sheet of aluminum foil to learning how to make a pipe from an apple, how to use weights and scales, how to research pharmacology at the university library, how to grow plants.

Most fun of all, pot taught us the guerrilla art of concealment, of disappearing into the fractal curves in the landscape: pockets of sagebrush, sandstone, and pine that have since been almost entirely obliterated by the tumorous development endemic to Southern California. Secret forts became stoner zones: Mars, Red Rocks, the Hobbit Hole, the Mushroom Tree. Like some pied piper of Pan, marijuana leads kids to places gone to seed—vacant lots, stream beds, canyons, underpasses, boundary zones where landscape becomes imaginative clay, suddenly collectivized in the ritual trinity of substance, vessel, and flame. While many drugs are "natural" in their origin, the worlds they conjure may seem artificial. But the cosmos pot opens up is distinctly organic (hence vegging out). You can hear it in pothead hip hop, a fuzzy echo as if some crunchy lichen has run riot over the mix. The resurgence of weed as cultural icon may not be a matter of returning to nature but recovering its flow in the urban milieu: how to slip through the cracks in the concrete, how to grow wilderness in the most degraded or rigidly stratified of circumstances. That's not a spoon or a needle or a bottle on all those caps around town. It's a leaf.

We drank loads too, almost as much for the sport of keg crashing as for the sloshy slapstick philosophizing it produced. And weed itself often devolved into a kind of beer. But psychedelics were always our Grand Guignol of phantasmic ecstasy. LSD turns the mind into a kind of silly putty, lifting images from a comic-book world and then twisting them alternately into hilarious caricatures or resonant archetypes. Kids can dig this, and certainly can ride with it better than most adults, who find the world unstable enough as it is. Because most of us were still cushioned in our parents' homes, my friends and I had a baseline security that allowed us to enter LSD's ontological house of mirrors with the proper plasticity. Like running hell-bent down the slippery rocks of a steep river bank, tripping makes for a certain balance in flux, an internal momentum easier for kids to achieve than their more brittle future selves.

We knew from Leary and Alpert the importance of set and setting, advice we both followed and blatantly ignored. Outdoor Dead shows were a cross between astral planes and romper rooms, but North County's unspoiled zones were the greatest backdrops. The summer we were gobbling all of Squiggles's white blotter, we'd time our doses to hit at sunset. We'd kick back on the coppery cliffs of Red Rocks beneath a hunchbacked pine and watch the sun melt into an immense, resplendent sea. The sky struck the total chord of the spectrum, from the crimson lump of the slipping orb through the violet haze of the canopy above. And to the east lay the distinct boundary where dusk stopped and evening began to sketch the uncertain hieroglyphs of the stars.

And then we'd plunge, in the aimless and reckless quest for the silliest of grails (a party, pot, a parent-free abode), arms open to the banal, tinny surface of suburban culture. Perhaps I became an apocalyptic psychonaut the night I entered a 7-11 with the knee-shaking awe of a UFO abductee, or learned to listen for the cosmic giggle in the babble of popular culture the night Weffles and I, toasted on some nameless blotter, visited Tuddy's downbeat seaside motel room. The place smelled like a cave, the carpet was stained with sticky grime, and Tuddy, an outpatient from a mental ward and one of the good-natured party animals we called aardvarks, was blotto. A half-empty case of Henry's or Mickey's or some other lousy lager sat on the formica table. We murmured weird communications, attempting to track the myriad and ridiculous paths other aardvarks had taken that night. Like the eye of a djinn, a thirteen-inch black-and-white TV stared down at us from the corner of the ceiling. It was showing *Animal Crackers*. Groucho took measure of our squalid scene, raised an eyebrow, and split the world apart with a wisecrack of gutter satori, as if someone had fished a smelly copy of *Mad* from a dumpster and folded it into a delicate origami swan that instantly took to wing, singing the elusive song of the psychedelic ineffable: "Hello, I must be going . . ."

It doesn't really matter what Groucho said. Acid doesn't give you truths; it builds machines that push the envelope of perception. Whatever revelations came to me then have dissolved like skywriting. All I really know is that those few years saddled me with a faith in the redemptive potential of the imagination which, however flat, stale, and unprofitable the world seems to me now, I cannot for the life of me shake.

Years ago, the weed and I pretty much parted ways. Some folks claim that pot chills them out, but in my brain it produces a bubbling, crackling connection-machine that generally sinks into the mire. Trivial objects, words, and glances stitch together webs of deep and intense meaning that uncomfortably thicken—one time a Greek salad in New Haven set off a rumination on the flows of Western history that overwhelmed my puny mind like a tidal wave. Pot makes a lot of people uncomfortably paranoid, in part because it produces enough connections to elicit the subterranean patterns of the conspiracy theorist, while not rewiring the self a la five grams of *Psilocybe cubensis*. Whether or not the sense that everything fits together is perceived as a holistic liberation or a dire trap depends a lot on how tightly you are clinging to your frame of mind.

For all their gifts, drugs create too many problematic relations: to their own absence, to habit, to money, to the dealer, to the down. They did nothing for my teen angst or my memory; for others, they were less forgiving. High school friends of great wit, intelligence, and spirit are now junkies, alkies, hopeless flakes, burn-outs, and, in more than one instance, a corpse. They were no more taken by drugs back then than I was. Today, I rave it up now and then, keep periodic appointments with the gibbering, serpentine, science-fiction All Being who resides in the hyper-dimensions of psychedelic space, and drink beer. I did not reject drugs; I cordially withdrew, making sure to leave the door ajar for whatever intriguing substances remain unchecked on my curriculum vitae.

But I take great satisfaction in the fact that many people, acquainted with either my writing or my person, assume that I'm a total stoner. For when I began to pull away from regular drug use, I realized that I didn't want to *do* drugs as much as to *think* drugs, to simulate their hyperconnections, magical causality, and semiotic drift as much as possible within my own mind. The French post-structuralists (and Castaneda fans) Gilles Deleuze and Félix Guattari, whose works produce the immanent patterning of psychedelic cognition, write that drugs can be understood at the level where "desire directly invests perception . . . and the imperceptible is perceived"—a liberatory goal indeed. But Deleuze and Guattari are fairly down on drugs themselves. To quote them quoting Henry Miller, the point is to get drunk on a glass of water.

In other words, sobriety alone does not have the tools to build sense and meaning from these vertiginous, data-dense End times. Level-headed thinking is no option when the ship is pitching to and fro—you either resist and puke, or ride with the galloping serenity of the mounted nomad. Perhaps Walter Benjamin was right: civilization is perpetual crisis, and my point of view is only an indication of that irreparable deviation my reason took over a decade ago. But for those of us who get stoned off dusk, who tinker with the simulacra of consciousness, who turn our minds into heads, the question is moot. Like that giddy flash of anxiety that hits the moment the blotter melts on your tongue, it's too late now. Here it comes.

1993

ORIENTALISMO

THE WANDERING SUFI

Peter Lamborn Wilson

Setting out in the late 1960s, the underground anarcho-Sufi scholar Peter Lamborn Wilson traveled abroad for over a decade, wandering from North Africa to India to Java. But he spent the bulk of his time in Iran, where he explored the heterodox nooks and crannies of Islam, a religion the West caricatures as fanatically monolithic but which Wilson's voluminous reading, Sufi practices, and face-to-face encounters with sorcerers, Satanists, and hash-smoking dervishes proved possesses one of the world's richest and most diverse living mysticisms. Wilson's expatriate days are over, but he remains a cultural and intellectual nomad—a true free-thinker.

Though the bulk of his work explores the historical and mystical dimensions of Sufism and Islamic heresy, Wilson has also translated books of Persian poetry, written on angels and early American spiritual anarchism, and penned science fiction and a few pseudonymous manifestos. Every other Tuesday, his free-ranging *Moorish Orthodox Radio Crusade* broadcasts on WBAI, and he lectures regularly at the New York Open Center and other local venues on topics ranging from hermeticism to Dada anthropology to "chaos linguistics" in the writings of Chuang Tzu. He's published high and low, from sci-fi zines to *Studies in Mystical Literature* to *Semiotext(e)*, which, as a member of the Autonomedia collective, he helps publish. And they still won't let him into a university library in New York.

As an underground intellectual, Wilson is particularly suited to tapping the underground streams of religious history—both the truths that canonical authorities keep hidden, and the shadows of truth that haunt history like phantasms. As Wilson demonstrates, heresies most often occur far from the legislating center, and his own heretical studies have put him knee-deep in apocrypha, secret histories, occult symbols, magic pamphlets, and popular art. These explorations not only move him from history into exoticism, but introduce a magical mode of writing: recombinant, luminous, fragmentary. As he writes in *Sacred Drift: Essays on the Margins of Islam*:

> In the world of apocrypha the Images of established religion and canonical texts acquire a kind of mutability, a tendency to *drift*, to reflect the subjectivities of the (often anonymous) visionaries who sift through fragments in order to produce more fragments . . . The world of apocrypha is a world of books *made* real . . . The apocryphal imagination turns "Tibet" or "Egypt" into an amulet or mantram with which to unlock an "other world," most real in books and dreams and dreams *of* books.

Wilson is more than willing to navigate this no man's land, but unlike many fringe thinkers, revisionists and spiritual autodidacts, he never lapses into kook logic or shallow rants. For an anarchist, he has a remarkably traditional respect for rigor and cautious argument, as well as a great love for the dusty bibliographies and arcane disputes of classic scholarship. Still, he hates the academic world, and thanks God that a trickle of family money keeps him "independently poor." This marginality grants him little status, for as he points out, "in America, the concept of an independent scholar is a null set." This is a shame, not only because Wilson's one of the few Americans writing about Islamic culture for a popular (or at least hipster) audience, but because his essays and lectures argue for the ultimate unity of imagination and intellectual investigation. Despite all his footnotes, Wilson is ultimately less interested in historicity than what he calls "poetic facts," insurrectionary images that puncture history. And he's more than willing to inhale on the opium smoke of exoticism to conjure them up.

Sacred Drift picks up the thread from his earlier collection *Scandal: Essays in Islamic Heresy*, which remains in many ways a more scandalous book. Along with discussions of Javanese shadow-puppets and the Assassins (the heretical order led by Hassan-i Sabbah, whose dictum "Nothing is true, everything is permitted" was famously imported by William Burroughs), *Scandal* includes material that even today's rather jaded audience would find heretical. Besides praising the mystical use of hashish (and including a recipe for the cannabis brew *bhang*), the essay "The Imaginal Game" offers a sympathetic portrayal of "sacred pedophilia," the practice of staring at beautiful boys interpreted as a kind of imaginal yoga.

Sacred Drift wanders through similarly marginal territory, from Islamic Satanists to some playful Rumi translations to a profound discussion of the problems of sexuality and authority in modern Sufism. But the heart of the book is the title essay, which uncovers the "nomadosophy" of heretical Islam via Situationism, Islamic travel narratives, and the delightful figures of the flying carpet and of Kzehr, the Green Man of the Koran. The spirit of this wonderful mosaic is best summed up by a line of Rumi that precedes the essay: "Journey forth from your own self / to God's Self—voyage without end."

"I admit to being a romantic," Wilson tells me as he lights up a Camel straight in his messy, funky apartment in Alphabet City. I had asked him about Said's famous critique of Orientalism. "Romanticism is definitely part of the problem he's identifying, and Orientalism in general does lead to fantasy. But fantasy—reveries, childhood dreams, fancies and magical images—is not entirely to be despised." It was by becoming infatuated with such exotic fantasies that Wilson first began his relationship to Islam—which is itself a perfect anticipation of the imaginative spiritual erotics he later found in Sufi poetry, in which the mundane self is annihilated through a radical romantic infatuation with the Other, the "Beloved."

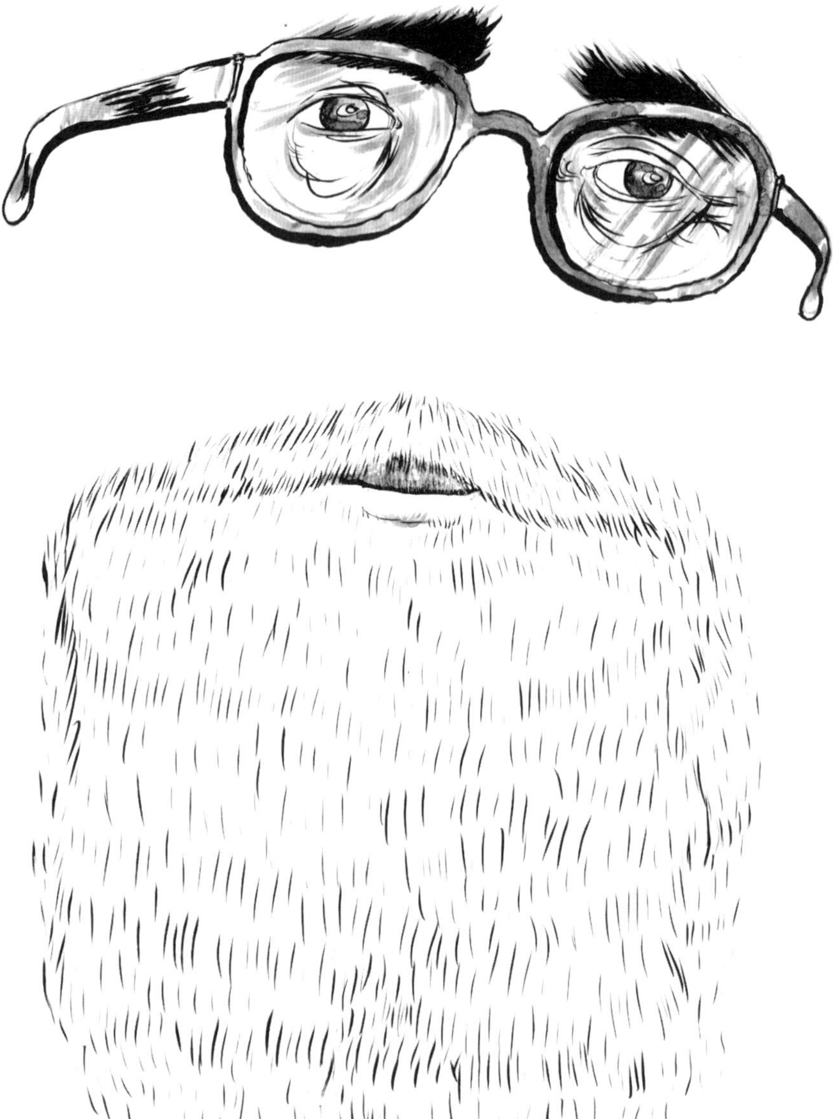

To describe his anti-colonialist embrace of the East, Wilson prefers the term *orientalismo*—an echo of the *tropicalismo* that freaked-out Brazilian intellectuals used to describe their mad cannibalism of First World culture in the late '60s. For him, the trick is not to shackle the nomadic imagination but to refuse "gaping at cultures or trying to appropriate their spiritual sap without paying any karmic dues." With his translations of Sufi poetry, collected in *The Drunken Universe* and elsewhere, Wilson gets around the problem of appropriation by co-translating with native Persian speakers.

Wilson derives his romantic image of cross-pollinating cultural exchange from the syncretisms, mutual poachings, and heretical countercultures that litter the history of religions. He points out that what he calls "fortuitous mistranslations" of one culture often mobilize "new insurrectionary modes of cultural thought" in another. A casebook example of "heresy as cultural transfer" is Beat Zen, one of the primal inspirations for the white drop-outs who inspired the countercultural tradition that Wilson himself still very much carries on.

> The first incursions of Zen into America were from Japanese of dubious orthodoxy—and I would even include D.T. Suzuki in that category. Then you had a lot of Americans who "didn't understand it," and they made their own thing out of their fortuitous mistranslation. Something about Zen filled the bill. In terms of Japanese scholarship, they were wrong. But in terms of the spirit, it seems they were right.
>
> What was happening was precisely what Zen itself calls "beginner's mind." After centuries, something radically new was happening to Zen, and unfortunately Zen was not able to appreciate it, because Zen soon moved in the Roshis. "Fine, fine, you're into Zen? Here's the real Zen." And the real Zen turned out to be just another fucking despotism. Even giving orthodoxy its due, they shouldn't have stamped out those embers. Because it had that benefit of beginner's mind, that sweetheart situation, Beat Zen made Buddhism what it is today: the biggest Oriental religion in America. That's

how you get things like the TV show *Kung Fu*. A lot of Oriental stuff seeped into that stupid show, and created a whole generation of people for whom it was part of their universe of discourse.

For Wilson, a more important instance of "heresy as cultural transfer" occurred in the early 1900s in the work of Noble Drew Ali, the African-American whose imaginative mixture of Masonry, esoteric Christianity, and his own visionary dreams of Egypt led to everything from Elijah Mohammad to hip hop's Five Percent Nation. As Wilson says, "Drew Ali's a real American prophet, the black man with a Cherokee feather stuck in his fez—the perfect image of everything I wish America were and isn't." In *Sacred Drift*, Wilson seeks the poetic fact of Noble Drew Ali, drawing not only from historical materials but from conversations with old-timers and pamphlets bought from incense-sellers in Times Square. "This is in fact the real opening of Islam in America. It's only long after that you find middle-class white people becoming interested in Sufism."

One of the those middle-class white persons was, as you might suspect, Peter Lamborn Wilson. He discovered the curious legacy of Drew Ali in 1964, when he met the hipsters who founded the Moorish Orthodox Church, an offshoot of Nobel Drew Ali's original Moorish Science Temple. In 1968, reacting to "the collapse of the political into spectacle," Wilson left America. Like many "feckless teenage hippies," he headed for India, but eventually got booted out for overstaying his visa. Rather aimlessly, he went to the Persian consulate in Quetta, Baluchistan, where he scored a year's visa for Iran. There he discovered not only that mysticism was alive and well in Persia but that he could earn a living in Tehran just by knowing English. "It's really still the only talent I have." As the cultural reporter for a little English-speaking newspaper, he had the freedom to explore fringe Islam as well as to meet the various avant-garde Westerners who passed through. Peter Brook gave him a job, and he almost slugged Stockhausen.

In 1974, a number of great Sufi scholars like Toshihiko Izutsu, Henry Corbin, and Seyyed Hossein Nasr, backed with money from the Shah's wife, founded the Iranian Academy of Philosophy, an institute devoted to Sufi research. Wilson's studies and translations continued there until the revolution.

> I went to a conference in Italy with an overnight bag and never went back. It wasn't really my fight exactly, and it tore my little world apart. Clearly, in retrospect, the Shah was a violent son of a bitch who didn't deserve to survive. But I would make an exception for Mrs. Shah. She's a very sweet lady and I owe her a lot of fun in my life so it would be churlish to make any remarks about her.

"I advise everybody to travel," says Wilson:

> And that in a somewhat Sufistic sense. As the Persians say, "A jewel that never leaves the mine never acquires polish." Of course, there's many ways to travel. There's tourism, there's traveling for business, joining a scientific expedition, visiting your relatives for the holidays. There's traveling in an army, which certainly is a very special way of moving across the face of the earth. All of these are different psychic modes.
>
> Travel for travel's sake is something very special. To be free and to learn are the only goals for the pure traveler. You've got to be strong, and keep your psyche polished and bright and open and ready to engage. If you look on travel not just as something that's happening to you but as something that you're doing, it requires the spiritual will the Sufis call *himmah*. You have to be aware of yourself as this free-floating zone unto yourself. You can give it a spiritual interpretation if you want, but it's incredibly real. Because it's really you in that hotel suffering from Montezuma's revenge. It's not an idea of you or a simulacrum of you. It's really your body there on the line—or at least on the toilet.

All this recalls the work of Hakim Bey, an intimate colleague of Wilson best known for his notion of the "temporary autonomous zone." As a surprisingly virulent concept/buzzword, the T.A.Z. has spread through the computer underground to *Time* magazine to the hippies at the Rainbow Gathering. Bey praises Wilson's contribution to Islam's anarchic spirituality, and Bey should know—he served as the court poet in a small sultanate in western Pakistan until an anarchist bombing incident forced him to flee to the U.S., where he now splits his time between New Jersey and a hotel in Chinatown. Reached at his Airstream in the Jersey wilds, Bey compares Wilson's take on spiritual travel to the T.A.Z.:

> Part of travel is running away as well as running towards. It's no terrible thing to run away from something if that thing is trying to destroy you, like the Empire of Work. In travel you are a kind of floating zone. You've got your whole little life with you in a suitcase. You become this bubble inside the cosmos running around, and you can make it autonomous or you can make it enslavement to misery depending on how much psychic energy you have.

For Wilson, there are tricks to travel.

> The people I met on the road who were really getting something out of it would be people who would settle down in Jakarta for a year and study batik. They had a love affair, and that's the difference. The tourist's not in love with any of this stuff.
>
> Another trick is to avoid places that have lost their aura by being mechanically reproduced through the medium of tourism, by fifty years of Cook tours and American Express and camera-clicking. All those things vampirically suck the life out of difference, or suck the difference out of the Other. Just going to obscure places makes a lot of sense, even if the big famous temples aren't there. I encourage people to go to busy Third World ports and industrial cities where tourists never go because there's nothing to see. There you often find traditional life far better preserved than the Disney World version of the exotic Orient that you're gonna buy for a tour.

Though this reliance on "authenticity" may strike some as the kind of naiveté vaporized by today's critical theorists, Wilson does not fear postmodern skepticism. "Baudrillard's a smart guy but he's a terrible traveler. His writings on America make that very clear. He seems to see only the ironies that he expected to see." When Wilson talks about authenticity he doesn't mean pure unmediated experience. "It's not at all the pure that I'm interested in. It's the Real, and everyday life is the arena of the Real." Wilson speaks of the Real not only as a Sufi might speak of it, but as an cultural interventionist who remains in fierce, and no doubt romantic, opposition to the nihilistic metaphysics of the spectacle.

> It's only now that we've reached the abyss of mediation that new paths appear. Of course they were always there, and actually involve a lot of archaic models. Travel plays a really important role in all this. It plays the opposite role of tourism, which nonetheless exists in a strange sort of dialog with travel, which goes along with travel at the same time and sometimes seems to actually become it. Tourism is a kind of travel that deconstructs difference. The kind of travel I'm talking about is to experience difference. It's something you do with the body—and probably ultimately the only really meaningful things you do are with the body. Unlike tourism, which is the prolongation of imperialist colonialism, the kind of travel I propose is a prolongation of the heretical margin. Every once in a while tourists are converted into travelers. They notice that besides the image of otherness that they're paying for there is a reality of otherness that they fall in love with. They're attracted to it, even erotically, and they walk out the tour bus and into the world.

1994

SAMPLING PARADISE

Goa Trance

It's one hour past midnight, and the jungle throbs with techno. The tropical breeze off the Arabian Sea is warm and wet. I stuff a wad of rupees into the outstretched palm of the auto-rickshaw taxi driver, and head toward the noise. I'm 350 kilometers south of Bombay, in India's coastal state of Goa, and I'm about to hit a rave.

The forest clearing swarms with bohemian backpackers and European hipsters strutting their cyberdelic stuff: holographic sneakers, flared fractal jeans, floppy Dr. Seuss hats stitched with the mirrored cloth of Rajasthan. The freaks gyrate around junky speaker stacks, soaking up the interstellar trance beats like they earlier soaked up the sun. A lithe Japanese girl dances by with a glowing plastic jewel affixed to her third eye, giving me and everyone else she encounters an omnivorous grin. An old Indian beggar passes through the crowd, the black lights turning his turban the color of moonlit bone.

The DJ booth lies at the edge of the clearing, set beneath low-hanging trees and cordoned off with bamboo. A large middle-aged hippie with white-boy dreads and a bearded, sun-burnt face stands behind the mixing table, pushing buttons and slapping DATs into two small decks wired through a pint-size mixer powered by a generator hidden in the bushes behind. Alongside stacks of black-matte cassettes stands a candle, a smoldering stick of incense, and a small devotional portrait of the Hindu yogi Shiva Shankar, sitting in the half-lotus position on a tiger skin.

"That's Gil," says one of the Indian locals mobbing the techno-shrine. "He's one of the best."

I had already heard about Gil from Genesis P. Orridge, who had filled me in earlier on the technofreak legacy of late-'60s London clubs like Middle Earth and UFO. "The basic premise was smoke and light shows, large quantities of ecstatic chemicals, and dancing like a dervish to accentuate your artificially induced mental state to a point that was equal to and integrated with an ecstatic religious state." When the scene decayed, the heaviest psychedelic warriors split, taking their musical alchemy with them. Some went to the Spanish island of Ibiza, while the more esoteric heads went east. Though Gil was from San Francisco, he had trodden a similar path. "You have to find him", Genesis told me. "He's one of the links."

But Gil is too lost in his craft to talk, and I merge back into pulsing psychedelic bardo of the dance floor. I've never seen people move like this: at the edge of their bodies, ceaselessly flowing, like Deadheads bonedancing in overdrive. Disembodied vocal samples float through the air like ghosts, triggering mindfucks left and right: "There are doors." "The last generation." "Everybody online?"

Craving touch-down, I head for Goa's gypsy version of a chill-out room. In an adjacent field, local village women have laid out rows of straw mats and piled them high with fruit and cigarettes and bubbling pots of chai. Scores of freaks flop out on the mats, smoking copiously by the light of kerosene lamps and sipping syrupy brew from scalding glasses.

I plop down next to a crowd of Brits. Pete is in pajama pants and an open vest, his aristocratic Tory features oddly framed by long scraggly hair. Hunched next to him is Steve, a skinny blond twentysomething rolling a spliff.

"Have you seen *The Time Machine?*" Steve asks me. "There's this noise that the Morlocks use to call the Eloi underground. That's exactly how it was five years ago when my friends and I first came to Goa. We heard this booming rhythm in the distance. We didn't know where the fuck we were, but we just crashed through the jungle with our torches. The sound was calling us. I got real paranoid that there was some alien intelligence directing the computers, like the Morlocks, summoning us to a place where they were gonna eat our souls."

Pete nods as if nothing his friend says could surprise him. "My first party, I just got the feeling I was in some spiritual Jane Fonda gymnasium," he says. "Boom, boom, boom, and everyone going into trance. It was quite alienating, actually."

"I just get a feeling of conspiracies, mass conspiracies, huge conspiracies," Steve counters, passing me the spliff. "We're under some bigger control at this point, and there's a lot more going on than we know." When the smoke hits my brain, I can almost see the plots thicken. I ask him how Goa differs from the raves in England. "Here people know about the history of freakdom, of free-form living. That vibe is carried forward with the music. In England it's not really freaky anymore. It's too organized. People are wearing the right kind of T-shirts, whereas here people will rip their T-shirts apart and run down the beach."

As the early sunlight streaks the sky, I leave the duo and head back to the dance floor. Dawn is Goa's sweetest moment. The bpm slows, and the night's bracing attack gives way to a smoother, narcotic trance. According to Goa's more shamanic DJs, the change of pace has a ritual function: after "destroying the ego" with the night's hardcore sounds, "morning music" fills the void with light.

The dawn light floats through the clearing like incense, and a deep resonating chant emerges on top of the lush, succulent beats: "Om Namah Shivaya." It's a mantra devoted to Shiva, the Hindu god of tantric transformation and hence something of a freak favorite. Slowly, a global rainbow emerges from the gloom: Australians, Italians, Indians; Africans in designer sweatshirts, Japanese in kimonos, Israelis in polka-dot overalls. A crowd of old-time Goan hippies ring the clearing, grey-haired and beaded creatures who dragged themselves out of bed just to taste this moment. As the dust fills my nostrils, I wonder whether Goa's raves were anything more than digitally remastered Be-Ins. Maybe something far more strange and ancient than beatnik dreams of the East was entrancing this crowd, something these old-timers knew but would not say.

As an Indian pothead I met in Mysore put it, "Goa isn't India." And Goa hasn't really been India since the Portuguese first colonized the place in the 1600s, when "Golden Goa" became a place a European man could really go to seed. Interbreeding with the locals was encouraged, and some adulterous Indian wives took to dosing their husbands with datura weed, rendering the men, as one early account put it, "giddy and insensible."

Goa remained in Portuguese hands until India seized it back in 1961, and the region was still more European than Asian in flavor when beatniks discovered its beautiful beaches a few years later. By the end of the '60s, hundreds of thousands of European and American freaks were streaming overland into South Asia, trying to find themselves in a country where it's easy to get lost. Though Goan beaches like Calangute and Baga didn't offer electricity, restaurants or much shelter, they did provide sweet relief from the overwhelming grind of travel in the East. Every winter a motley tribe of yoga freaks, hash-heads and art smugglers would gather, until the growing heat and the threat of the summer monsoon pushed them further on. Goa was like going home for the holidays, and the freaks celebrated: Christmas, New Year's, and especially full moons.

I asked one grey-haired French Canadian freak about these backwater bacchanals. He hadn't been in Goa since the '70s, but was passing through after returning his dead Tibetan lama's ashes to Dharamsala. "They were very free" he said, raising a lascivious eyebrow. Free enough to have the local Catholic nuns up in arms, scandalized by orgies and nudity and rumors of hippy waifs breast-feeding monkeys. Less than a decade after the Portuguese finally left Goa, the land had been invaded by Christian Europe's footloose pagan spawn.

By the time I arrived, underground Goa was well on its way towards becoming a bohemian Club Med nestled amidst rice patties and palm trees. As any Lonely Planet guidebook will tell you, Anjuna is one of Goa's last hippie holdouts, but most of Anjuna's available housing had been rented out by regulars months before. After hours of wandering along cool sandy paths, I found a two-dollar room: a mat on a stone floor, no windows, a bare bulb. Hunkered down next door was a crew of vacationing Indian men, drawn like many middle-class Indians to purview Goa's exotic (and frequently bare-chested) freak fauna. They sold Compaq computers to missile developers in Hyderabad, a full day's drive to the east. "We like the hippies! They're in their own world! Do you know where the party is?"

With its bucket shower, scorpions, and outhouse (not much more than a chute into a pig trough), my abode was hardly plush. But like the saddle sores you might get at a dude ranch, such rough edges keep the straight tourists at bay and add an adventurous texture to the delicious lethargy that Anjuna otherwise affords: free parties, great drugs, jumbo prawns, cold beer, cool bikes for rent.

Along with Xavier's restaurant, where the beatnik pioneer Eight-Finger Eddie sits every night like some ancient mariner, Anjuna's greatest tourist draw is its Wednesday flea market. What began decades earlier as a lazy venue for local vendors and destitute hippies has swollen into a glorious seaside mall. Wandering past acres of blankets and bangles, vests and singing bowls, spices and raw chunks of amber, I felt like some reincarnated Portuguese trader armed with American Express. The freaks have their own section, where travellers sell blank DAT tapes and Drum, Stussy tank-tops and original rave-ware. I wasn't surprised when an expatriate American fashion photographer told me that some of the East's traveling technofreak designers made up to a 1000 dollars a day on the streets of Tokyo, money they just poured back into their nomadic drift.

Goa is only one stop on the hippy trail that three decades of drop-outs, drug lovers and mystical travellers have carved into the East. But Goa is perhaps the only boho roost where techno is as ubiquitous as faded blue jeans. The electronic beats seep out of half the houses and all the cafes, morning, noon and night. In three weeks' time, I heard Pink Floyd once. I did not see one acoustic guitar.

For a certain underground breed of DJ, Goa is an esoteric Mecca, and they flock from every corner of the globe—New Zealand, Japan, Israel, Italy, France. Established music-makers arrive with their fall crop of trance tracks for exchange and tasting, while rising stars train like athletes and perform as much for their fellow DJs as the crowd. The Orb's Alex Patterson has passed through, the famed London remixer Youth is a regular, and Sven Väth—Frankfurt's techno Kaiser—fell in love with the place.

I run into Väth at the Shore Bar, an open-air seaside cafe with the ambience of Amsterdam-by-the-beach. It's dusk, and the sun slips like a swollen egg into the Arabian Sea as fishing trawlers crawl along the horizon. With his pale bald dome, soul patch and slightly devilish eyes, Väth looks like a techno Mephisto. As an acid jazz take of "I'm In With the In Crowd" bubbles in the background, Väth tells me how surprised he was with Goa's hip musical edge when he first visited a few years ago. "One of the first Goa DJs, Laurent, came up and said how much they liked my early, 16-bit recordings. Hardly anybody knows those records!"

Väth's been back to India every year since. On his previous visit, he recorded DAT samples that showed up on *Accident in Paradise,* whose strongest cuts are now in regular rotation. "The Goa sound is a very special deep trance," Väth says. "It's a serious thing. These people are not kids, this music is a part of their lives. Now when I produce or DJ in Frankfurt, I try to give the people there this kind of feeling. In India I fill my energy, and in Europe I put it out." This year, Väth lugged 150 kilos of turntables and vinyl into India just so he could make a real Goa party.

DJs are the maestros of the information age, and not just because the discs they spin are largely electronic creations. Freed from the gravity of faces and fixed names, underground dance music finds its essence in constant mutation and total overproduction. Sifting through hundreds of records a week, DJs define themselves in part by what they comb out of the data overload. That's why many act like spies, taping over record labels, or buying all available copies of a favorite record. DJs are made of information. But in Goa, where the inability to mix makes selection particularly important, they tend to drop their guard and swap tapes.

A few of those tapes are brewed locally. Johan is a young German producer who looks like Anthony Kiedis with a brain. He lives in a huge house in a small inland village, his room containing little more than a bed, a batik print and his gear: Macintosh PowerBook, Akai sampler, keyboard, DAT deck. I'd heard two of Johan's intense tracks on the Dragonfly label's *Project II Trance* (under the name Mandra Gora), which along with Juno Reactor's *Transmissions* and the *Ethnotechno* and *Concept in Dance* compilations, is the best stateside introduction to Goan trance. But Johan doesn't like to DJ—he's one of those hardcore power dancers who treat the night as one long track. "With a combination of good music, a good spot and good dancing, it's like a cosmic trigger goes off," he says of Goa's greatest rites. After a night of such cosmic gyration, Johan would return to his studio, download his vibes, dump the bytes onto DAT, and pass the tape onto his DJ friends. "It was like a perfect feedback loop."

When Johan first arrived in Goa six years ago, the techno-trance scene was totally off the map. Synchronicities abounded. "It was like a poker game no one could follow." But these days he's starting to sell his stuff in the West, and though he plans on setting up a large Goa studio as soon as he can figure out the right bureaucrat to bribe, he's pessimistic about the future of the East's nomadic underground. "Soon we'll have a global digital network where everyone will know where everybody is all the time." He looks me in the eye as only a German can. "What you're here to write about is already dead and gone."

Väth and Johan are friendly enough guys, but many Shore Bar insiders set themselves apart from the rave tourists (and journalists) with the same kind of snobbery you find in London or New York. Given the mystical legacy of freak India, the cliques here have a mystical air, like they're pushing the envelope of consciousness right before your eyes. As Raja Ram, an old moustached prog rocker-cum-techno musician, told me, "You have to become a neuronaut to understand this music. We've gone from flint-rock to the moon landing in a few thousand years, and now we're on the edge of the world opened up with information machines. This is a new inner space we're exploring."

One of these inner astronauts is Ollie Wisdom, whose Bamboo Forest party was the best of the season. Ollie's one of Goa's rising stars, an ex-Goth from a circus family who learned the DJ ropes on the Thai island of Koh Pha Ngan. I had decided not to artificially stimulate myself for his party, so I crawled into bed, setting the alarm for 5 a.m. But the Bamboo Forest was only a few hundred yards away, and the bass beats warped my dreams. Two glowing Tibetan eyes appeared before me in the dark room, and led me up a moonlit mountain path to an old, white-bearded yogi. He said that reality was like a television set, and then he showed me how to surf the channels. I zapped between technicolor twilight zones until an immense metaphysical boredom set in. "Techno is the sound of the universe being created and destroyed every second," he said.

I woke up woozy as hell, but dragged myself out of bed and headed down the jungle path, past cool, dark trees and rows of Enfield bikes and mopeds. Rounding a large banyan tree, I found a Mad Hatter's acid test of a party: banners of Shiva and blaxploitation hussies hung in the breeze; patches of bamboo coated with a rainbow swath of luminescent paint glowed in the black light; a phallic purple pillar stood in the center of the dance floor, crowned with a pumpkin-sized quartz crystal. As hardcore techno pounded, someone set a large wooden pentagram on fire, and in the witchy light I could see a large pyramid lashed together with bamboo in the distance. From inside, Ollie lorded over the crowd, decked out in shiny silver pants and Jetsons shades. He rolled his hips, flipped through DATs, pressed buttons like one of Raja Ram's neuromancers.

When Ollie's final cut faded around 11 a.m., I picked my way through the iridescent bushes and approached him with notebook in hand. Bad move. He was sitting in a circle outside the DJ hut, sharing a smoke with a man whose short hair was twisted up into two chartreuse Martian devil-horns. I asked if I could set up an interview. He and his friends turned on me with maniacal disgust, like I was a Mormon covered with dogshit. "Nooooo! Go away!"

One DJ I did manage to nail down was Gil, the dread-headed Kris Kringle who spun at the hilltop party. When he DJs in San Francisco and other Western cities during the summer monsoon, he's known as Goa Gil—only one of the items that makes Gil less than well-loved by today's younger DJs. Gil lives in a spacious brick house behind the

Orange Boom restaurant and alongside a pile of rubble he calls a temple. "Come in, come in," he barks before I even introduce myself. A large collage of rave flyers, psychedelic posters and photos of Hindu holy men covers one wall.

Just as I start to get comfortable, Gil's pretty young French wife Ariane—herself the child of Goan freaks—begins interrogating me. "Why are you writing an article for? You're going to spoil everything." She complains about a piece in *i-D* magazine that resulted in floods of Brits. "Now we get the Americans and all the hip-hoppers coming," she whined. I assure her that the hip-hoppers have better things to do. She grabs her sunglasses, and storms off to the beach.

But Gil knows he has a story to tell, so he tells it. Growing up in Marin County in the '60s, Gil took the bus down to the Haight after school. He fell in with Family Dog, the loose freak collective that sparked the psychedelic concert scene before Bill Graham moved in with dollar signs in his eyes. In 1969, fed up with "rip-offs and junkies and speed freaks," Gil bought a one-way ticket to Amsterdam. He then made his way overland to India, where, among other things, he discovered the sadhus.

Hymns in the ancient Vedas describe these wandering holy men as long-haired sages who lived off the forest, covering themselves with ash and drinking the elixir of the gods. Today, some of India's hundreds of thousands of sadhus are strict ascetics, some are simply beggars, and some resemble Hindu Rastafarians. These impressive, bloodshot souls wander about, wearing their hair in long dreads and finding spiritual sustenance in charas, India's yummy mountain hash. Before they smoke the clay pipes called chillum, the sadhus cry out "Bum Shiva!" the way Rastas bark "Jah!"

Not surprisingly, the freaks took to the sadhus. Gil went whole hog, living in caves, wearing orange robes, and coaxing the Kundalini up his spine. But he still found his way to Goa's firelit drum circles every winter. Despite persistent false rumors that the Who or the Stones or the Beatles left their gear on the sands of Calangute, the source of Goa's music machines was a fellow named Alan Zion, who smuggled in a

Fender PA and two tape decks overland.

According to Gil, these parties are the direct ancestors of raves. Techno historians already know that English working-class kids brought raves back from Ibiza, the cheap vacation island off of Spain whose weather, slack and lack of extradition treaties made it a Goa-style hippy colony decades ago. While many DJs shuttled between Ibizan summers and Goan winters, some claim that the more authentic lineage of electronic ecstasy belonged to the East. As Genesis P. Orridge put it, "The music from Ibiza was more horny disco, while Goa was more psychedelic and tribal. In Goa, the music was the facilitator of devotional experience. It was just functional, just to make that other state happen."

And Goa went totally electronic in 1983, when two French DJs named Fred and Laurent got sick of rock music and reggae. At the same time Derrick May and Juan Atkins created the futuristic disco-funk called "techno," Fred and Laurent used far more primitive tech—two cassette decks—to create a schizo's brew out of New Wave, electronic rock, gay Eurodisco and experimental industrial bands like Cabaret Voltaire and the Residents. They slipped electro-pop like New Order and Blanc Mange into the mix, but only after cutting out all the vocals. It was heady shit, and soon hipsters started slipping them underground tapes from the West.

Gil and his friend Swiss Ruedi quickly joined in, but the techno transition was not smooth. The freaks were attached to their Bob Marley, their Santana, their Stones. Ruedi had to enlist a bodyguard to ward off a rock fan's blows.

"How can you listen to the same music for fifteen years?" Gil now booms. "I used to love the Dead when I was growing up, but I can't listen to that stuff anymore. It sounds like cowboy music." Gil thinks that music is always flowering, but that the juice moves through different genres, always one step ahead of the record companies. "Now it's in techno. Music has gone through a complete cycle. It started in ancient times with tribal drumming, and now it's come back to tribal trance techno. Where do you go from there?"

Gil starts pacing about, wildly gesticulating. "I'm basically just using this whole party situation as a medium to do magic, to remake the tribal pagan ritual for the twenty-first century. It's not just a disco under the coconut trees." He pauses to light up a Dunhill. "It's an initiation."

Gil slaps on two remixes he made while visiting San Francisco. The band is Kode IV, a German duo who brag about producing tracks in five minutes and which Gil was to join later in the year after one of the members died. He blasts the tunes, and towers over me as he identifies the samples: a sadhu's "Bum!", the Pope, Aleister Crowley. Then he plays the "Anjuna" remix of the cut "Accelerate," towering over me as he repeats word for word a long sample cribbed from some flying saucer movie: "'People of the earth, attention,'" he booms over the beat. I'm deeply stoned by this point, and his eyes bore into mine, and for a moment I feel like he's channeling the message to me directly from the aliens, like I'm finally getting the key. "'This is a voice speaking to you from thousands of miles beyond your planet. This could be the beginning of the end of the human race.'"

Ariane walks in, breaks the spell and bad-vibes me out of the house. Gil follows me outside, trying to explain the reasons for her underground protectionism: the rising pollution, the clueless young DJs, the sharp rise in prices. Gil shakes his head. "We came here so long ago, to the end of a dirt road and a deserted beach. It was like the end of the world. And now the whole world is at our doorstep. The communications lines are open. Where do we go from here?"

If Gil had listened a little harder to the music he loves to spin, he would have seen it all coming, because techno is the sound of one world shrinking. The media tsunami that gave backwater hippies like him DAT players and computerized music has also brought fax machines and MTV and journalists to their hideaway. Gil's stuck in the paradox of the technofreak: you can't drop out and plug in at the same time. The underground is now networked, and you can't escape the feedback loop for long. You might even call it karma.

British club kids can now fly straight to Goa for around 500 bucks, and many arrive with nothing more than cash in their pockets, suitcases stuffed with party clothes and a desire to get "off their face." They care nothing for India, its art or music or deep spirituality. What had been a magical release valve for expatriates intoxicated by the East has become a thing in itself. "These new people have no idea," one silver-haired French sarod player who first came to Goa in the early '70s told me. "They didn't come overland, they didn't have to find their own food, and they never really got lost."

Most of Asia's hardcore gypsy freaks don't come this way anymore. They've drifted far south, to primitive spots not listed in the Lonely Planet guidebook. At the same time, Goa's state and local government have begun maneuvering for tonier tourists and five-star hotels, even though many locals prefer to get their rupees straight from the relatively noninvasive freaks. As the cops crack down on drugs and parties, Goa's underground is caving in. All this scene really needs is great weather, weak currency and a degree of invisibility (or permeable law enforcement). Goa-style parties have already popped up in Bali, Thailand, Australia and the valleys of the Himalaya. But as the grid invades Anjuna, one of the last pockets of freakdom's mystical and stridently non-commercial trance-dance culture may fade away like the moon at dawn.

I decided to hunt down Laurent, the French DJ who had pioneered the electronic parties back in '83 and had alternately been described to me as a burn-out and a genius. Gil hadn't been too encouraging. "He probably won't talk to you. He's very mysterious." But he told me where Laurent could be found every day: in the last chai shop on Little Vagator, playing backgammon.

So I puttered my unhip little TVS moped towards the cliffs overlooking the lush coves of Vagator beach. I clamored down bluffs packed with coconut trees and tall hippy teepees, marveling that the temporary shelters of the nomads the Europeans called "Indians" were now housing European nomads in India. Down on the sand, a scruffy Rajasthani man was giving camel rides to blond kids with names like Shakti, while their bronzed parents played paddle-ball or soaked up the rays. Packs of young fully clad Indian men strolled by, middle-class guys from Bombay who piled on Goan tour buses for the sole purpose of glimpsing European tit. I watched their sheepish, furtive eyes; I watched the sun-bathing tourists pretending they hadn't themselves become a tourist attraction.

The last chai shop on the beach was a grimy hut filled with folks who looked as weather-beaten as the long wooden tables they hunched over. Some played backgammon, others sipped orange juice and chai, and everyone smoked like the Amazon. A sour-faced Indian girl serving up a bowl of porridge and honey pointed to Laurent: a scrawny guy in a Japanese print T-shirt, tossing a pair of dice. Gaunt and bloodshot, his teeth stained and bent, the man looked like a hungry ghost.

Laurent gave a caustic laugh when I asked to interview him. While we talked, he kept slapping the tiles with his partner, a balding, middle-aged Brit named Lenny. "Art does not pay so I am forced to gamble," he explained in a throaty Parisian accent thick with sarcasm. He fiddled with my Sony mini-tape recorder, clearly bent on soaking this little episode for all the humor it was worth.

"The spy in the chai shop," mused Lenny as he drew heavily on a cigarette. Laurent cracked up, his laugh quickly degenerating into an asthmatic coughing fit.

"You know, it used to be very bad here for spies," Laurent said, with a cocked eyebrow indicating mocking concern. I couldn't tell, but it seemed like he was referring to two journalists who had been slipped heavy knock-out drugs some years before.

Despite his heavy sarcasm, creepy laughs, and constant hints that he'd tell me more if I gave him a lot of money, I took a liking to Laurent. He reasserted Goa's contribution to rave culture—"This is the source of the source"—but he was low-key about it all. No mysticism, no nostalgia. He gave his friend Fred the credit for first mixing electronic tapes at the parties, but said his friend's style was too bizarre for the crowds. "Nobody liked it. Then I played and made it so people liked it. And now people like it all over the world."

Laurent paused, and looked me in the eye. "Here you make parties for very heavy tripping people who have been travelling all over the place. You have to take drugs to understand the scene here, what people are thinking."

Some pals walked over, and Laurent began to carry on three conversations in three different languages. Meanwhile, the game with Lenny came to a head, and Laurent was losing. He stood up, rolling the dice with macabre drama.

I was getting frustrated. Could this sarcastic wraith gambling for pennies in a burned-out shack be the father of raves? One tale I heard had it that Laurent got his start DJing because he had been an unrepentant leach. Figuring to put him to good use, someone handed him a tape deck and said "Make party music." And the same source said that Laurent was the most brilliant DJ he'd ever heard, doing things with cassette tapes that blew away most vinyl-spinning DJs in the West.

Laurent let slip that he still had some of his early party tapes, and I pressed to hear them. "Ah, this would be very, very expensive," he said, curling his lip. "We must draw up a contract." Then he turned away from me and racked up another game.

One hazy, hot afternoon, I was hanging around the Speedy Travel agency waiting for a fax. A steady stream of freaks bought tickets for Hampi. "It is a very ancient place," a bronzed Dutchman rolling a Drum told me, describing what sounded like a Hindu Stonehenge 300 kilometers to the east. "I hear some German with a bus will throw a full moon party in the temple there."

A week or so later, a creaking local bus spits me out at Hampi Bazaar. I'm worn to the bone. The dusty main street is lined with trinket shops, cheap restaurants, and packs of sad-eyed kids with their outstretched hands and mantras of "Rupee! Pen! Chocolate!" At the end of the bazaar stands a massive 160-foot gopuram, a gaudy pyramid with the melted curves of a drip sand-castle.

Hampi is not an "ancient" place—the Hindu city fell to rampaging Moslems during Queen Elizabeth's reign. But the ruins that spread out for miles around the small, freak-filled village exude a haunting, archaic calm. Green parakeets roost in silent temples encrusted with jesters and monkey gods. Rice paddies line the nearby Tunghabhadra river, which snakes past huge mounds of desert boulders. Across the river, a number of sadhus tend Shiva shrines and pass the pipe with hearty Caucasians who have turned their backs on the minimal comforts of the village and gone totally caveman.

Hampi is far mellower than Anjuna. I waste away my afternoons flopped out on the shaded mats at the Mango Tree, a peaceful outdoor cafe on the banks of the lazy river. The cafe's mandatory "Smoking Psychotropic Drugs Not Allowed" sign is cloaked by a poster, so all you can see is the word "Smoking." Sometimes the white sadhus from across the river show up, with their orange robes and mala beads and fading biker tattoos. A few days before the full moon, a noticeably trendier crowd moves into town: nattier threads, better cheekbones. Rooms fill to capacity, kids sleep on roofs or in temples. Finally a huge tour bus drives up and parks in the dusty bazaar. Slogans blaze across the side: Techno Tourgon, LSD 25, Shiva Space Age Technology. Jörg the DJ has arrived.

When I finally catch up with Jörg, it's the day of the full moon. "Come in, come in," he says as I climb onboard. The BBC has just finished interviewing him, and the man is beaming, his blue eyes glowing with an intense lucidity. A huge dancing Shiva statue dominates the dashboard, and Jörg's taut naked belly is tattooed with an image of the Shaivite yogi Shankar.

Jörg is pure freak, too maniacally enthusiastic to cop a snobbish DJ attitude. "I used to be a typical heavy-metal rock'n'roller. Now I am addicted to techno," he says in his heavy German accent. "For five years' time now I listen to nothing else. Except meditation songs in the morning."

Like many technofreaks, Jörg's first Goa party was nothing less than a conversion experience. "You can laugh, but it was like seeing a keyhole to God," he says in a hoarse voice. He's been back and forth to India ever since, selling land cruiser parts at the Chinese border, DJing parties around Kathmandu, dipping in the Ganges with the sadhus at the holy city of Haridwar. The last time he made the overland trip from the West, he was cruising through Iran in the middle of the night, trance blasting, multi-colored lights flashing along the side of his Techno Tourgon. The police pulled him over. He stepped out the door, wearing a pair of goggles ringed with blinking lights. They trained machine guns on him.

It dawns on me that Jörg is in some fundamental sense insane. But like a reincarnated Neil Cassady, he rides his lunacy the way he guides his bus along India's suicidal roads—with spontaneous grace.

"I'm a little bit extremist," he admits, grabbing a cigarette from a pack lying next to a crumpled photo of Bhagwan Shree Rajneesh. The previous year, after a month in Goa packed with drugs and dancing, and with hardly any DJing experience, Jörg set up his gear in Hampi's underground Shiva temple and threw the archaeological area's first rave. "After that party I feel like this big hole. I sat for another month under a tree. Nothing inside anymore." He fiddles with the 5-inch Sony mini-discs he uses instead of DATs. "But believe me, to be empty and open to everything is exactly the right position when you come to India. You have to improvise."

And today, just hours before moonrise, Jörg's still improvising. After spending days finding the right official to bribe in order to throw a party, he made his case. "We talked for hours. We got to know each other very well. Then he said no."

So in the fading sunlight, Jörg decides to cross the river into another district. He and his crew lug their gear down the river's edge, and load the equipment into the same round, leather-covered basket boats the Portuguese explorer Paes noted when he passed through Hampi in the sixteenth century. Darkness descends upon them, and they have no idea where they're going.

Hours later, hundreds of us ferry across the river in the same leaky boats. We thread our way past crumbling walls and along paths lined with ominous palms, following a trail of lanterns a mile or so onto a treeless plateau of moony rock. We glimpse black lights in the distance, hear the dull thud of techno. No chai ladies tonight. We're partying in Bedrock.

Jörg crouches over his machines beside a large boulder dry-painted with the appropriate symbols for the night: peace, OM, anarchy. Though his music was old, his mixing rough and his generator tepid, Jörg soon sinks the dancers into the groove. I start taking snapshots. Unlike Goa, where blissed-out hippies can transform into ferocious assholes at the sight of a camera, nobody seems to care. An Indian sadhu passes through the crowd, talking with a grizzled Italian in orange robes who occasionally whipped out a conch shell and blew. Who is the holy man? I wonder. Who is the pothead?

After a bug-eyed Jörg leads us careening through an eon's worth of cartoon wormholes, dawn finally arrives, dusting the rocks with pale purples and rusty reds. Fairy-tale temples emerge in the distant mist, but it's no hallucination. Jörg climbs up on a rock and pumps his fist, exhorting us into a supreme embrace of the moment. It is nighttime, daytime, alltime, and as the rising sun and the setting moon touch the horizons on either side of us, the heavenly bodies perfectly balance the land on which we dance. Like great sex, great parties move the earth.

I climb up some huge boulders to get a view of the high and wholly bizarre scene. A young Japanese man with a bandana sits smoking atop a slightly unsteady rock. "Go slow," he softly warns as I sit down gingerly on the rock face. "Go natural." Abé lives in Tokyo, but doesn't like it much. "People forget nature-mind," he says, gesturing above to the morning's crystal blue dome.

Then it hits me. There's nothing "natural" about the sounds echoing off the rocks. These melodies and beats are created, recorded, and reproduced in the digital ether of electronic circuitry. Techno's frenetic data-dense intensity seems totally contrary to Abé's air of bodhisattva calm. "So do you really like this music?" I ask him.

"Yes," he says, tapping a hollowed-out coconut mixing bowl hanging from his neck. "I like primitive sounds."

And that's the paradox of the techno-freak. As we hurtle into the twenty-first century, these transient refugees from the First World have poached the info tech that's speeding up the march of progress and made an abrupt about-face towards the archaic. Technology is mobile, so they drag it to the rocks and jungles. Technology loves connection, so they sync it with the ancient wheel of the heavens. Technology simulates, so they make it mimic the fear and splendor of shamanic trance. The Goan beaches that spawned this ecstatic digital primitivism may be lost to media hype and packaged tours, but the hardcore technofreaks will just lose themselves in the porous Third World landscape. After all, the full moon follows you everywhere you go.

1994

CAMEO DEMONS

The Sun City Girls

Alan and Rick Bishop are two halfbreed desert rats on the cusp of middle age who live in Seattle and make music, when they do, in a trio called Sun City Girls. Rick's on guitar, Alan plays bass and sings, but the brothers play with lots of other things as well: double-reed pipes, gamelan, puppets, language, demons, audience expectations, states of consciousness. The third Girl is named Charlie Gocher, and he's a scraggy Californian transplant the Bishop boys first met in the open-mic scene in Phoenix over twenty years ago. Gocher plays drums—open, slippery, consternating drums—and he writes and occasionally lets loose some mighty ornery post-Beat rants.

The Bishop brothers are addicted to third world travel, and have been so since they first hit the Moroccan hinterlands in 1984. Gocher joined a Bishop expedition only once, during a 1989 trip through Indonesia. One night in Yogyakarta, a seaside city on the coast of Java, the trio stumbled into an itinerant Kuda Kepang group, a family troupe that entertained the crowds with a ferocious, gamelan-fueled mixture of magic tricks, hobby-horse theater, and glass-eating, fire-breathing performance trance. Whenever tourists stopped, the leader cracked a bullwhip next to their heads and scared them off.

The Girls, characteristically, held their ground. Years before, when they first hit the stage with their peculiar mix of sardonic rock, outsider improv, and hippie mysteriosa, they could only get gigs at punk shows, and the crowds responded to their baffling sets and bizarre costumes with anger and violence. The band came to aggressively taunt these people, dishing out verbal abuse, sarcastic musical moves, and the occasional cup of urine. Guys like that can certainly deal with a stingless lash from a Javanese heavy. They could even see where the dude was coming from.

So every night the three young men would wait for what they called "the call of the wild": the distant madcap clang-clang-clang-clang that would lead them through the crowded city to the Kuda Kepang crew. After two weeks of this, they had almost become part of the family, with Charlie banging out percussion as Alan fed lightbulbs to the kids, their mouths a repulsive mass of lacerations and kerosene burns. You could say a sort of transmission occurred. Alan describes it simply as "the best show ever."

A month and half later, the Girls were on a boat, heading through the Strait of Malacca on their way to the Sumatran city of Medan. With nothing better to do, the trio asked the boat's lounge act to hand over their electric instruments for a set. The band ripped through what one might call a "typical" Sun City Girls set: "House of the Rising Sun," "Esta Susan En Casa?" from *Horse Cock Phepner*, and a sun-baked skronk-jam peppered with abrupt stops and starts. The Indonesian audience clapped at the beginning of every song, and then clapped again at the end. Like nearly all Girls performances, this one was recorded, and Rick reports that at one point on the tape you can hear a patron lean over to his companion and proclaim: "Ah, this is American jazz!"

Purists might have trouble with this description, although SCG are more than capable of pounding out Duke Ellington and Paul Bley tunes. But if jazz means a deep commitment to improvisation, and if improvisation means having the guts to force the hand of chance, then Sun City Girls are most certainly jazz.

They are most certainly not purists. Sun City Girls traffic with bizarre miscegenations, self-indulgent trash, and hardcore mystic exotica. Their sometimes garish album covers attack the eye with devils, yonis, sacred transvestites, and nubile native jailbait. Lyrics, song, and album titles—"Naga Smoke Signals," "The Genghis Necro-Nama-Khan," *330,003 Crossdressers from Beyond the Rig Veda*—can sound like the spontaneous verse of young *poètes maudits* tanked up on *National Geographic* cheesecake and *A Pictorial History of Magic and the Supernatural*. This lurid romance with the Other fuels some of their most incandescent sounds as well, a music of transport that explores Middle Eastern, Southeast Asian, and South American atmospheres with a passion composed equally of informed pleasure and the heedless appropriation of the strange. Looking high and low, far and wide, the Sun City Girls have sought the wellsprings of the weird, of what H.P. Lovecraft called *outsideness*, and when they have found them, they have taken what they wanted. On that boat in Indonesia, they got to give some of it back.

Sun City Girls released the first of their countless recordings in 1984, and since that time they have become probably the most prodigious, uncompromising and caustically esoteric band in the American post-punk underground. Musical chameleons, they have performed tantric space jams, out jazz, riff rock, Sumatran pop covers, spaghetti-western soundtracks, and haunted folk songs worthy of Harry Smith. But they started out simply jamming, back in that trailer park in Tempe, Arizona, their three instruments creating a whirlwind of noise that Alan compares to a nuclear explosion.

"It was like we discovered this switch," he says. "Without really playing together very long we were listening and improvising and hitting synchronicities that we didn't even think were possible. Within a twenty minute piece, we were stopping on dimes, not even looking at each other, fifteen times. Rick and I would hit eight or nine straight notes, the exact same notes, with Charlie accenting them. How the fuck is that done?"

According to *Forced Exposure*'s Byron Coley, Sun City Girls were "the first truly crazy band to emerge from the shards of hardcore. At first they seemed almost like a goofus prank being played by post-core stoners, but by the time that *Torch of the Mystics* was released, they were absolutely amazing and obviously pure of heart." When Majora released *Torch* in 1990, Coley helped spread the news, and the album's astral cabaret of voodoo folk jams and dark ethno-psychedelic rites remains the band's most celebrated release. According to Coley, Sun City Girls laid the foundation for today's new American sub-underground. "Without these french-fried, grass-skirted motherfuckers it would all sound like Merzbow."

Sun City Girls also became some of the most original performers in American rock. Simultaneously wanting to shock, amaze, and irritate, the Girls used the stage as a platform for snotty tricks and bravura experiments that tested both themselves and their audiences. One night they played nothing but an extended version of a single soul tune; another night they executed a perfect cover of Jodorowsky's *El Topo* soundtrack; and sometimes they just ditched their instruments altogether. Once, opening for fellow travelers Thinking Fellers Union Local 242 at San Francisco's Great American Music Hall, the trio donned cheap Radio Shack wireless mics, plopped down on the stage, and improv'd a group of hobos waiting for a train while a prerecorded fifty-minute tape of crickets ground toward the inevitable whistle moan. Their longtime sound engineer Scott Colburn came on and danced a tramp jig, while Gocher sprayed peach air freshener in the air and threw marshmallows around, ruining the carpet.

"That's classic Sun City Girls," says Colburn. "You get what you get."

With their monster touring days behind them, a Sun City Girls gig is a rare affair that draws the converted. In November of 2003, I was lucky enough to catch an unadvertised all-acoustic show at the Rendezvous, a jewel box theater in Seattle's Belltown that looks like a padded cell for mad Napoleons. Their first gig in over a year, the Rendezvous show celebrated their twenty-first anniversary as a trio. It also served as a warm-up for an upcoming performance at the Java Jive, a tiki dive in Tacoma, Washington, that's shaped like a coffee cup and known for whore karaoke and the occasional strip show with live monkeys.

As the bird-like Gocher slipped behind his modest kit, a bearded and shade-wearing Rick began a snarly song about "the audience who's come here to dream." Alan passed through the crowd of hirsute and scruffy musos like an androgynous Uncle Fester, pouring from a bottle of Old Crow straight into people's mouths—a ritual I later learn he lifted from Burmese spirit mediums. Between covers of "Midnight at the Oasis" and "Heart Full of Soul," the trio played some of the misanthropic folk tunes Alan has recorded for his Alvarius B solo project, and which make him as proud as anything he's done. Perhaps for my benefit, they play a game-show spin-off of *The Wire*'s "Invisible Jukebox," with Rick plunking out songs on a ukulele-toned kid's guitar, as Alan handed out mint-condition LPs—23 Skidoo, Duke Ellington, *The 50 Guitars of Tommy Garrett*—to whoever could name the tune.

Inevitably, perhaps, the mysterious Sun City Girls "X Factor" struck. During one of Gocher's cubist drum rambles, a thick and tipsy nouveau jock walked into the theater, clad in a sweatshirt, Yankees cap, and nu-metal facial scruff. Booker, as we subsequently learned this apparition was called, had no idea what was going on, but he nonetheless clambered onstage and demanded that Gocher kick up some funkier beats. In response, the drummer brought his brushes down to a whisper. Booker kept at it and Charlie grew cranky: "I do what I want to do. Not what I'm told." Charlie then stood up and told Booker to take over on drums, but the fellow turned to the audience instead and started beat-boxing. Charlie and some audience members led the suburban B-boy offstage as Alan started pulling spastic jujitsu moves around this ghost of their punk-rock past. As Alan said later, "We must have conjured him up."

The Sun City Girls' inner sanctum takes up one half of a former theater on a low-rent commercial strip in Seattle's Ballard district. Their entrance room is filled with slacker shrines and towering shelves of LPs carefully filed away in crisp plastic sleeves. Alan's office is off to the side, and further on is the huge blue room that serves as the main rehearsal/hangout space. Here American Spirits are endlessly smoked. From the walls hang a collection of curious stringed instruments:

banjos, mandolins, a Burmese harp, a Russian balalaika, a thrift store score called an Orie Tone. A Kali poster is slapped onto the side of an upright piano that belongs in a saloon, with Holst's score for "Dance of the Demon" displayed on a nearby music stand. On the floor lies the crumbling gamelan orchestra that a Javanese puppet troop dragged around Indonesia for twenty-seven years before Alan got it at a Folklife Festival auction. A red devil mask leers from above.

I am barely over the threshold of this strange place when I catch the title of a burned CD-R sitting on Alan's desk: *Broken Hearted Dragonflies*. The man immediately starts telling me about these fat Burmese insects whose chests routinely explode. Alan's wife, who is Burmese and "from another planet," says they are called broken-hearted dragonflies, and Alan has written the phrase onto a friend's recording of Thai insect squalls whose intense electronic tones, I soon learn, vibrate with an almost nauseating menace. "Maybe I'll put it out," Alan says, as he finally turns the volume down. "But I probably couldn't move more than 500 copies."

Alan wears a backwards baseball cap tugged tightly over a close-cropped skull that accentuates his thin elfish ears. He is hefty and slightly wall-eyed, and has the somewhat disconcerting habit of not always looking at you as he speaks. He's not the cagey hipster I expected. With his amusing, smart-ass patter, he comes off like a friendly hustler who wants to sell you an eighteenth-century *kilim* or tell you where the best ping-pong shows in Bangkok can be found. I'm not surprised to learn that for twelve years, Alan worked for one of the largest ticket brokers in the world, a business he compares to *The Sopranos* without the violence.

Alan's restless energy and immense drive lies behind the manic productivity of the Sun City Girls, who have left a huge and serpentine trail of recordings in their wake. Scott Colburn's online discography lists fifty full-length releases, and Alan estimates that only a couple of hundred people have heard more than half of their hydra-headed catalog. And they like it this way. In the early '90s, when stalwart '80s outsiders like Sonic Youth or the Butthole Surfers were cashing in on the capital-infused expansion of indie rock, the Girls quit Majora, founded their own Abduction label, and continued releasing 1000-copy runs of LPs and CDs that went out of print more or less quickly and more or less stayed that way. Believe me, you don't need to collect them all. And you couldn't do it if you tried.

"We have the luxury of a huge backlog of recordings," explains Alan, who is an obsessive archivist. "Why press 5000 copies of one record and sit on 3500 when you can run five different projects that sell out? It's just basic business. Don't put your money into boxes in the closet." This strategy has certainly led to lots of self-indulgent crap, but the Girls' hyperactive catalog is of a piece with the band's overarching improvisatory ethos. "We make hard decisions and we make 'em quickly and we move on," says Alan. "The downside of that approach is that there is too much for people to digest. The upside is that it's fearless. We don't sit around and analyze the fact that we're releasing this or that. So we leave a few diamonds by the roadside and we leave a few heaps of pterodactyl shit as well. Its like a big wagon with sparklers and fireworks going off with a trail of dust behind it."

Alan's gig as a legal ticket scalper helped the Girls maintain the curiously profane purity of their sub-commercial style. "It was never our intention to ever make much money as a band, even from day one," he says. "We made a pact: If we ever wind up on MTV we gotta shoot ourselves." But in the summer of 2003, Alan quit his day job to devote himself full-time to SCG and related projects. "I work every day," he says. "I'm relentless. I want to do as much as I can in five or ten years before I get fed up with the bullshit that this society puts out and relocate to a place that's less predictable and ridiculous."

There is plenty on his plate the day I visit. Hisham Mayet, a friend and cohort who goes by the handle Frank Sumatra, has just gotten back from Libya with 12 hours of footage taken at the Ghadames music festival. Mayet also snagged a box of North African 45s from his family's basement in Tripoli, and these discs need to be combed through, the nuggets burned onto CD-R and added to the archive, where they may become fodder for a future Girls tune or a release on their new label,

Sublime Frequencies, which is devoted to releasing CDs and DVDs of unusual international music and culture. The first batch of releases includes three CDs of music captured during the band's 1989 visit to Indonesia: *Radio Java* is a surreal fever dream of spliced commercial broadcasts; *Night Recordings from Bali* features field recordings of raw and giddy village gamelan; and *Folk and Pop Sounds of Sumatra Vol. 1* culls the choicest cuts from their collection of sometimes nameless street-side cassettes, and which includes at least one tune that the Girls have covered, with more passion, as a single. The jewel in the batch is *Nat Pwe: Burma's Festival of Spirit Soul,* an hour and a half DVD devoted to Burma's nats: godlike spirits of the dead who take possession of transvestite mediums, consume liquor and cigarettes, demand fistfuls of cash, and grant boons.

The Bishop brothers hope that Sublime Frequencies will fill a gap in what Alan calls "international recordings," presenting unusual documents with a passionate informality rather that the clinical dissections of Smithsonian/Folkways or the high-tech fetish of lots of world fusions. "It doesn't have to be funded," says Alan. "You don't have to go to school to learn how to record or to learn how to interpret a foreign culture or bring it back and spin it for someone. You don't need to have five hundred microphones, you don't need to gather up these people for recording sessions and pay them a thousand dollars a piece. As far as I'm concerned, its open season, and you record what you want to record."

"It's disappearing too," adds Rick. "It's good to get it while you can."

By the standards of multicultural propriety that shape the discourse of "world music," the Sun City Girls are, well, rather crude. *Folk and Pop Sounds of Sumatra Vol. 1,* for example, offers only vague credits and no compensation to the original artists. Alan insists he tried to track down the publishers, to no avail, and he adds there is no money in it anyway. "When it starts selling like fucking Outkast I'll fly to Medan and start handing out Benjamins to anyone who looks like these guys."

More disturbing is the absence of the prose and packaging that usually mediate international recordings. The *Nat Pwe* DVD comes with a short bibliography and some brief explanation, but the film itself offers no informative voice-over. Combined with some very long takes, the lack of an anthropological filter is uncomfortable, invoking the raw bafflement and delirious boredom that travelers taste when they find themselves confronting something beyond their ken. This confrontation is key to the Sun City Girls. Theirs is an ethnographic surrealism that stalks the marvelous, using the encounter with confounding and unusual human practices as a neuron-pumping portal into the outside. Their surrealism can be coarse, even prurient, and calls to mind the *Mondo Cane* world of international shockumentaries that were popular in the 1960s. Interspersed with the Nat Pwe footage, for example, Rick has included phantasmagoric clips of snake handlers, drunks, toothless kids, merry-go-round beasts, and lots of disarmingly cute girls. Occasionally the camera's gaze will rest on faces whose return stares suggest a smoldering hostility, a resentful recognition of recording's fundamental theft.

However "problematic," the Sun City Girls' relationship to third world music culture is an extension their own dark romanticism of travel. "We're always looking for the end of the line," Alan says. Most tourists seek otherness, of course. But in the words of Peter Lamborn Wilson, tourism deconstructs difference while true travelers experience it. Tourists (and many consumers of "world music") buy prefab images of the exotic, but travelers fall in love—or become entranced. Without a doubt, such enchantments run the risk of Orientalism. But there are many babies in that bath water. How many of us become armchair Orientalists when the headphones are on?

During one of our chats, Alan invited me to take a turn at the gamelan. I crouched down, and, fumbling about, asked him how to play it. "My philosophy is that there is no set way to play any instruments," he told me. "Obviously there's a sense of respect for how to play something like the gamelan. But to give in to that respect you don't do right by tradition. Tradition is not about slavish imitation. The last thing I want to see is a bunch of fucking white guys playing Javanese gamelan proper. It's disrespectful."

The term struck me as odd. Many people, after all, would consider the Girls' psychotronic appropriation of native instruments and non-Western languages distinctly disrespectful. So I asked him what he meant.

"They are being disrespectful because they are not evolving the situation. They are not rolling the dice. They are copying, just following somebody else's rules. That's not what you find in these situations." Instead, Sun City Girls risk insensitivity, political incorrectness, and crappy music to evolve the situation, and their punk disdain for multicultural pieties paradoxically allows them to extend the creative logic of folk appropriation. That's why you can't always tell the difference between the "ethnic" tunes they make up and the "ethnic" tunes they cover, and why Alan babbles in languages he does not understand, and why their version of the insidious "Lambada" meme of the late 1980s is without a doubt the most moving you will ever hear. Call it underground world music, or underworld music, a place of creative misunderstandings and mutual fascination.

And it is mutual. Before heading to Taungbyon to film the Nat Pwe last summer, Rick and Alan bought two eight-dollar guitars and entertained Burmese folks along the way. They improv'd plenty, but after being hounded for weeks, they finally broke down and learned to perform their most requested tune: "Hotel California." They knew that when it comes to the desires that inflame human music, you just can't kill the beast.

This matter of Orientalist appropriation is further complicated by the fact that the Bishop boys have the Orient within, coded into their DNA and the tenderest layers of their memory banks. Their grandfather was a Druze named Jamil Salman, and he left Lebanon as a kid to tap rubber in the Brazilian Amazon. After saving enough money, he returned to the Levant and brought his family to the States, where the boys' mother was born. Alan and Rick grew up in Michigan, which has one of the largest concentrations of Arabs in America, and Lebanese friends and family would often gather at Salman's house on the weekends to party. The boys remember slick small-time businessmen in funny suits hanging out in their grandfather's tapestry-lined basement, sucking on hookahs, consuming sweetmeats and coffee, and playing music into the night—pop songs and long instrumental jams. Salman was a master oud player, and also took turns on shroud fiddle, dumbek, and various double-reeded horns.

When Rick started playing guitar, he acted as any red-blooded Midwestern boy should and worshipped Jimmy Page, Richie Blackmore, and the almighty Nuge. But at a certain point he stopped aping and started just fucking around. An early cassette of solo acoustic stuff drips with metal, but there's no order or obvious structure to the riffs, and weird Middle Eastern melodies keep wafting through. "That's just from growing up with that stuff," he says. But even though these sounds bubbled up from his ethnic matrix, Rick still appreciates them as a mode of imaginal transport rather than personal identity. "Middle Eastern music is not caged in by having to have the guitar here, the drums there, the voice over there. Regardless of what notes you're playing, it's the overall feel of the music, the atmosphere, that's important. It puts you in, for lack of a better term, an exotic place."

For the Bishop brothers, the exotic is a kind of birthright, a point at once of origin and the obliteration of the ordinary self. Their grandfather's home dripped with mystery as well as music, an old world atmosphere of creepy wonder that helped spark the brothers' later fascination with the nether regions of spirit and the sacred forces that surround sex, death, and the utterly deranged. Salman was also a Freemason, and encouraged his grandsons to join a junior Mason's club called the Order of DeMolay. The elders would bring the boys into the temple, sit them down between pillars on a black-and-white checkerboard floor, and whisper things in their ears. "We didn't know what was going on," says Rick. "It wasn't until later that we found out who Jacques de Molay was, that he was head of the Knights Templar and burned at the stake for heresy. We went: Yah! We have a history again!"

For Rick, that toy initiation blossomed into a lifelong love affair with the occult. The Orientalist vibe of Masonry led him into Egyptology, and from there he moved into Crowley, sexual ritual, Haitian voodoo, tantra. "I don't claim any powers," he says with a grin. "I just keep reading, keep taking it in. I figure I'll remember it when I need it." Along the way, he also started collecting esoterica, and for years he has made a most modest income buying and selling items like Jacques Collin de Plancy's *Dictionnaire Infernal,* Michael Allen's *The Cult of Kumari: Virgin Worship in Nepal,* and the 1913 edition of Budge's *Book of the Dead.*

Rick is very much a younger brother. Though friendly, he is more reserved and pensive than Alan, and dresses in a surprisingly slobby manner that the wag behind the great *Blastitude* webzine compared to a high school basketball coach. What's going on inside is clearly what counts. There is a curious humility about him, as if he lives in the awareness that, as he said at one point, "if certain things didn't happen in the past, I could be working at Wal-Mart now and going to church on Sundays." Instead, he lives in a freak scholar bachelor pad above the band's rehearsal space. Django CDs are piled next to a collection of goofy ithyphallic monsters from Bali. A futon lies near a shrine filled with exotic personal power trinkets and bookshelves packed with esoterica. The front wall of his office is lined with tactical pilot maps of Assam, the northeastern Indian province that is his next travel destination. He wants to visit the Kamakhya temple in Guwahati, a Shakti hot spot where the yoni of Shiva's dismembered first wife was said to have fallen. He hears that tribal witches gather there, near a cunt-shaped cave that regularly "bleeds" rust-colored water.

Rick, you see, is a devotee of Kali, the black tantric goddess often pictured with a protruding tongue, a necklace of human heads, and the lingam of Shiva erect beneath her femme fatale thighs. Images and statues of Kali saturate his space. "She kinda lives here," he says, a little sheepishly. "The whole tantric thing interests me, not just the sexual symbolism but the graveyard symbolism. There's something about the gore of it all. I'm not into going out and hacking up people, but there's something about that imagery that's really powerful."

Rick got his best hit of that gore when he visited a Kali temple outside of Kathmandu. The priests chopped the heads off small goats, hugged the bodies like submachine guns, and directed the spurting blood onto the statues of the goddess. Soon the floor was covered with blood. "It smelled kinda good actually. In the corners where the blood would roll off there were all these marigolds that were blocking the drain and these dogs came up and licked up all the blood. These beautiful little five- or six-year-old girls in solid white just walked in the blood. Then they hauled the rest of the goat off to the family and they ate it. It's a whole family event."

Bishop reminds me that, to the people who know her, "our lady of the cremation ground" also serves as a compassionate mother goddess. But the eldritch dark still sets the dominant tone of Rick's spiritual universe. "I'm fascinated with the demonic," he says. "Demons get a bad rap, but they're real. That's the key. I believe that spirits and demons are real, in whatever abstract or physical sense you want to put it in. Nobody gets that much publicity if they're not real. Demons are everywhere. I think I've been a demon before. I bet you have too. I bet we're all demons."

Rick Bishop may have made his pacts with the beyond, but the question before us now is how such activity informs the music of the Sun City Girls. As Rick talked about his devotion to Kali, I asked him about the ritual practices he undertook—always a tricky issue for Westerners.

"I can't approach it like a Hindu because I haven't done the studies a Hindu would do," he said. "But it doesn't matter. There's still a connection. So if I want to worship Kali—and it would be bad for me to say that I never do—I'm gonna do it when I know I have to do it. And I'm gonna improvise. It could be silent inside, it could be through her images, it could be with incense or whatever. There's no order to it. I don't do it three times a day because, well, I don't have to. I don't have to do it at all. But sometimes I do.

"It's kind of the same way with our music. Sure we don't always improvise, but if you're gonna play music and improvise, just like you might perform a ritual, you're gonna try to approach it in a certain way. It's always good to not know. If you approach the thing in an established way, you're assuming that you have to do it that way because that's what's required. But if you just play off the energy at the time . . ."

"It's strange," says Alan. "When the three of us are on stage and we're in it and we're on it and the electricity is moving, we get this thing going to where it's an unexplainable phenomenon of energy. It's like traveling overseas: how far you wanna go? We trust it, we live for it at times. And it's an addictive thing." The longer they have played together, the more this "invocational phenomenon" seems to occur. "I sometimes don't know where some of this stuff comes from. Are we just receptors channeling personalities? Are some of the more flamboyant characters from the last five thousand years just pirating right through?"

Anyone familiar with Alan's singing would have to offer a qualified yes, as his vocal chords are regularly hijacked by a range of strange and androgynous entities: a moonshine-swilling hick, a sarcastic guttersnipe, an Indonesian banshee, and a hilarious two-bit wise guy named Uncle Jim. "Often I fall into characters that I've already evolved and it's comfortable," says Alan. "But sometimes if the path is open I can invoke some character I've never invoked before." In the beginning of the aptly-named eleven-minute title track of *Cameo Demons and their Manifestations*, for example, Alan randomly coughs. Then he starts dredging phlegm from the back of his throat, a nauseating deep hiss that mutates into a Gollum-like wraith whose infernal whispering channels the pitch black below as eerie close-miked shaman rattles pan back and forth through the mix.

Then there's the matter of the garbled or fake tongues that Alan spews during some of the band's "international" tunes. Alan knows bits of Indonesian, Spanish, and Burmese, but he's not particularly facile with languages and some of his singing is outright glossolalia. "Sometimes I'm singing exact words from a language and sometimes I'm not singing words from any language," he says. "And sometimes I'm singing my own language of before birth and after death." Alan guesses this peculiar skill started when he was a kid, making fun of Chinese or the Arabic he heard at home, but now it has blossomed into an expressive art beyond linguistics—a vocalization of the unsayable. That's also why Alan prefers to listen to music sung in languages he doesn't understand. "I like things that are undefined. It's the same attraction to travel, to going out as far as you can go. Whether it's in your face or very subtle, I'm looking for the undefined."

I wonder how desperate this search may become. The world today is experiencing a claustrophobic saturation of mediation and control, as the totality of human existence is recoded into a grid of data that saps the romantic imagination and blocks the ancient avenues to the beyond with cheesy simulacra and manufactured fear. And so I ask them whether their search for the undefined, for the space before birth and after death, is harder to achieve these days.

"Maybe," says Alan. "Everything seems to be closing in. There's a spin out there that people aren't as free, that there's too many rules, too many obstacles to be able to express our selves. It seems harder to get to the folkloric knowledge that could be far superior to what this reality we supposedly live in has to offer. I don't think we're really that restricted though. I think it's all still there and can be tapped into. But perhaps too many people have the power now to convince us that it's not possible."

In such a world, it's good to keep the doors of perception as wide open as possible, if only for the otherworldly perspective it provides. "When I look at Attorney General John Ashcroft and company, I'm looking down at them," says Rick. "I refuse to give them power. Sure they could come at me anytime. But until they come knocking at the door, I'm going to put myself above them. When it's all said and done and we move on, it's not gonna mean anything. I'm only planning for the next whatever-it-is, the next life, the next big flash. The big bright light, whenever it comes."

2004

THE GONE WORLD

The Secret Museum of Mankind

One afternoon, in the same anthropology section of San Francisco's Austen Books where I scored cheap editions of *Conversations with Ogotemmeli, The Gift,* and a rare copy of Herskovitz's *Life in a Haitian Valley,* I stumbled across a mighty bizarre volume known as *The Secret Museum of Mankind.* Lacking page numbers, pub date, or any editorial information beyond the name of an obscure press (Manhattan House), this apparently mid-1930s volume consists of a couple thousand captioned "photographs" of traditional folks from the four corners of the globe. I say "photographs" because many of these portraits and scenes have been retouched as blatantly as the average *Weekly World News* cover shot, and a few are basically cartoons.

Such absurd distortions are appropriate, because *The Secret Museum* is no-bones exotica, reflecting early pop anthropological obsessions with racial typology, hygiene, and nipples of color. Nevertheless, these simultaneously gaudy and fading images are powerful, arresting, and impressively strange: a Congo woman's globular scarifications, a Burmese tyke smoking a cheroot, a group of Arunta tribesmen doffing Seussian wizard-caps. Herein you can find South Sea cannibals, Kirghiz nomads, and the "Fuzzi Wuzzi Woman of the West," whose gravity-defying hairstyle belongs on a Pedro Bell Funkadelic album cover. You can't even accuse *The Secret Museum* of being Eurocentric—one section includes Dutch milkmaids, crossdressing Irish straw boys, and Canary Island "troglodytes."

The Secret Museum's captions are a hilarious blend of clueless condescension, cheery racialism, and loopy fashion critique, and they require no post-colonial fake books to deconstruct. ("Her disk-sewn neckband and rope of beads are the chief pride of this Ainu maiden whose grotesque tattooed mustache cannot quite destroy her ingenious youthful charm," reads a typical entry.) Since these captions are basically data-free, the only frame provided for the photos comes from our own raw fascination. Stripped of anthropological machinery, these faces simply amaze; some recall friends and lovers, while others stare out like bizarre carven idols from some pulp otherworld. At the same time, the hack artists who helped flesh out *The Secret Museum* don't let us forget that these "photographs" are halfway projections of the rootless American eye. But our pleasure persists nonetheless, or mine anyway, at once a guilty Orientalism and a dreamlike embrace of the universal human carnival.

Fans of traditional non-Western music know this paradoxical pleasure well. I say fans and not scholars, for there's always fantasy in fandom, while ethnomusicology is too often a dry sport of pinning butterflies. The information crammed into today's non-pop world music CDs is our fetish, a promise that all ghosts of exotica will be exorcised, all nomadic imaginings fixed in a briny, anthropological pickle. Preservation is a valuable and necessary goal, but too often suffocates the more errant power of other people's music to send us tripping out of ourselves.

When the record collector Pat Conte named his recently debuted compilation series of rare and remastered "ethnic" 78s after *The Secret Museum of Mankind* (it's also the name of Conte's enormous personal collection; his WBAI radio show is called *The Secret Museum of the Air*), he wanted to highlight the spectral and romantic spell induced by these crackly tunes rather than their considerable documentary significance. After all, the original 78s were created not by intrepid field scholars like Alan Lomax but by early record companies eager to stimulate enough pleasure to induce people the world over to buy record players. As with the blues and hillbilly sides cut in the States, most of the recordings collected on *The Secret Museum* were made in the field, with the subsequent discs sold back to local communities or to immigrant pockets in the West. And while it's impossible to know how the performers felt about being captured on wax, they certainly weren't building a career for a mass market or preserving their authentic folkways. Being recruited by the record companies was probably more like getting your best cow photographed—the resulting souvenir became a source of pride, pleasure, and community honor.

Recorded in places as far-flung as Kazakhstan, Rapu Nui, and Cape Breton, the performances collected on the first two volumes of *The Secret Museum* are almost entirely excellent, making this one of the more consistently rewarding compilations in years. The cuts range from 130-bpm Macedonian fiddle jaunts to Puerto Rican Christmas tunes, from Abyssinian religious chants to ominous Japanese court music, from down-and-dirty klezmer to the psychedelic minimalism of a Javanese "new song." The instruments include Ukrainian sleigh bells, Sardinian triple pipes, Vietnamese moon lutes, and Ethiopian one-string violins. Though some of these tunes were little more than entertaining ephemera for the folks who made them, Conte's choices sound like masterworks today, a profound and playful artistry lurking beneath their alien vernaculars.

Falling in love with these tunes can be dangerous—one risks both the politically dubious spell of exotica and the postmodern heresy of recognizing universal emotions in these distant sonic subjects. But when I hear Smyrna's Rita Abatzi sing a mournful cafe dirge over spare instrumentation worthy of Joy Division, or the Swedish master Eric Sahlström play an airy, bittersweet strain on his medieval-era keyed fiddle, or Trinidad's Lord Invader rail with vindictive mirth against "hooliganism" over the exuberant clarinet in his "Old Time Cat-O'-Nine," I hear the basic beats of the human heart.

That's not to deny the bizarre shit herein. Sardinia's Efisio Melis pulls a Rahsaan Roland Kirk on his triple pipe: while a drone cycles miraculously without a breath-stop, his hyperactive pastoral dance builds to a chaotic cluster of insanely trilling birds. Master Manahar Barve's "Gungru Tarang" is a simple Indian folk tune played on harmonium and violin, but the melody is echoed by suspended clusters of differently tuned bells that sound like astral cloudbursts or the resonating sighs of sylphs. And the strangest cut doesn't come from the jungles of Borneo or the steppes of inner Asia, but from France. On "Jabadao de Quimper," the Bretagne duo Les Freres Sciallour plays a squealing folk-metal leprechaun jam on their eerie little druid pipes.

Walter Benjamin claimed that mechanical reproduction leeched the aura from art, an aura that in indigenous music is nothing less than the lived spirit of passing time. Before recording (or musical notation), even the oldest musical forms were contemporary or not at all. The magical glue that unifies *The Secret Museum*'s otherwise disparate recordings is the afterimage of that aural aura, of the moment when technological reproduction and the commodity form had just begun to capture and irreparably reconfigure the evanescent flux of musical memory. Only the most smug technophiles would deny the autumnal tone this poaching lends these cuts, a melancholy deepened by the knowledge that nearly all of these musicians must be dead, and most of their lifeworlds severely eclipsed.

But false nostalgia is a sucker's game, and it's mushy-minded to interpret the greasy fingerprints of colonialism that gum up these cuts as signs of tyranny and loss. After all, in the hands on non-Western musicians, imperialist flotsam like violins, clarinets, Christian choruses, and pump organs offer opportunities for syncretic mutation, from the unmistakably African polyphony of Nigeria's Eleja Choir to the flattened bridge used by a Rajahstani violinist to allow for drones in "Jat Song." Even though the harmonium's lack of microtones does violence to Indian modes (and pissed off purists in its day), this Victorian contraption had become, by the time Professor Narayanrao Vyas recorded his ecstatic hymn to Krishna's mom, one of India's most definitive popular instruments.

Folk music has never been pure; its creative mutations, cannibalizations, and cross-cultural thefts make up its living continuity as much as the conservative retention of rhythms and tunes. Certainly "Kapirigna," a manic Afro-Portuguese/Sinhalese street romp recorded in Ceylon, is as "authentic" as it is scrambled. But what about "Naidasay Toy Pusoc," a Spanish-tango-inflected Filipino tune recorded in L.A. by a Visayan Islands duo using the newly invented dobro? Beats me.

I just keep coming back to that spooky technological aura, the snap crackle pop of weathered 78s that defines early recordings the way washed-out videotape defines '70s sitcoms. Today, computerized signal-processing is getting pretty good at remastering these old platters. But one man's noise is another man's message, and though the rarest of Conte's cuts were initially "more noise than music," he wisely chose to leave his remastered tunes somewhat scuzzy. Besides preserving more of the original recording, this remaining surface noise spills the dustbin of history into the digital clean room of today's musical universe. When I hear the scratchy samples of Tricky, Portishead, or the Mo' Wax crew, I hear entropy, death, and vinyl ancestor-worship. But when I listen to the nightstorm of static that bathes G. Kurmangaliev's Kazakhstani lute or Sa Zen Ga Zhiu Luh's serpentine Tibetan melody, I hear nothing less than the immense but muted roar of all strange, lost, and forgotten music, the long-ago strains of humanity's joyful noise.

1995

BURMESE DAZE

My Date with a Transvestite Spirit Medium

I do not have children, which saddens me a bit, for I would like some day to tell my offspring of the time I met Valiant Lord Kyawzwa, the Burmese guardian god of rogues and vagabonds, on the hot and dusty planes of Mandalay. We were traveling in the month of August, J and I, and the sky was low and heavy with monsoon. Our guides had brought us to the town of Taungbyon, famed throughout the land for its exuberant *Nat Pwe*—a week of endless overlapping rites that honored, propitiated, and feted the Thirty-Seven Nats, Burma's earthy and melodramatic pantheon of all-too-human spirit beings.

The crowded central footpath through Taungbyon was flanked by food stalls, tea shops, and globalist collages of T-shirts and cheap jeans. A labyrinth of smaller paths radiated outward from this main artery, and beckoned us with clanging gongs, drum beats, and otherworldly folk-pop squealings—the sonic signs that the nats were in the house, or, more accurately, inside the bedecked and spangled bodies of Burma's incomparable spirit mediums. Following one of these paths, we stumbled upon a group of smiling women who invited us to join them inside a small stall set up next to a particularly boisterous orchestra.

We settled down on the raised platform, joining what turned out to be a small and informal session with a spirit medium, or *nat kadaw*, who sat cross-legged before a lacy altar wearing a glazed, otherworldly look in his eye. Most of Taungbyon's mediums are, in some manner or another, transgendered—"ladyboys" in the local parlance. The nat kadaw before us was clearly a man, though he was dressed in an effeminate array of pink and white chintz and wore a fetching orange bandana topped with a few crisp low-denomination units of Burmese kyat (pronounced "chat"). The medium smiled at us and silently directed someone to give us some fried chicken legs, stringy and vaguely repulsive, which I dutifully munched down for the both of us. The ladies moved aside, and encouraged me to shuffle up the medium, who gifted me with the first glug of what would become, by the end of the day, a veritable stream of Grand Royal whiskey.

Though I did not know it at the time, chicken and whiskey signify the presence of Ko Gyi Kyaw, also known as the aforementioned Lord Kyawzwa, at least according to one the few documents on nat worship I have managed to scare up. Lists of the Thirty-Seven Nats are notoriously incomplete and contradictory; they are often composite figures, with multiple names, and there are well more than thirty-seven. Though the Burmese use the term nats to refer to both heavenly devas and local nature spirits, the Thirty-Seven "Great Nats" are a spectral crew of former human beings, some quasi-historical and some obviously folkloric, who linger on in an astral antechamber of the earth, refusing to vacate the premises. They are a colorful lot, packed with princes and beauties, and nearly all left our world in wretched and excruciating circumstances, like self-immolation or leprosy or death by tiger. I can't tell from my research whether Ko Gyi Kyaw died of drink or was buried alive, but his life course was firm, its debauched credo—which conjures

Hafiz and 50 Cent in equal measure—captured in this sample from one of his ritual songs:

> Do you not know me? Have you not seen me at cockfights? Have you not seen me letting off fireworks? Many times have I fallen prostrate in the gutter, drunken with my wife's wine, and many times have I been picked up by the loving hands of pretty village maidens.

I needed my photo taken with this guy. So I ponied up 500 kyat and sidled next to Ko Gyi Kyaw's temporary vessel for a shot. Egged on by the ladies, I put my arm around the medium's shoulder. His whole body trembled, a jittery pulse that reminded me of the characters in old Betty Boop cartoons. Taungbyon's mediums are performers first and foremost, but this guy seemed to be deeply tranced out. Nobody—at least nobody *normal*—was home.

Our stall was well placed to take advantage of the nearby orchestra, which was, as the kids say, going off. One drummer gripped a stick in either hand, rooting the rhythm with a primitive pulse, while another guy devoted himself to smashing cymbals together with seemingly careless ferocity. The heart of the orchestra was a circular drum station that allowed the bandleader to pivot around and strike twenty-odd small drums tuned with some sort of gooey clay. Two similar wheel-like consoles were devoted to brass and bronze gongs, tuned more or less to a major scale, with an odd half-step here or there. The shimmering and hysterical melodies of these gongs scampered dizzily over the monkey-mind clank and clatter of the drums, with further bewitchment supplied by an ear-splitting oboe and wailing, mildly distorted vocals. It was the most madcap music I have ever heard, a brash and giddy bumblebee romp that called to mind a garage-rock gamelan orchestra banging out the soundtrack to some delirious and exotic Warner Bros. cartoon—call it *Daffy Does Devil Worship*.

Dancing to these jarring and jittery beats, which shifted gears like Zappa at his wackiest, a bespectacled middle-aged woman in our stall became as one possessed. She started shaking, then began a sluggish stumble-dance, and finally dropped to her knees on the raised floor of the stall. A couple of older women immediately stopped their grooving and attended the woman with looks of great concern; later I learned they were attempting to prevent whatever nat had entered her body from staying too long and burning out her psychic circuits, or even killing her. Then, just as quickly as the entranced woman had slipped out our realm, her conventional personality returned. She had journeyed up to Taungbyon from her home in Yangon and looked like she worked in an appliance shop or some other vaguely middle-class endeavor. "I was just hearing the music," she explained. "I don't remember . . ."

A few moments later, the nat kadaw, responding to no obvious signal or ritual resolution, hopped up, shed his sprinkly ritual garb, and returned to the standard Burmese male gear of a skirt-like longyi and a button-down shirt. He walked away without engaging the devotees, his gig as Ko Gyi Kyaw finished for the moment. As J and I wandered off, the nearby orchestra reached one of its delirious crescendos, a sound capable of waking the dead—or, perhaps more accurately, of those who continue to live through us.

I first heard about Taungbyon from Alan Bishop, the bass player and impresario behind the Sun City Girls. Alan first went to Burma in 1993 and has returned six times. He married a Burmese woman, and his adopted daughter, Thiri (pronounced "Theory") helps create the charming and garish cover art for the bizarro world music CDs and DVDs that Bishop releases on his indispensable Sublime Frequencies label. He showed me footage of Taungbyon's Nat Pwe, and it looked like Southeast Asian voodoo. My reaction was immediate and unbidden: This I have to see.

Visiting Taungbyon meant visiting Burma, however, and visiting Burma gave me—a seasoned but hardly intrepid traveler—a creeping feeling of unease. This mild sense of dread emanated as much from the opprobrium of political incorrectness as from fears of guerrilla bombs or anal parasites. One of a very small number of old-school military dictatorships left in Asia, Burma—renamed Myanmar in 1989 by the ruling State Law and Order Restoration Council (these days known as the State Peace and Development Council)—remains a pariah state that practices forced labor, massive censorship, and a corrupt and criminally irresponsible economic policy. In other words, Burma resembles most developing countries, except for the fact that its generals don't play ball with multinational corporations or, by extension, most nation-states. The famous democracy activist Aung San Suu Kyi, currently under house arrest in Yangon, long ago asked foreigners not to visit the country, and many potential western tourists, especially from English-speaking countries, continue to honor her request. But many Burmese who hunger for democracy disagree with Suu Kyi on this point, arguing that foreign visitors provide a flow of desperately needed dollars to ordinary Burmese and also make violent mass repression less likely—at least in the parts of the country that tourists and their cameras are allowed to visit. With Alan's encouragement, J and I decided to take the plunge, though the news that forced labor helped refurbish some key tourist destinations, like the Mandalay Fort, hardly quelled my anxiety.

Burma's air of the forbidden only thickened when the Myanmar embassy in Bangkok mysteriously rejected my application for a visa, which I had submitted via the travel agents on the horrible Khao San Road, a Lonely Planet limbo where all self-styled "travelers" eventually wind up whether they want to or not. The visa police, it seemed, had zeroed in on one particular letter of the English language scrawled on an old Indian visa glued into my passport: "J." As in journalist. So we dutifully hoofed it to the embassy, where, after bathing in the wan fluorescent lights for hours and suffering an occasional insulting outburst from a sniveling French asshole who insisted that Americans had no business traveling anywhere at all, we were informed by a flabby-faced gent with a dull green uniform and poor English that journalists were simply not allowed into Burma. Persisting, we talked with Miss Miu, a young educated woman with sexy librarian glasses who suggested I type up and submit a formal promise that I would dig no dirt during my stay.

The fax, written with pointless irony, did the trick, and a week later, I got my visa. The lure of the tourist dollar, it seems, can still tickle the fancy of a paranoid military junta.

Buffaloes, Toe called them, as we drove into Yangon. Toe had hopped unbidden into the passenger seat of our cab as we were hustled into the vehicle following an elaborate hand-off between numerous airport touts and starched-shirted operators whose choreography I can by no means reconstruct. A sharp-eyed and wiry guy, Toe spoke openly about the country's woes and the corrupt lugheads in power. "They do not watch CNN, they do not know media, they are just buffaloes fighting in a field, eating, sleeping, getting rich."

As you might have guessed, Toe also turned out to run a tour agency, Ko Tar Travels & Tours, and he offered to hook us up with a car and driver during our stay. Most western tourists in Burma avail themselves of a car and driver, and occasionally an additional guide. The practice is inexpensive, convenient in a land starved for infrastructure, and turns over fewer dollars to the government, which owns and operates the rails, which Toe called "the buffalo train." With their beat-up cars and convoluted English, Burma's freelance cabby guides have now paved an ad-hoc tourist circuit through the country, one that is regularly plied by the French, Germans, and southern Europeans who made up the vast majority of the country's western tourists. As first-time visitors, J and I were happy to follow most of Toe's recommendations—Inle Lake, Kalaw, the Pindaya Caves, and the world-class Pagan. All we insisted on was a side trip to Taungbyon during the climax of the festival, which finds its close at the fullness of the moon.

Jasmine flowers dangled from the rear-view mirror of our dented white sedan, which was driven by a gruff-looking middle-aged guy with fat aviator shades. He had previously served as a captain with Burma's merchant marines, sailing across the globe and seeing far more of the world than most Burmese, and this was his first trip working the tourist circuit. He spoke little English, smoked at every stop, and laughed with sardonic good humor. I scribbled down his name, but we just called him "the Driver," after the nameless James Taylor character in Monte Hellman's classic road movie *Two-Lane Blacktop*.

In the passenger seat, taking up the Dennis Wilson role, was Thi Ha, who called himself Lion. A youthful fortysomething who had been plying the tourist circuit since he was a teenager, Lion had an infectious grin, a pronounced limp, and a temperament that veered between boisterous good humor and a sullen brood, the latter of which was not infrequently triggered by the Driver's philosophy of manual transmission. Because he usually acted as a driver rather than an official licensed guide, Lion was not overflowing with facts and figures, which was occasionally frustrating but largely a relief. Like many folks his age, Lion had spent some hard years in prison after the massive democracy demonstrations of the 1980s, but seemed more sad than bitter. He was good folk.

On the way out of Yangon, we drove by Shwedagon Paya, the holiest pagoda in Burma, an enormous golden Hershey's kiss topped with a tinkling finial peppered with sapphires, emeralds, rubies, and diamonds. As we passed the paya, the Driver lifted both his hands off the wheel and offered a short and somewhat alarming bow. A creeping feeling of uncanniness grew inside me. Was it the billboard advertisements for Dagon beer, an alarm for any Lovecraft fan? Or could it be the garish yellow pancake makeup, derived from the thanaka tree, that Burmese women applied in sometimes fantastic designs across their faces? Then I realized that what had unnerved me was the total absence of multinational branding, as if the crumbling city lay in some parallel dimension not yet colonized by Coke and VISA and McDonalds.

We headed north towards Mandalay through leagues of rice patties, stopping for the night at Mother's House hotel, where we watched Burmese music videos, including a delirious homage to a tractor factory that featured pom-pom wielding cheerleaders. Go team! The next day we turned east, climbing up terrible roads into the mountains that cradle Inle Lake, probably the most popular destination for domestic tourists in Burma. Before arriving at the lake, we stayed a night in Kalaw, a lush mountain town of pine trees and bougainvillea gardens and military

training facilities. After disturbing dreams, I awoke early in the morning and took a walk. The glass shards that covered the bell-shaped pagoda in the center of town sparkled in the rising sun, its square base decorated with four elven-eared devas that represented the heavenly strain of nats. Across the street, nestled in the trunk of a sprawling banyan tree, a coarse and far more earthly nat stood within a locked shrine.

As I turned from this rough idol and made for the mosque on the south side of town, I was greeted by two grizzled characters lounging against a wall, the sort of folks we called "tuddies" in high school. One guy was large and fleshy, and made a stark contrast to his scrawny buddy, who sported an Islamic beard and a long thin early riser cheroot. The mouths of both men were a crimson holocaust of betel rot. The big fellow was drunk, and was dead set on letting me know, in no uncertain terms, just how fucked up his country was. "We are under the boot, like Germany, like Gestapo," he growled as his mute and grinning friend enthusiastically bobbed his head in agreement. "They have taken away our human rights. You should tell the BBC." So for a moment, dear reader, please pretend that you yourself are the BBC.

Inle Lake is a long and luxurious body of water nestled between two soft mountain ranges. The area was gorgeous, and, more to the point, relaxed. The traffic in the main town was still largely restricted to bicycles and scooters, and there was enough of a tourist infrastructure to produce a decent Italian restaurant but not so much that it spoiled the scene or the goodwill of the folks who lived and modestly prospered there. The lake itself was peppered with floating gardens, villages on stilts, and fisherman who steer their boats with their feet—an image that serves as the icon of the region, like gondoliers in Venice. One inevitable but worthwhile stop was the Jumping Cat Monastery, a gingerbread teak compound that hovers over the lake atop rust-red stilts and houses felines that smug and vaguely disdainful monks have trained to leap through hoops on command.

Lion had a good friend in Inle town named Linn, who served as a freelance trekking guide while also waiting tables at the Italian joint. One morning, after we visited a village market overflowing with pickled tea, jackfruit tar, and pornographically flayed fish, Linn took us into the mountains. He sported floppy Converse trainers he had scored from a European client, and a baseball cap that evoked a runty Tiger Woods. Like Lion, his good humor was leavened with a sad and somewhat traumatized air. At one point during our muggy hike through fields of turmeric and tobacco, we passed a young peasant couple and their small grubby child. After they were behind us, Linn stopped, his eyes brimming with tears. He came from a poor village himself, and though he tried to educate the villagers about medicine and birth control, he knew there was little hope of vanquishing Burma's vicious circle of rural poverty and ignorance.

Later we were invited to a meal at Linn's home. We expected to eat *en famille*, but instead found ourselves a twosome at a candlelit table on their dirt driveway. I was already feeling the first rumblings of the gastrointestinal bummer that would trouble me the following few days—the result, I expect, of the delicious pickled tea we had eaten for lunch at the mountain village. But I valiantly dug in, and enjoyed our best exposure yet to Burma's hybrid and rather unspectacular cuisine: a pepper soup, sprightly greens, sweet-and-sour veggies, thickly curried prawns, and weird chunks of fried fish.

Afterwards, we were taken inside and shown the family nat shrine, which prominently featured an altar for Maha Giri, the Lord of the Great Mountain. Shrines to Maha Giri appear in every Burmese home, or at least those that still traffic with the nats. A small curtain was drawn before the Lord, here embodied by a coconut tied with a red kerchief. The reason for the curtains is that, when Maha Giri was a mortal hero, the King of Tagaung ordered him tied to a champa tree and burned alive, and so he does not care to see light at night.

I related this bit of lore to my hosts, having gleaned it from a grimy reprint of Maung Htin Aung's *Folk Elements in Burmese Buddhism*, which I had scored in a no-less grimy shop in Yangon. My datum made enough of an impression on Lion that he joined us at the table with a bottle of whiskey and talked about the nats. Lion estimated that only thirty percent of Burmese believe in the nats. He was brought up within the other seventy percent; though many Burmese worship the Buddha alongside the nats, Lion's parents believed that the dharma was incompatible with such popular supernaturalism. The strain between the two faiths goes back a millennium, to the imposition of Theravada Buddhism by Pagan's sanctimonious King Anawrahta in the eleventh century. Anawrahta disliked the nats, but was unable to suppress their worship; and so, like the Catholic church in the heathen colonies, he assimilated them. Against the riot of popular lore and orgiastic rites that preceded the dharma, he codified and established thirty-six nats, headed by Maha Giri, at his central paya in Pagan. Anawrahta then crowned the posse with a thirty-seventh nat—the deva Indra—and thereby symbolically placed the nats under the Buddhadharma.

Lion explained that many Burmese worship the Buddha in order to guarantee a good future life, while they propitiate the nats in order to reap rewards and avoid calamity—much of it caused by the nats—in this world. Lion then admitted that he began serving the nats after he hooked up with his wife, whose mother was a strong devotee. Nats often communicate in dreams, so when Ko Myo Shin came to Lion one night while he slept and said, "I want to be in your home," he went out the next day and bought a shrine. In exchange for taking on some of Ko Myo Shin's restrictions—she does not care for either beef or pork and wants her devotees to abjure the same—Lion was eventually gifted with dream transmissions of some winning lottery numbers. But the nats can also be as petulant as children, and their propitiation is a two-edge sword. One day Lion fell off a low wall and inexplicably broke his leg, which healed badly and continues to cause him chronic pain. He blames the whole incident on the shirt he wore that day, a black rocker T with a buffalo head on it. Lion believes the garment offended a nat named Popa Medaw, who has a thing about buffaloes and the color black.

As the cries of the crickets and bullfrogs rose to a deafening keen in the Inle air, Lion, now in his cups, revealed that he once lived with a ladyboy who had embarked on the path of the nat kadaw. Lion learned some of the ritual nat dances from his friend, and became quite proficient at a few of them. He insisted that lots of mediums were in the game just because they liked to dress up and dance (and, presumably, to make some decent money). Only a small number of nat kadaw, he claimed, were the real deal, capable of genuinely invoking and holding these powerful spirits in their bodies without going crazy or becoming sick. As the evening wound to a close, I could not resist asking what the deal was with all the crossdressing. Lion's answer was crisp: "Nats prefer ladyboys!"

A week later, J and I were packed in the car with Lion and the Driver, inching our way past the wide fields of rice patties that lie north of Mandalay. We had left our grotty urban hotel mid-morning, as the touts for the taxi-vans filled the air with cries of "Taungbyon! Taungbyon!" Vehicles piled with eager passengers were already pulling away, hoping to avoid the traffic that would later choke the route to the nearby town. Along the way, we found the road lined with beggars and cripples and clumps of people attempting, with widely varying degrees of conviction, to extract road tolls and donations, the latter elicited with heavily reverbed bullhorn entreaties and small children tossing "coins" (no longer part of the money system) inside silver bowls. Even before we reached town, with windows rolled up against the dust, we sensed the crackling, eternally returning energy of festival. A few dreamtime shivers struck my spine, and I recalled the pothead rush of anticipation I felt as a teenager arriving at Grateful Dead parking lots—that electric sense of a luminous collective secret about to open to all.

J and I left Lion and the Driver in the parking lot, where they would wait like bored soldiers for half a day. We walked into a dusty, unkempt scene that resembled nothing so much as a South Asian county fair. The main streets—thankfully devoid of cars—were lined with stalls offering gelatinous sweets, flowers, cassettes, greasy treats, and shoddy goods. Kids ran around gobbling candy, and a manually-operated Ferris wheel loomed behind the village's central paya, the attraction's upper struts lined with young men prepared to generate momentum by hurling their bodies earthwards while holding on to the spokes. Inside a roomy nearby stall, behind a single rickety turnstile, a troop of large stick puppets fought out a gory domestic drama to a prerecorded soundtrack of spooky B-movie chords and heavily distorted Burmese piano doodles. Outside, the piles of coconut husks and banana leaves—the refuse of a brisk trade in offerings—reminded us that this low-key rural carnival was in some sense sacred. But there was no heaviness of purpose among the crowds, no gloomy pilgrim piety, no religious mania.

The casual, boisterous atmosphere saturated Taungbyon's central paya as well, where crowds decamped on the floors of open halls glittering with mosaics of silvered glass. The pagoda plays a crucial role in the story of the Taungbyon brothers, the two nats who lord over the town and its annual pwe. Shwepyingyi and his brother, possessed of the amazingly similar name of Shwepyinnge, were the sons of Byat-ta, a "mighty man of endeavor" employed by King Anawrahta. Byat-ta, along with his brother Byat-wi, had been discovered floating in a seaborne basket by a monk. While he was raising the orphan boys, who had Indian features and were considered Muslim, the monk chanced upon the corpse of one of Burma's myriad alchemists, who spent their time concocting elixirs of immortality and fighting magical battles over the fruit maidens they liked to fuck. Knowing the extraordinary powers imparted by cooked alchemist flesh, the monk promptly roasted the dead body. He then commanded Byat-wi and Byat-ta to guard the corpse while he fetched the king. But the young brothers could not resist the aroma of the flesh, and so gobbled the entire alchemist, becoming superheroes in the process.

Anawrahta grew to distrust both brothers and eventually killed them. But after murdering Byat-ta and his ogress wife, the king took pity on their two sons and raised them in the court. Because the boys had inherited some of their father's superpowers, they were later ordered to lead the king's army into China to seize the empire's Buddha relics, which Anawrahta believed would help him banish the nats from Burma. Unfortunately, the lazy brothers brought back a jade replica of the Blessed Molar instead of the real deal. Later, when the king ordered the brothers to help construct the pagoda at Taungbyon, the two men decided to play marbles instead. This was too much for Anawrahta, who castrated the guys with a magic spear and let them bleed to death.

From beyond the veil, the brothers, now nats, continued to hassle the sovereign, and the king eventually made them the spiritual lords of Taungbyon. The annual pwe held in their name grew and grew, and when a later sovereign, King Mindon, proclaimed that he would cancel the festival, the two nats made his balls swell until Mindon relented.

Passing through the thronged halls of the paya, where a few missing bricks intentionally recall the brothers' fateful goof-off, J and I entered a crowded courtyard and plopped down on a mat beneath the scant shade of a scrubby tree. It was hot. An old woman danced nearby—mad, possessed, or both—and a troop of uniformed authorities moved through the crowd, snarling at people and taking notes on an immense form attached to a clipboard. Almost instantly, we were absorbed into a group of folks sitting in the shade of a stall besides us, waiting for their turn at dancing and propitiating later that evening. They seemed like an extended family or friend network—ordinary folks just having a picnic. A few attractive young ladyboys sat mincing in their midst, integrated into the scene in a manner unimaginable in the West. They fed us greasy rice fried with cardamom, even greasier fish, and fat purple banana coconut treats. J swapped an arm band for cheap gold chains and bracelets, and I performed for the crowd by rolling some of the loose Virginia tobacco I had purchased in Bangkok, a wise move which saved me from the ignoble fate of smoking foul Chinese cigarettes.

We left our new friends and walked towards the Ferris wheel. Along the way, we passed a small crowd intently clustered around some curiosity we could not see. Even before I peered over their heads, I felt the foreshock of the bizarre, and indeed the curiosity in question turned out to be a magnificently deformed kid with an enormous peanut-shaped head almost the size of a horse skull. From the yellow dress it seemed this person was a girl. Though her handlers did not seem be gouging the crowd for kyat, the pitiable being was clearly on display, as she lay on a cot in the shadow of an umbrella, beaming beatifically into the void. I was tempted to videotape this strange and in some way touching scene, but some force stayed my *Mondo Cane* hand. And, with this shocking sight having inadvertently opened our minds to the weirdness always within our midst, we passed from the paya and made our way toward the maniac beats and wailing reeds of the distant orchestras, calling down the ghosts.

Around 1710, Alexander Hamilton, a British seaman visiting Burma, wrote in his journal about the oracles who performed at a sacred feast he attended. Though the event he described could have reflected another popular tradition, it sounds an awful lot like a nat pwe.

> I saw nine dance like mad folks, for about half an hour, and then some of them fell in fits, foaming at the mouth for the space of half an hour; and, when their senses are restored, they pretend to foretell plenty or scarcity of corn for that year, if the year would prove sickly or salutary to the people, and several other things of moment, and all by that half hour's conversation that the furious dancer had with the gods when she was in a trance.

While such powerful possession cults still exist in Southeast Asia, the rituals at Taungbyon now seem rather tame compared to Hamilton's account, with formal dances replacing epileptic jitters and mantic drool. Today's mediums still dispense predictions, although advice on love or money has replaced the corn forecasts of yore. However, in one crucial way, the tradition Hamilton saw has not changed at all. When it came to the gender of the oracles, the captain wrote, "Hermaphrodites, who are numerous in this country, are generally chosen, if there are enough present to make a set for the dance."

For one curious week in August, Taungbyon is tranny city, although you would not know that from reading some of the sources. *Burmese Supernaturalism*, first published in 1967, is probably the most thorough book on the subject available in English; within its pages, author Melford Spiro goes into fascinating detail about Taungbyon's nat kadaw. He claims, though, that they are almost entirely women, while "experts at Taungbyon estimate that 3 to 4 percent are male"—most of which, he adds, are homosexual or transvestite. Now, the realm of the transgendered is tough to clarify and categorize; given the endless permutations and tangles over nomenclature, biology, and sexual orientation, the liminality of the dual sexed makes itself known in all discourses that approach the subject. Nonetheless, I can't imagine who Spiro's "experts" are, or how the author could have missed the signs familiar to any tranny fan. Because if Taungbyon's nat pwe today is anything like the pwes Spiro visited in the 1960s, ladyboys—whether crossdressers or more hormonally driven hermaphrodites—dominate the sacred congress between nats and human life.

In the modern West, people celebrate tranny culture, when they do, because of the way the transgendered scramble and expand forms of sexual identity and erotic possibility. But many traditional cultures have recognized that transgendered folks—whether "homosexual" or something more ambiguous—also have a sacred and numinous power. From the primal hermaphrodites of Chaldean and gnostic myth to the mystic crossdressers of South Sulawesi to the Native American "Two-Spirit," who often serves as both an oracle and healer, transgendered people have the power to pass between the worlds, to draw down the gods, to penetrate and contain the cosmic mystery sustained by the primal polarity between masculine and feminine. On the most mystic level, the transgendered being embodies the *coincidentia oppositorum*, the union of opposites captured in the alchemical androgynes of German spiritualists like Jacob Boehme and Franz von Baader, and later of Jung. Here the anatomical wonders of the ladyboy—monstrous to some—are spiritualized into a "perfect man," an Adam Kadmon characterized by a primal wholeness that lies beyond gender.

The sacred hermaphrodite is a crossroads being. Holding masculine and feminine in her left and right hand, he is also characterized by another, more vertical polarity: between the "higher" spiritualized androgyny of perfect union and the polymorphous eroticism of the sexual depths. So while Burma's nat kadaw certainly serve an oracular and even sacred function, they are also hip-deep in the erotic. According to Spiro, who makes curious asides about the temptations of "bottom-pinching" stirred up by Taungbyon's crowds, the nat kadaw are frequently initiated into their roles through sexual visions. Like medieval incubi, nats often approach their future servitors in dreams, seducing and then fucking them. Many people so approached marry their nats ritually and become mediums—*nat kadaw* means "nat spouse."

For most, there is not a lot of choice in the matter—nats are capricious and vengeful players, and it takes a lot of guts to reject their advances. Sometimes the nats allow their new spouses to continue ordinary sexual relationships, but mostly they jealousy demand fidelity. From a more sociological perspective, the call of the nat serves as perfect cover for individuals born into Burmese society who do not confirm to standard heterosexual identities; the role of the nat kadaw offers "the third gender" an avenue toward status and financial power otherwise nearly impossible to achieve. At the same time, they continue to carry a transgressive and threatening sexual charge—though the nat kadaw are respected for their oracular skills, they are also suspected of being promiscuous sluts or even prostitutes.

To J and me, the nat kadaw largely seemed like voodoo voguers, exuberantly kicking up their heels in the superstitious limelight. After squeezing through the crowd that thronged one pwe enclosure, J and I were approached by a friendly character wearing a baseball cap and a lime-green Hawaiian shirt decorated with dolphins. With the proud air of a successful entrepreneur, he invited us to join his extended family inside the enclosure for the next pwe, which he had sponsored. A sponsor like him might pay around two hundred bucks to rent the stall and hire the orchestra and the mediums, who often accompany the sponsor from his home town (the orchestra stays put as different mediums and sponsored groups come and go). The sponsor's fee does not include the whiskey or cigarettes consumed by the nats and occasionally dolled out to the devotees who crowd the floor between the orchestra and the altar. Nor does the fee cover the wads of crisp, small denomination bills that the mediums in turn throw at the crowd, who lunge for this "lucky money" like contestants at a game show.

J and I followed the sponsor into a dark, musty room that abutted the enclosure, where the two nat kadaw he had hired, bedecked in elaborate head gear and lacy white robes tied with thick red sashes, were quietly waiting for their turns on the stage. The boss medium must have been in her fifties, a shriveled and leathery ladyboy, imperiously fanning herself in the gloom. Her partner was younger, moon-faced and attractive, her prettiness marred only by severely betel-rotted teeth, although whether this imperfection is seen as such by the Burmese I cannot say. As I posed for a photo with these two ladies, the Hottie reached behind my back, grabbed my hand, and placed it firmly on her hip as she gave me an alluring glance. When we parted, the imp of the perverse who lies within us all could not resist giving her hip an unseen squeeze.

We were ushered into the main pwe enclosure, a large blue stall surrounded by fences on three sides, its roof strung with multicolored Christmas lights. The altar was crowded with a handful of mannequin-sized idols, tons of flowers and bananas, and a small Buddha in the corner, reminding those who cared to notice who was theoretically in charge. Things got rolling when the Boss performed a stylized sword dance for Maha Giri. Small flags decorated with rabbits and moons were then trotted out and twirled, and finally the two mediums faced the altar and lightly flagellated themselves with bunches of green ferns as they offered up little hip shimmies. A long series of dances followed, with each medium alternately taking the lead. The Boss or the Hottie would call out the tunes associated with various nats, the appropriate ritual implements would be placed in their hands, and then they would dance—curious moves that simultaneously invoked the nats, propitiated them, and allowed those disincarnate beings to temporarily get a groove on. At regular intervals, the two mediums would toss lucky money at the small crowd, which was mostly made up of women sitting cross-legged on the ground. The devotees offered up warm cans of soda to the nats, or liberally sprayed their living vessels with cheap perfume—treats that soon gave way to London cigarettes and Red Sea rum. Others would rise and pin bills to the lacy robes and glittery headdresses of the nat kadaw. Large denominations were likely to elicit private words of advice, which usually concerned the appropriate nats to propitiate for success in love or business. As they accumulated kyat on their costumes, the mediums took on the character of androgynous birds, their feathers composed of one of the more comical currencies on the planet.

The nat kadaw certainly commanded all the attention, but they were not exactly in charge. Their ringleader was a rail-thin young man who acted like the pimp-daddy manager of a pair of soul divas, keeping one eye on the clock and the other on the cash. He looked like a genie, the nails on his right hand as long as claws, his many rings a garish brand of mystic bling. Radiating the condescending pride of a hustler, Mr. Bling seemed completely unmoved by the presence of the sacred forces in his midst. Without a smile, he collected notes from the crowd in a small silver pot that he then handed to the Boss, who proceeded to dance the gambling dance of Ko Gyi Kyaw, magically suspending the pot between her hands like an ace juggler.

As the rum continued to flow, the Hottie began to direct her attentions toward yours truly, and the mischievous squeeze earlier in the afternoon flowered into full-scale public flirtation. I knew all bets were off when she came up to me, demurely turned her head away, and invited me wordlessly to kiss her neck, which the imp of the perverse performed with alacrity. The act produced gleeful cheers from the crowd, including the profoundly amused J. When I next turned toward the orchestra, one of the male singers—a sweaty, vaguely feral guy whose thinning hair was pasted to his forehead—caught my eye. Through winks and gestures, he let me know that the real trick when offered nat neck was not to kiss but to inhale. He mimed a sniff that embodied, at least at that drunken moment, a heartfelt prayer for carnal deliverance and release. Ten minutes later, after the Hottie had bestowed a soft peck on my cheek, she again offered me her neck. I took the fellow's advice and huffed. And there, in that late afternoon air, thick with particulate matter and sweet perfume and pungent sweat, I was delivered unto an aromatic pureland, some far field of ambrosial incense and flowering trees where the Buddhas teach by scent alone.

The rite closed with a long series of false denouements, as the nats refused—characteristically, I would learn—to disembark from their vessels of flesh. The Hottie kept calling more tunes, although it was no longer clear whether she was guided by the spirits of the nats or the ethanol. Calming down his ladies, dabbing off their sweat in a vain attempt to keep them looking regal, Mr. Bling seemed to grow annoyed, although his irritation may have been as ersatz as outrage at a WWE meet. As the orchestra mimed a rock band in an eternal drum roll climax, one woman—responsible for much of the cash flow throughout the afternoon—went into trance: flailing limbs, wiggly eyes, wacky-assed dancing. After the mediums had brought her back, the Hottie tried to do something with the money the possessed woman had earlier given her. The proceedings were obscure, but the woman leapt up and began arguing passionately with the Hottie, until the Boss and Mr. Bling came over to straighten things out.

At this point, the most powerful supernatural force that animated these rites came to the fore: cash. Many of the folks around me had scrimped the entire year in order to splurge at the nat pwe, believing that their offerings would bounce back to them in the form of luck or lottery numbers or good business. Now the liberal economy of the earlier "lucky money" phase, with its free-for-all distribution of small bills, gave way to a more retentive logic, as the mediums paused amid their chaotic dancing to count their accumulated cash with the finesse of bookies and dole out chunks to the singers and the orchestra. Clearly unsatisfied with the numbers, the nats aggressively focused on the further extraction of cash from their devotees, affecting an attitude of haughty privilege no doubt designed to stimulate the superstitious awe of their temporary acolytes.

As wealthy Westerners, we were inevitably drawn into this monetized game of seduction and command. I had been recording the event with both a Sony video camera and a small Canon Elf, and I happily handed over a small wad to the various musicians I had recorded. But I was not satisfied with the footage I had shot of the Hottie, and so, in order to coax her to perform for the camera, I kept slipping more money into her garb, soon switching from kyat to single dollar bills. As she wised to my game and began to deliberately turn away from my camera, I realized that this exotic Burmese possession rite had become something much more akin to a strip show. Given all the attention and money I had paid to the younger medium, I should not have been as surprised as I was when a jealous Boss stepped up and aggressively demanded three dollar bills. As this transaction occurred, the Hottie started rifling through J's bag in search of more greenbacks, and only narrowly missed the twenty that J had expertly palmed. Yanking out a copy of Orwell's *Burmese Days*, the Hottie looked utterly disgusted and threw down the book.

Finally the orchestra quit and the crowds dispersed. The Hottie approached me and coyly cupped her hand near her mouth, as if feeding herself rice, and I realized she wanted to eat with us, or me at any rate, or me and my wallet. But before my imagination could grapple with the quantum wave form generated by this invitation, Mr. Bling put the kibosh on the whole affair, whisking away his nat kadaw in the blink of an eye. J and I wound up eating with some of the people who manned the pwe stall. They served us rice and vegetables and a dish featuring Burma's classic stinky fish sauce, which should certainly be sampled by all lovers of Marmite. We had great fun as these disarmingly friendly folks schooled us on how to eat the clumpy sauce-soaked rice with our hands, a procedure that involved flicking the moist clump of kernels into your mouth using your thumb as a kind of shovel. As I practiced this move, I briefly thought of the Hottie, while I most likely picked up the bug that, once again, wreaked havoc on my gut.

Sated and still blazing from the pwe, J and I wandered through the early evening, surrounded by droves of young trannies, flirty but sweet, dressed to the nines. These ladies were not channeling the ghosts of ancient heroes but were here to strut their own stuff, and they lovingly vamped for our cameras, which to my eternal horror had run out of juice. Though J and I were still sloppy from our earlier slugs of nat whiskey, we finished off our own bottle, huddling in the dark as the crowds thickened around us. Over the next few hours, we dipped into a handful of pwes, and I tried and failed to track down the one great tape by a Burmese metal act called Iron Cross. After visiting the main nat temple, where we stumbled over a drunken propitiator flopping around a pile of ferns beside the booming speaker stacks, we called it a night. Lion had pleaded with us not to stay after dark, but the crowd seemed perfectly mellow as we returned to the car. Then Lion and the Driver whisked us away, relieved less for our safety, I suspect, than that their long day was finally done.

The night before we departed from Yangon, we stayed in a hotel near the Shwedagon Paya so we could walk up to the holy site in the early morning. Shwedagon crowns a steep hill and is approached by four long stairways that lie in the cardinal directions. We chose the north approach, which does not have an escalator or elevator and is crowned at the top by a guardian ogress. There she sat, like a proud and hideous fishmonger's wife, surrounded by an enormous pagan array of green bananas. Someone had stuck a burning cheroot between her fleshy lips.

Shwedagon is a world-class sacred spot, a peaceful palimpsest of Burmese spirituality, with equal measures of supernatural pop, alchemical esoterica, and energized Theravada Buddhism. The paya itself sits in the middle of a fourteen-square-acre platform that hosts an impressive array of pagodas, platforms, pavilions, shrines, and 3-D murals. The crowded, helter-skelter deployment of these structures, as well as the riot of eras and styles they represent, give the site an eclectic, urban feel despite the pervasive air of gentleness and calm. That morning the place was crowded with ordinary folks, and their range of attitudes and practices, from silent meditation to the ritual bathing of rodent idols, suggested a casual democracy of the spirit.

The paya itself sat like a Buddha at the center of the square, an enormously fat and pointy bell topped with a gold-plated umbrella that tinkled distantly in the breeze. The gold leaf that coats the massive form was mostly muted beneath the overcast skies, though occasional blasts of skin-crisping sunlight brought the surface to blazing life. The stillness embodied by the paya reminded me of the implacable tranquility of the great Gothic cathedrals, but rather than the medieval sense of hushed interiority, this huge tapered thing was all surface, sitting squarely in the midst of the bustle, its windowless mass embodying an architecture of meditation. I climbed up a small platform near the paya, and sat silently among the astrologers and shop-keepers, meditating on the melancholy of departure.

As we hustled back to our hotel to collect our luggage and leave, we counted the small amount of kyat that remained in our pockets. Rounding a corner near the hotel, we came upon a young man holding a cage filled with sparrows. Five hundred kyat, the last of our lot, would buy us the right to release three birds and thereby stock up on some merit, an empty but poetic act of exchange that seemed as good a way as any of dispensing with this nearly worthless paper. The guy placed two birds in my hand, and they immediately took to the air. Then he set one sparrow on J's open palm, delicately lined like an old soul's, and the bird just sat there, perfectly content, like there was nowhere to go. But our flight would not wait, and so J softly shook her hand, and the sparrow rose into the glowering skies.

2006

INVOCATIONS

KLINGON LIKE ME

The dealer floor of the latest Star Trek Creation Convention is closed, the day's security work is done, and in a darkened Ramada Inn conference room, the Klingons prepare for their ritual, Tera'daq Tlhinganghom'mey. The hulking creatures, all members or allies of the Karizan Empire, file past a table in silence, depositing their energy weapons in a pile. Incense chokes the room as twelve aliens, both male and female, take their seats around an altar. Candlelight reflects off the latex ridges of some foreheads, and the soundtrack of *Bram Stoker's Dracula* plays on a nearby tape deck. The impressively built Mok walks counterclockwise about the altar, brandishing a hammer of Thor as he invokes the heroes of old and demands their presence at the gathering. The candles shake as he slams the hammer on the table. "We are between the worlds," he announces.

A huge, balding man enters, supporting himself on a cane. He is Korghas, supreme commander of KLAW, the Klingon Legion of Assault Warriors. Like many of those present, Korghas is not in garb, but he radiates *klin*, that volatile essence of the Klingon. KLAW and the Karizans have fought bitter fanwars in the past, but now an uneasy peace exists between the clubs. Korghas watches with amused dispassion as Mok, the Karizan Orm, or high priest, formally dissolves all standing alliances and freezes the current membership—Klingons can neither join nor leave the club. Suddenly a shout rings out, and a violent coup attempt against the Imperitor Kargh Restarc ensues. Cries of "petaQ!"

and "cheese-grater head" fill the air, and role-playing dice hit the carpet like broken bones. When the smoke clears, Kargh stands tall.

Afterwards, the Klingons gather for a toast of Romulan ale. The blue ooze tastes distinctly like schnapps.

The specter of the geek haunts Star Trek fandom. Few have forgotten the *Saturday Night Live* skit where William Shatner, playing himself at a convention, proclaimed to a passel of bespectacled weenies that they should "get a life." And Trekkers know that the vast majority of mundanes—fanspeak for those of you who do not grok—put them in the same boat as computer junkies, *Dungeons & Dragons* devotees, and sci-fi paperback gluttons: a bunch of maladjusted, pimple-faced wonks.

But even a glance at a con will reveal that Trekkers are ethnically and generationally diverse, are as likely to be female as male, and display no more incidence of acne than the crowd at a Depeche Mode concert. While encouraging much trivial consumption and claustrophobic socializing, the con also creates what the Sufi underground anarchist Hakim Bey calls a "temporary autonomous zone." Loosening themselves from the mundane demands that nail the adult world in place, fans are free to playact, lust over aliens, and make goofy puns. But this free zone requires lots of work too: Fans churn out reams of zines and fiction, build models of battle cruisers and phasers, stitch together costumes, and perform filksongs (slang for frequently parodic fan songs). And most fans share a good degree of irony and humor about their "weekend-only world."

And some dress up like ferocious, scowling aliens who like their combat brutal, their conversations blunt, and their sex ferocious. Dress-up Klingon fan clubs were born in 1974, when Robert Asprin formed the Klingon Diplomatic Corps to provide security at cons, but the race has really been rearing its gnarly head of late. The Klingon language, tlh-Ingan, a self-consistent tongue concocted by the linguist Mark Okrand for the third Star Trek movie, has lately drawn strong interest from fans and the press, and has led to a best-selling dictionary, a language tape, the semi-academic zine *HolQeD* and a summer camp. Besides proliferating at cons, members of the passionate and noble race have been spotted in the darker corners of New York City dance clubs. A sample of dialogue from Worf—the resident Klingon of *Star Trek: the Next Generation*—opens a recent album by Orbital, a popular techno group. And Los Angeles Laker James Worthy was granted his wish to play a Klingon. He appeared as a six-foot-nine mercenary in a recent *ST:TNG* episode.

Though many things to many people, Klingons are not geeks.

Prince Keon of the Kreene line makes his home in the sovereign Klingon states of the Darkhold Nebula of the Karizan Empire, a small enclave of about seventy star systems hidden in the dark matter of an ion-storm nebula. There he and his people lurk, swiping technology from anyone foolish enough to slip into their space: Romulan, Klingon, Federation. Like many Klingons a large individual, Prince Keon is a hybrid, a kind of energy vampire bred from Klin blood and a mysterious breed—possibly genetically engineered—discovered in his father's day.

Prince Keon is also twenty-nine-year-old Lenny Greene, a long-haired ex-Army man of great good humor who resides in Long Island, where he drives a bus for mentally handicapped kids. "Basically Long Island is under my command," he says with a grin. His Klingon sash is peppered with various fan pins, the Karizan stella, security badges, and an army decoration for proficiency with grenades and rifle ("that's for real"). In Germany, Greene was part of the Dirty Thirty force who would mobilize to protect "the army's big stick": truck-mounted Pershing missiles. Alongside the simulated drills Green would perform as part of his duties, he participated in Starship tactical role-playing games. Military service also exposed Greene to Neopaganism, the contemporary practice of reconstituting Europe's pre-Christian nature religions. He chuckled when I raised an eyebrow in surprise. "Oh, there are lots of pagans in the armed forces."

Having already participated in a "war machine," Greene was attracted to both the code of honor and the pragmatic, no-nonsense worship that marks Klingon warrior society. "The Klingons are very similar to the Norse, the Japanese samurai, Genghis Khan. It makes sense—if you're taking from those people, not only are you gonna take their organization, but you're gonna take the basic concept of their religion."

Ambassador Khristine Arengar Azhir plops down next to Keon and cools him off with a Japanese fan. He starts to massage her stockinged feet. "We're a crazy lot," she says to me. "Like one big happy dysfunctional family." A pale brunette with large glasses, a stick-on dragon tattoo, and a button that reads "To Hell with the Prime Directive I'm Going to Kill Something," Khristine wears decidedly kinky garb—along with a short black skirt, black stockings, black fingernail polish, and pumps, Khristine's "showpieces" include a cat-o'-nine-tails, a riding crop, and a knife jammed into her red garter (it's actually a key chain).

The twenty-three-year-old unemployed billing clerk from Queens proceeds to explain the "hodgepodge smorgasbord" of Neopagan elements that go into the Tera'daq ritual, fingering the pentagram and the Bajoran symbol that dangle from her neck. "Mostly this is for show. We would have fog machines if we could afford it."

"We're not really doing anything," Keon insists. "When we do Tera'daq we are in character. Once you close the door, you're it. Once you walk out the door, you're back in your normal life. When I play my character it's sort of like a different person, but it's part of myself, something that no one can take away. Klingon is what's inside you. You have to let it out."

Khristine found that getting in touch with her inner Klingon was not only fun, but also empowering. "One of the reasons I became a Klingon was that I was going through a bad relationship and it helped me build self-confidence. I like interacting with people, growling at them and stuff. It's healthy for me," she says. "It keeps me sane, actually. A lot of people here are paramedics or work in law enforcement and public safety. Stressful jobs. This is a way to act out. 'Cause they see the darker side of reality."

With their Siberian swagger and their talk of empire and conquest, the Klingons on the original *Star Trek* series obviously represented the

Soviets. But by the mid-'80s, glasnost forced Paramount's hand, and in the sixth Star Trek film the Klingon Empire and the Federation moved towards peace. The Star Trek movies also opened up Klingon subjectivities—literally. For the first time, we saw the dark, cramped interiors of Klingon ships and met the Imperial race—the Klingons with the walnut ridges on their foreheads. As one fan put it, Klingons were no longer "just guys painted brown with a Fu Manchu mustache." But perhaps most importantly, the movies gave us the harsh, guttural Klingon tongue—which, years before *Dances With Wolves*, was respectfully subtitled.

By the time *Star Trek: the Next Generation* takes place (seventy years later), the Klingons have formed a tentative alliance with the Feds. *ST:TNG* added a further twist by placing a Klingon on the bridge (like many Klin fans, doing security). Raised by humans, Lieutenant Worf constantly struggles with his split identity, and some of *ST:TNG*'s best episodes, Worf wrestles with—and gives into—the call of his Klingon blood. By casting Worf and many Klingons with African-American actors (most notably, Tony Todd as Worf's brother Kurn), *ST:TNG* added an alien dimension to TV's tentative engagement with cultural difference. Taken solely as racial allegories, Klingons come off as galactic gangsta rappers with Afrocentric pride—like most liberal and mainstream representations of ethnicity, a thoroughly problematic blend of stereotypes and positive imagery.

But as good myth-weavers know, the potency of myth lies in the magic of ambiguity. Myth derives its power from twilight, from straddling the here and there, like those optical illusions in psychology textbooks that signify different images depending on how you look at them. Strong myth has room for many specific and contradictory functions, political or otherwise, but it always opens up into another secret garden. No matter how much you allegorize Klingons, as Russkies or black nationalists or creatures from the id, they are compelling because they retain a certain nomadic volatility—what the zine *Katra* calls "outliness."

The Karizan Klingons who gathered in the Ramada Inn are even more iconoclastic than most Trekkers, and their ritual conjures meanings only hinted at on the screen. Like Greene, most of the members of the club are Neopagans, part of a small but thriving tribe of folks who have concocted an earthy, polytheistic religion out of nature worship, boho sensibilities, the recovery of the Goddess, and the Wiccan revival cobbled together by Gerald Gardner and other British witches in the mid-1900s.

The Karizans are not alone in their heathen fandom—while Neopagans groove to lunar cycles and the ancient wheel of the seasons, and conjure forth archaic pantheons within a decidedly pre-Enlightenment aesthetic, a significant chunk of this magical community are also serious sci-fi fans. Both fans and witches share a very concrete sense of the power of the imagination, seen not as an elite realm restricted to "artists" (or TV producers) but as a vital phantasmic faculty that links the realms of fantasy with the here and now. Most of us lose this vigorous sense of imagination when we age, but both fans and Neopagans learn to recover it, feed it, manifest it. There are more differences between fandom and Neopaganism than similarities, and even the Karizans insisted that the Tera'daq ritual was a "show-piece"—not a real Neopagan ritual but a way to play with their magical leanings within the Trek mythos. But by performing their spiritual sensibilities in the trappings of a TV show, the Karizans also revived the oldest derivation of the word "fan:" *fanaticus*, a devotee of the ancient mystery cults.

Panayiotis K. Venetis enters the Ramada room where the Karizans take their breaks from working security. "It's a cluster fuck out there," he says, plopping down. Bearded and built like the Norse thunder god whose hammer he wears around neck, Venetis radiates an intelligent and heroic charisma. As K'Thor, leader of the Karizans, many considered him a power-mad demagogue before he staged his own ouster.

"It's no coincidence that a lot of people who are first-generation immigrants are kinda schizophrenic and get into subcultures," says Venetis, who grew up attending Greek parochial school and hearing the tales of the heroes of old. "You're receiving contradictory feelings between your upbringing and the culture you're transplanted in, which is giving you a whole new set of messages. So you gotta wend your way through that and not go crazy."

Attending the Bronx High School of Science, Venetis became aware of Neopaganism. "It seemed to be something invented rather than something that survived from antiquity. So I figured I might as well invent my own worship." While working as a rehabilitation counselor in City Hospital, he decided to form a Neopagan group that would mix European lore with the precepts of warriorhood he had been gleaning from his martial arts practice. "I had been exposed to role-playing, so I wanted to use that as a way of experiencing the mythology a little more directly than just reading or writing it."

Finding that Norse mythology was alien to most of his group, he decided to use more familiar aliens instead. "At that time, the movies were portraying the Klingons in a very Viking manner, as independent raiders with a warrior culture, so it was very easy to adapt that to the mythical structure I was working on."

When Venetis and his crew started going to cons in character, they stirred up a lot of controversy. "We were Neopagan so we brought a lot of Neopagan elements. It was theatrics, but a lot of people here are born-again Christians and we used to freak them out." Rumors of sex orgies and blood sacrifice began circulating, so the Karizans began weaving together the most outrageous tales in their zine *The Void Warrior* and then admitting to them. "We deny nothing" was their battle cry.

In *The Practice of Everyday Life*, the French theorist Michel de Certeau describes the tactics used by popular readers as poaching. Excluded from the meanings legislated by critics or academics, "readers are travelers; they move across lands belonging to someone else, like nomads poaching their way across fields they did not write, despoiling the wealth of Egypt to enjoy it themselves." As Henry Jenkins points out in *Textual Poachers*, his solid study of media fandom, de Certeau's model lends itself to TV readers as well. "Within the cultural economy," Jenkins points out, "fans are peasants, not proprietors." Everything they touch is copyrighted, and even their best-loved products can be canceled.

Fan fiction writers weave their stories from the threads Hollywood leaves dangling, creating both an overarching consistency to their favorite shows and a body of off-kilter, contradictory tales of parallel universes, time slips, and love affairs the series writers would never dare suggest. Going far beyond the parameters of the original series, this labor of love transforms the passivity of watching TV into a creative, and sometimes critical, practice. Cultural studies folks have begun to pay attention to media fandom, which involves shows as diverse as *Starsky & Hutch, The Avengers* and *Beauty and the Beast,* as well as *Star Trek* (which draws both media and sci-fi fans). For obvious reasons, these scholars are particularly drawn to fan stories which depict Kirk and Spock (and other buddy teams) getting it on with each other—though the focus of such "slash" fiction, written almost exclusively by straight women, says as much about the academia as it does about fandom.

For these stories, like other products of fandom, become meaningful only in the context of community. Fan writing, with its sampling, genre conventions, and relative lack of emphasis on individual authorship, produces not so much definitive stories as a shifting collective body of lore. Beefy zines like the *Klingon Agonizer* contain not only fiction but also recipes, sewing instructions, technical specs, poems, con reports, and filksongs, like the "The Earthly Klinbillies," with melodies cribbed from TV shows. Only one of many tactics fans use, lore helps carve out a distinctly popular space within the bowels of the culture industry. Perhaps the best demonstration of this peasant logic is the con itself—a seasonal festival of play and excess that would fascinate Bakhtin. The term filk describes this logic perfectly—fandom is filched folk culture.

Perhaps the intense vitality of some Klingon groups—though they represent a small portion of Trek fandom—arises from the fact that they already imagine themselves to be pillaging nomads. Comparing the Karizans to KLAW and Federation clubs, Lenny Greene almost scoffs. "You've got some groups who will only adhere to what has been canonized by Paramount. Or they use FASA as their Bible (FASA is a role-playing game company that issued a plentiful book on Klingons). That's good for people who like their conformity, and the Feds are very conformist. They don't like us because we are so different. We take the ball and run with it."

Appropriately, the religious imaginations of the Karizan folks are in step with the folk bricolage of fandom. Greene defines himself as an "eclectic solitary"—meaning he is not in a "traditional" Wiccan coven. He uses bits of Asian, Amerindian, and Wiccan lore. "Lately there is a bit of Norse flavoring. I just mesh all this stuff together in my own mind to find what works. It's a practical, common-sense approach." Greene left KLAW not only because it was too conformist and hierarchical in style, but also because the founder was a hard-core Baptist. "We all know about the old days," he says with a knowing grin.

Noting that many Paramount folk attend conventions, Greene insists that the Karizan emphasis on Klingon ritual has influenced *ST:TNG*'s portrayal of Klingon culture. "They're sort of borrowing from us. Hollywood is not that creative; they steal most of their ideas. We don't mind, because they give us kudos for this." Greene's proof, such as it is, is a mention Commander Sisko of Deep Space Nine made of "some girls down on Karizan" and the placement of a Karizan insignia on Galron's seat in an episode of *ST:TNG*. "You can't see it unless you have a crystal-clear copy," Greene says. The truth of the debt doesn't really matter. In the symbiotic world of fandom and culture industry, no one controls the meaning of the Klingons—though if push comes to shove, Paramount owns them. As Greene said, "There's a feedback. Paramount feeds off fandom, fandom feeds off Paramount. It's a wonderful cycle."

Decked out in boots, a golden sash, and Klingon bustier, her long black hair falling loose aside remarkable forehead ridges, Admiral Ka'Hil Zantai Dok'Marr, the Legion Sub-Commander of KLAW, is costumed far more impressively than any of the motley Karizans. After I declared myself a *Village Voice* reporter and requested an interview with Ka'Hil, a hulking marine glowered at me and pulled her aside. It turned out that some renegade KLAW member had moved to Florida had founded a zine called *The Pillage Voice*, and the Klingon was concerned for the safety of his commander.

Though she's been a fan since she was a kid, Ka'Hil—Ines Peek—only recently became involved in Klingon, after surviving an accident in which she lost her husband. "I was in a wheelchair, with no prospects of walking again. I was about to kill myself. I was suffering from insomnia, and the TV was on twenty-four hours a day. At midnight, Channel 11 used to show the old *Star Trek* series. I was getting razor blades to kill myself, and Kirk, just by a twist of fate, was making one of his impassioned overacted speeches about the sanctity of human life. It just stopped me in my tracks."

Born and raised in the Bronx, Peek comes across as a strong, self-controlled person with a great deal of clarity about the division between fandom and the world. "In real life, I'm Ines Peek, but today I'm not. I'm Ka'Hil, with everything that entails. If you saw me in corporate America, you'd be very surprised," she says with a rare smile.

Peek likes the Klingons because "they are very honor-bound and very pragmatic. I've had a life where being tough meant surviving, and I like the Klingon toughness and survival instincts." This also explains her attraction to the hierarchical structure of KLAW. "I started out as a lowly commander on somebody's ship in charge of communications, and now I'm vice president of the Legion. Ka'Hil is very no-nonsense, spit'n'polish, very physical. She got through with no family connections."

Unlike the Karizans, KLAW demands a great deal from their members—everyone has to make their own latex forehead ridges, for example. "It's enormously creative," Ka'Hil says. "People who never wrote a letter to their mother are all of a sudden writing Klingon stories and poetry. We have Klingon cuisine. We eat a lot of seaweed and strange mushrooms, and we serve the meal with no silverware, and people are belching at the table."

Very diplomatically, Ka'Hil acknowledges the acrimony and back stabbing between her club and the Karizans. "But we finally all sat down and said, 'Look, there is no judgment here. It's IDIC'"—a reference to the commonly held Vulcan philosophy of Infinite Diversity in Infinite

Combination, an ethos as Spinozan as it is multicultural.

All small groups share small group politics, from garden clubs to anarchistic collectives. But Klingon fans have the advantage of being able to act out their highly volatile system of alliances and fanwars on the level of myth as well as club organization. The day following our interview, Ka'Hil approached me in order to keep me abreast of the latest developments. It seems that when we spoke, Ka'Hil was contemplating leaving KLAW. "But my honor bound me to speak to you as a member of KLAW." Later that night, Korghas accepted her resignation in a hotel suite. "I turned my back on him and my crew and walked away. After that my crew made their own decisions to follow or not. Then we all went back in the room and had some pizza."

Kyxak Solazarn enters the Karizan security room. With long cornrows, a strikingly attractive face, a "pure vinyl" suit, tights, and a con hand stamp on her breast, Kyxak embodies the Valkyrie/Amazon archetype of the Klingon female. A Bajoran calls out, "Women with Klingon ridges drive me wild!" She bares her teeth and growls.

Later I track down Solazarn, who works in engineering on Admiral Ka'Hil's ship *Puqbe' K' Ramjep (Daughter of Midnight)*. "Kyxak is independent, pretty much what you'd call the misfit of the group," explains twenty-six-year-old Danielle Thompson, who lives "and will probably die" in Jackson Heights, Queens, with her daughter Olivia.

Like her commander, who is also African-American, Thompson insists that race had nothing to do with her attraction to Klingons. "No! In Klingon society, there's no such thing as black and white. You're either Imperial, with the forehead, or you're irrelevant." She grins. "Even if you're a fusion (mixed-race), you're treated as one of the group. There's no such thing as me, me, me.

"Role playing gives me a chance to act out my fantasies. When I was a kid I used to think about being from a different planet, traveling the stars, being someone other than Danielle Thompson, this only child. I kept telling myself, these aren't my real parents, I'm from some other planet and my real parents are going to come pick me up soon. So I developed a real fascination with space and exploration."

She likes working security as a Klingon because "You get to have attitude. You get to walk up to other people and tell them what to do and not explain why. And if you bump into someone you don't have to say 'I'm sorry'—two words we never say. It's pure power."

I point to her riding crop. "Oh that? That's just something to hold on to. When I'm doing crowd control, its just an extension of my arm. As far as domination, I don't need this."

1994

CALLING CTHULHU

H.P. Lovecraft's Magickal Realism

> In this book it is spoken of . . . Spirits and Conjurations; of Gods, Spheres, Planes, and many other things which may or may not exist. It is immaterial whether they exist or not. By doing certain things certain results follow . . . —Aleister Crowley

Consumed by cancer in 1937 at the age of 46, the last scion of a faded aristocratic New England family, the horror writer Howard Phillips Lovecraft left one of America's most curious literary legacies. The bulk of his short stories appeared in *Weird Tales*, a pulp magazine devoted to the supernatural. Within these modest confines, Lovecraft brought dark fantasy screaming into the twentieth century, taking the genre, almost literally, into a new dimension. Nowhere is this more evident than in the loosely linked cycle of stories known, somewhat problematically, as the Cthulhu Mythos. Named for a tentacled alien monster who waits dreaming beneath the sea in the sunken city of R'lyeh, the mythos encompasses the cosmic career of a variety of gruesome extraterrestrial entities that include Yog-Sothoth, Nyarlathotep, and the blind idiot god Azathoth, who sprawls at the center of Ultimate Chaos, "encircled by his flopping horde of mindless and amorphous dancers, and lulled by the thin monotonous piping of a demoniac flute held in nameless paws."[1] Lurking on the margins of our space-time continuum, this merry crew of Outer Gods and Great Old Ones attempt, in story after story, to invade our world through science and dream and horrid rites—and, just possibly, through the medium of pulp fiction.

As a marginally popular writer working in the literary equivalent of the gutter, Lovecraft received no serious attention during his lifetime. But while most 1930s pulp fiction is nearly unreadable today, Lovecraft continues to attract attention. In France and Japan, his tales of cosmic fungi, degenerate cults, and seriously bad dreams are recognized as works of bent genius, and the celebrated French philosophers Gilles Deleuze and Felix Guattari praise his radical embrace of multiplicity in their magnum opus *A Thousand Plateaus*.[2] On Anglo-American turf, a passionate cabal of critics fill journals like *Lovecraft Studies* and *Crypt of Cthulhu* with their almost talmudic research. Meanwhile both hacks and gifted disciples continue to craft stories that elaborate the Cthulhu mythos, while fans gather at Lovecraft conventions like the NecronomiCon, named for the most famous of his forbidden grimoires. Like the science fiction writer Philip K. Dick, H.P. Lovecraft epitomizes the cult author.

Lovecraft fans do exhibit the unflagging devotion, fetishism, and sectarian debates that have characterized religious sects throughout the ages. But Lovecraft's cult status has a curiously literal dimension. Many magicians and occultists have taken up his mythos as source material for their practice. Drawn from the darker regions of the esoteric counterculture—Thelema and Satanism and Chaos magic—these Lovecraftian mages actively seek to generate the terrifying and atavistic encounters that Lovecraft's protagonists stumble into compulsively, blindly, or against their will. Secondary sources for this Lovecraftian magic include three different "fake" editions of the *Necronomicon*, a few rites included in Anton LaVey's *The Satanic Rituals*, and a number of works by the loopy British Thelemite Kenneth Grant. Besides Grant's

Typhonian O.T.O. and the Temple of Set's Order of the Trapezoid, magical sects that tap the Cthulhu current have included the Esoteric Order of Dagon, the Bate Cabal, Michael Bertiaux's Lovecraftian Coven, and a Starry Wisdom group in Florida, named after the nineteenth-century sect featured in Lovecraft's "The Haunter of the Dark." Solo Chaos mages fill out the ranks, cobbling together Lovecraftian arcana on the Internet or freely sampling the mythos in their chthonic, open-ended (anti-) workings.

This phenomenon is made all the more intriguing by the fact that Lovecraft himself was a "mechanistic materialist" philosophically opposed to spirituality and magic of any kind. Accounting for this discrepancy is only one of many curious problems raised by the apparent power of Lovecraftian magic. Why and how do these pulp visions work? What constitutes the authentic occult? How does magic relate to the tension between fact and fable? As I hope to show, Lovecraftian magic is not a pop hallucination but an imaginative and coherent interpretation set in motion by the dynamics of Lovecraft's own writings, a set of thematic, stylistic, and intertextual strategies which constitute what I call Lovecraft's magick realism.

Magical realism already denotes a strain of Latin American fiction—exemplified by Jorge Luis Borges, Gabriel García Márquez, and Isabel Allende—in which a fantastic dreamlike logic melds seamlessly and delightfully with the rhythms of the everyday. Lovecraft's magick realism depicts a more convulsive eruption, as ancient and amoral forces violently puncture the realistic surface of his tales. Throughout his work, Lovecraft constructs and then collapses a number of powerful polarities—between realism and fantasy, book and dream, reason and its chaotic Other. By playing out these tensions in his writing, Lovecraft also reflects the transformations that darkside occultism has undergone as it confronts modern thought in such forms as psychology, quantum physics, and the existential groundlessness of being. And by embedding all this in an unusually original mythos, he draws the reader into the chaos that lies "between the worlds" of magick and reality.

A PULP POE

Written mostly in the 1920s and '30s, Lovecraft's work builds a somewhat rickety bridge between the florid decadence of *fin de siècle* fantasy and the more rational demands of the new century's science fiction. His early writing is gaudy Gothic pastiche, but in his mature Cthulhu tales, Lovecraft adopts a pseudodocumentary style that utilizes the language of journalism, scholarship, and science to construct a realistic and measured prose voice, which then explodes into feverish, adjectival horror. Some find Lovecraft's intensity atrocious—not everyone can enjoy a writer capable of comparing a strange light to "a glutted swarm of corpse-fed fireflies dancing hellish sarabands over an accursed marsh."[3] But in terms of horror, Lovecraft delivers. His protagonist is usually a reclusive bookish type, a scholar or artist who is (or is known to) the first-person narrator. Stumbling onto odd coincidences or beset with strange dreams, his intellectual curiosity drives him to pore through forbidden books or local folklore, even as his empirical turn of mind blinds him to the nightmarish implications that the reader readily perceive. When the mythos finally breaks through, it often shatters the protagonist, even though the invasion is usually more cognitive than physical.

Lovecraft did not just tell tales—he built a world. His mythos stories all share a liminal map that weaves fictional places like Arkham, Dunwich, and Miskatonic University into the New England landscape; they also refer to a common body of entities and forbidden books. A relatively common feature in fantasy fiction, these metafictional techniques create the sense that Lovecraft's mythos lies beyond each individual tale, hovering in a dimension halfway between fantasy and the real. It's no accident that one of the more successful role-playing games to follow in the heels of *Dungeons & Dragons* takes place in Lovecraft Country. While most role-playing adventure games build their worlds inside broadly based genres (heroic fantasy, cyberpunk, Arthur's Britain), *Call of Cthulhu* is staged in Lovecraft's 1920s America. Players become "investigators" who track down dark rumors or heinous occult crimes that gradually open up the reality of the monsters. *Call of Cthulhu* is an unusually grim game; the best investigators can do is to retain sanity and stave off the monsters' eventual apocalyptic triumph. Nonetheless, the game has proven extremely popular, its success due no doubt in part to the considerable density of Lovecraft's original metafiction, a density that the game itself further magnifies.

Lovecraft himself multiplied and deepened the mythos by encouraging his friends to write stories that take place within it. Writers like Clark Ashton Smith, Robert Howard, and a young Robert Bloch complied. After Lovecraft's death, August Derleth carried on this tradition with great devotion, and today, dozens continue to write Lovecraftian tales. With some notable exceptions, most of these writers mangle the myth, often by detailing horrors the master wisely left shrouded in ambiguous gloom.[4] The exact delineations of Lovecraft's cosmic cast and their apocalyptic time line remain murky even for those devoted to a great deal of close reading and cross-referencing. But in the hands of the Catholic Derleth, the extraterrestrial Great Old Ones become elemental demons defeated by the "good" Elder Gods. Forcing Lovecraft's cosmic and fundamentally amoral pantheon into a traditional religious framework, Derleth committed an imaginative and interpretive error. For despite the diabolical aura of his creatures, Lovecraft generates much of his unique power by stepping beyond good and evil altogether.

THE HORROR OF REASON

Lovecraft largely abandoned the religious underpinnings of the classic supernatural tale, turning instead towards science to provide frameworks for horror. Calling Lovecraft the "Copernicus of the horror tale," the fantasy writer Fritz Leiber Jr. wrote that Lovecraft was the first fantasist who "firmly attached the emotion of spectral dread to such concepts as outer space, the rim of the cosmos, alien beings, unsuspected dimensions, and the conceivable universes lying outside our own space-time continuum."[5] As Lovecraft himself put it in a letter, "The time has come when the normal revolt against time, space, and matter must assume a form not overtly incompatible with what is known of reality—when it must be gratified by images forming *supplements* rather than *contradictions* of the visible and measurable universe."[6]

For Lovecraft, it is not the sleep of reason that breeds monsters, but reason with its eyes agog. By fusing cutting-edge science with archaic material, Lovecraft creates a twisted materialism in which scientific breakthroughs returns us to the untamed abyss, and hard-nosed research revives the factual basis of forgotten and discarded myths. Hence Lovecraft's obsession with archeology; the digs which unearth alien artifacts and bizarrely angled cities are simultaneously historical and imaginal. In 1930 story "The Whisperer in Darkness," Lovecraft identifies the planet Yuggoth (from which the fungoid Mi-Go launch their clandestine invasions of Earth) with the newly discovered planet called Pluto. To the 1930's reader—probably the kind of person who would thrill to popular accounts of C.W. Tombaugh's discovery of the "ninth planet" that very year—this factual reference opens up Lovecraft's fiction into a real world that is itself opening up to the limitless cosmos.

Lovecraft's most self-conscious, if somewhat strained, fusion of occult folklore and weird science occurs in the 1932 story "The Dreams in the Witch-House." The demonic characters that the folklorist Walter Gilman first glimpses in his nightmares are stock ghoulies: the evil witch crone Keziah Mason, her familiar spirit Brown Jenkin, and a Black Man who is perhaps Lovecraft's most unambiguously Satanic figure. These figures eventually invade the real space of Gilman's curiously angled room. But Gilman is also a student of quantum physics, Riemann spaces, and non-Euclidian mathematics, and his dreams are almost psychedelic manifestations of his abstract knowledge. Within these "abysses whose material and gravitational properties . . . he could not even begin to explain," an "indescribably angled" realm of "prisms, labyrinths, clusters of cubes and planes, and Cyclopean buildings," Gilman keeps encountering a small polyhedron and a mass of "prolately spheroidal bubbles." By the end of the tale that he realizes that these are none other than Keziah and her familiar spirit, classic demonic clichés translated into the most alien dimension of speculative science: hyperspace.

These days, one finds the motif of hyperspace in science fiction, pop cosmology, computer interface design, channeled UFO prophecies, and the neo-shamanism of today's high-octane psychedelic travelers—all discourses that feed contemporary Chaos magic. The term itself was most likely coined by the science fiction writer John W. Campbell Jr. in 1931, though its origins as a concept lie in nineteenth-century mathematical explorations of the fourth dimension. In many ways, however, Lovecraft was the concept's first mythographer. From the perspective of hyperspace, our normal, three-dimensional spaces are exhausted and insufficient constructs. But our incapacity to vividly imagine this new dimension in humanist terms creates a crisis of representation, a crisis that for Lovecraft calls up our most ancient fears of the unknown. "All the objects . . . were totally beyond description or even comprehension," Lovecraft writes of Gilman's seething nightmare before paradoxically proceeding to describe these horrible objects.

Lovecraft has a habit of labeling his horrors "indescribable," "nameless," "unseen," "unutterable," "unknown," and "formless." Though superficially weak, this move can also be seen a kind of macabre *via negativa*. Like the apophatic oppositions of negative theologians such as Pseudo-Dionysus or St. John of the Cross, Lovecraft marks the limits of language, limits which paradoxically point to the Beyond. For the mystics, this ultimate is the ineffable One, Pseudo-Dionysus's "superluminous gloom" or the *Ain Soph* of the Kabbalists. But there is no unity in Lovecraft's Beyond. It is the omnivorous Outside, the screaming multiplicity of cosmic hyperspace opened up by reason.

For Lovecraft, scientific materialism is the ultimate Faustian bargain, not because it hands us Promethean technology—a man for the eighteenth century, Lovecraft had no interest in gadgetry—but because it leads us beyond the horizon of what our minds can withstand. "The most merciful thing in the world, I think, is the inability of the human mind to correlate all its contents," goes the famous opening line of "The Call of Cthulhu." By correlating those contents, empiricism opens up "terrifying vistas of reality"—what Lovecraft elsewhere calls "the blind cosmos [that] grinds aimlessly on from nothing to something and from something back to nothing again, neither heeding nor knowing the wishes or existence of the minds that flicker for a second now and then in the darkness."[7]

Lovecraft gave this existentialist dread an imaginative voice, what he called "cosmic alienage." For Fritz Leiber, the "monstrous nuclear chaos" of Azathoth, Lovecraft's supreme entity, symbolizes "the purposeless, mindless, yet all-powerful universe of materialistic belief." But this symbolism isn't the whole story. For as DMT voyagers come to suspect, hyperspace is haunted. The entities that erupt from Lovecraft's inhuman realms seem to suggest that in a blind mechanistic cosmos, the most alien thing is sentience itself. Peering outward through the cracks of domesticated "human" consciousness, a compassionless materialist like Lovecraft could only react with horror, for reason must cower before the most raw and atavistic dream-dragons of the psyche.

Modern humans usually suppress, ignore, or constrain these forces lurking in our lizard brain. Mythically, such forces take the form of demons imprisoned under the angelic yokes of altruism, morality, and intellect. Yet if one does not believe in any ultimate universal purpose, then these primal forces are the *most* attuned with the cosmos precisely *because* they are amoral and inhuman. In "The Dunwich Horror", Henry Wheeler overhears a monstrous moan from a diabolical rite and asks "from what unplumbed gulfs of extra-cosmic consciousness or obscure, long-latent heredity, were those half-articulate thunder-croakings drawn?" The Outside is within.

CHAOS CULTURE

Lovecraft's fiction expresses a future primitivism that finds its most intense esoteric expression in Chaos magic, an eclectic contemporary style of darkside occultism that draws from Thelema, Satanism, Austin Osman Spare, and Eastern metaphysics to construct a thoroughly contemporary magic. For today's Chaos mages, there is no tradition. The symbols and myths of countless sects, orders, and faiths, are constructs, useful fictions, games. That magic works has nothing to do with its truth claims and everything to do with the will and experience of the magician. Recognizing the distinct possibility that we may be adrift in a meaningless mechanical cosmos within which human will and imagination are vaguely comic flukes (the "cosmic indifferentism" Lovecraft himself professed), the mage accepts his groundlessness, embracing the turbulent self-creating void that is himself.

As we find with Lovecraft's fictional cults and grimoires, Chaos magicians refuse the hierarchical, symbolic, and monotheist biases of traditional esotericism. Like most Chaos magicians, the British occultist Peter Carroll gravitates towards the Black, not because he desires a simple Satanic inversion of Christianity but because he seeks the amoral and shamanic core of magical experience—a core that Lovecraft conjures up with his orgies of drums, guttural chants, and screeching horns. At the same time, Chaos mages like Carroll also plumb the weird science of quantum physics, complexity theory, and electronic Prometheanism. Some darkside magicians become consumed by the primitive forces they unleash or grow addicted to the dark costume of the Satanic anti-hero. But the most sophisticated adopt a balanced mode of gnostic existentialism that calls all constructs into question while refusing the cold comforts of skeptical reason or suicidal nihilism, a pragmatic and empirical shamanism that resonates as much with Lovecraft's hard-headed materialism as with his horrors.

The first occultist to explore these modern mysteries was Aleister Crowley, who shattered the received vessels of occult tradition while creatively extending the dark dream of magic into the twentieth century. With his outlandish image, nefarious texts, and his famous Law of Thelema ("Do what thou wilt shall be the whole of the Law"), Crowley called into question the esoteric certainties of revelation and lineage, and was the first magus to give occult antinomianism a decidedly Nietzschean twist. Unfettered, this occult will to power can degenerate into a heartless elitism, and the fascist and racist dimensions of both twentieth-century occultism and Lovecraft himself should not be forgotten. But this self-engendering will is more exuberantly expressed as a will to Art. In many ways, the occultism that exploded during Crowley's time was an essentially *esthetic* esotericism. A good number of the nineteenth century's more inspiring magicians were poets, painters, and writers, Symbolists and decadent Romantics who dabbled in Satanism, Rosicrucianism, and esoteric societies. The Hermetic Order of the Golden Dawn was infused with artistic pretensions, and Golden Dawn member and fantasy writer Arthur Machen was one of Lovecraft's strongest influences.

But it was Austin Osman Spare who most decisively dissolved the boundary between artistic and magical life. Though working independently of the Surrealists, Spare also based his art on the dark and autonomous eruptions of subconscious material, though in a more overtly theurgic context.[8] Today's Chaos magicians are heavily influenced by Spare, and their Lovecraftian rites express his simultaneously creative and nihilistic destruction of limitations. And as the spawn of role-playing games, computers, and pop culture, they celebrate the fact that Lovecraft's secrets are scraped from the barrel of pulp fiction.

PROOF IN THE PUDDING

In a message cross-posted to the Internet newsgroups alt.necromicon [*sic*] and alt.satanism, Parker Ryan listed a wide variety of magical techniques described by Lovecraft, including entheogens, glossolalia, and shamanic drumming. Insisting that his post was "not a satirical article," Ryan then described specific Lovecraftian rites he had developed, including this "Rite of Cthulhu":

> A) Chanting. The use of the "Cthulhu chant" to create a concentrative or meditative state of consciousness that forms the basis of much later magickal work.
> B) Dream work. Specific techniques of controlled dreaming that are used to establish contact with Cthulhu.
> C) Abandonment. Specific techniques to free oneself from culturally conditioned reality tunnels.

Ryan goes on to say that he's experimented with most of his rites "with fairly good success."

In coming to terms with the magical power embedded in Lovecraft, one quickly encounters a fundamental irony: the cold skepticism of

Lovecraft himself. In his letters, Lovecraft poked fun at his own tales, claiming he wrote them for cash and playfully naming his friends after his monsters. While such attitudes in no way diminish the imaginative power of Lovecraft's tales—which arguably lie outside the control and intention of their author—they do pose a problem for the working occultist seeking to establish Lovecraft's magical authority.

The most obvious, and least fruitful, answer is to find authentic magic in Lovecraft's biography. Lovecraft's father was a traveling salesman who died in a madhouse when Lovecraft was eight, and vague rumors that he was an initiate in some Masonic order or other were exploited in the *Necronomicon* cobbled together by George Hay, Colin Wilson, and Robert Turner. Others have tried to track Lovecraft's occult know-how, especially his familiarity with Aleister Crowley and the Golden Dawn. In an Internet document relating the history of the "real" *Necronomicon*, Colin Low argues, perhaps with tongue in cheek, that Crowley befriended Sonia Greene in New York a few years before the woman married Lovecraft. As proof of Crowley's indirect influence on Lovecraft, Low sites this intriguing passage from "The Call of Cthulhu":

> That cult would never die till the stars came right again, and the secret priests would take great Cthulhu from His tomb to revive His subjects and resume His rule of earth. The time would be easy to know, for then mankind would have become as the Great Old Ones; free and wild and beyond good and evil, with laws and morals thrown aside and all men shouting and killing and reveling in joy. Then the liberated Old Ones would teach them new ways to shout and kill and revel and enjoy themselves, and all the earth would flame with a holocaust of ecstasy and freedom.[9]

Going out on a limb, Low claims this passage is a mangled reflection of Crowley's teachings on the new Aeon and *The Book of the Law*. In an article in *Societé*, Robert North also states that Lovecraft referred to "A.C." in a letter, and that Crowley was mentioned in Leonard Cline's *The Dark Chamber*, a novel Lovecraft discussed in his *Supernatural*

Horror in Literature. But so what? Lovecraft was a fanatical and imaginative reader, and many such folks are drawn to the semiotic exotica of esoteric lore regardless of any beliefs in or experiences of the paranormal. From *The Case of Charles Dexter Ward* and elsewhere, it's clear that Lovecraft knew the basic outlines of the occult. But these influences pale next to *Vathek*, Poe, or Lord Dunsany.

Desperate to assimilate Lovecraft into a tradition, some occultists enter into explanations of mystical influence by disincarnate beings. North gives this Invisible College idea a shamanic twist, asserting that prehistoric Atlantian tribes who survived the flood exercised telepathic influence on people like John Dee, Blavatsky, and Lovecraft. But none of these Lovecraft hierophants can match the delirious splendor of Kenneth Grant. In *The Magical Revival*, Grant points out more curious similarities between Lovecraft and Crowley: both refer to "Great Old Ones" and "Cold Wastes" (of Kadath and Hadith, respectively); the entity "Yog-Sothoth" rhymes with "Set-Thoth," and *Al Azif: The Book of the Arab* resembles Crowley's *Liber Al vel Legis: The Book of the Law*. In *Nightside of Eden*, Grant maps Lovecraft's pantheon onto a darkside Tree of Life, comparing the mangled "iridescent globes" that occasionally pop up in Lovecraft's tales with the shattered *sefirot* known as the Qlipoth. Grant concludes that Lovecraft had "direct and conscious experience of the inner planes," the same zones Crowley prowled, and that Lovecraft "disguised" his occult experiences as fiction.[10]

Like many latter-day Lovecraftians, Grant commits the error of literalizing a purposefully nebulous myth. A subtler and more satisfying version of this argument is the notion that Lovecraft had direct *unconscious* experiences of the inner planes, experiences which his quotidian mind rejected but which found their way into his writings nonetheless. For Lovecraft was blessed with a vivid and nightmarish dream life, and he drew the substance of a number of his tales from beyond the wall of sleep. In this sense, Lovecraft's magickal authority is nothing more—or less—than the authority of dream.

So what kind of dream tales are these? A Freudian could have a field day with Lovecraft's fecund, squishy sea monsters, and a Jungian analyst

might recognize the liniments of the proverbial shadow. But Lovecraft's shadow is so inky it swallows up the standard archetypes of the collective unconscious like a black hole. If we see the archetypal world not as a static storehouse of timeless godforms but as a constantly mutating carnival of figures, then the seething extraterrestrial monsters that Lovecraft glimpsed in the chaos of hyperspace are not so much archaic figures of heredity than the avatars of a new psychological and mythic aeon. At the very least, it would seem that things are getting mighty out of hand beyond the magic circle of the ordered daylight mind.

For the Chaos magician, reality can coherently present itself through any number of self-sustaining but mutually contradictory symbolic paradigms (or "reality tunnels," in Robert Anton Wilson's memorable phrase). Nothing is true and everything is permitted. By emphasizing the self-fulfilling nature of all reality claims, such a perspective creatively erodes the distinction between legitimate esoteric transmission and total fiction.

This bias toward the experimental is found in Anton LaVey's *Satanic Rituals,* which includes the first overtly Lovecraftian rituals to see print. In presenting "Die Elektrischen Vorspiele" (which LaVey based on a Lovecraftian tale by Frank Belknap Long), the "Ceremony of the Angles," and "The Call to Cthulhu" (the latter two penned by Michael Aquino), LaVey does claim that Lovecraft "clearly . . . had been influenced by very real sources."[11] But in holding that Satanic magic allows you to "objectively enter into a subjective state," LaVey more emphatically promotes the ritual power of fantasy—a radical subjectivity which explains his irreverence towards occult source material, whether Lovecraft or Masonry. In naming his Order of the Trapezoid after the "Shining Trapezohedron" found in Lovecraft's "The Haunter of the Dark"—a black, oddly angled extraterrestrial crystal used to communicate with the Old Ones—LaVey emphasized that fictions can channel magical forces regardless of their historical authenticity.

In his two rituals, Michael Aquino expresses the subjective power of "meaningless" language by creating a "Yuggothic" tongue similar to that heard in Lovecraft's "The Dunwich Horror" and "The Whisperer in Darkness." Such guttural utterances help to shut down the rational mind (try chanting "P'garn'h v'glyzz" for a couple of hours), an idea also elaborated by Kenneth Grant in his notion of the Cult of Barbarous Names. After leaving the Church of Satan to form the more serious Temple of Set in 1975, Aquino eventually reformed the Order of the Trapezoid into the practical magic wing of the Setian philosophy. For Stephen R. Flowers, the current Grand Master of the order, the substance of Lovecraftian magic is precisely an overwhelming subjectivity that flies in the face of objective law. "The Old Ones are the objective manifestations . . . of the subjective universe which is what is trying to 'break through' the merely rational mind-set of modern humanity."[12] For Flowers, such invocations are ultimately apocalyptic, hastening a transition into a chaotic age in which the Old Ones reveal themselves as future reflections of the Black Magician. "There are no more Nightmares for us," Flowers wrote to me.

This desire to rebel against the tyranny of reason and its ordered objective universe is one of the underlying goals of Chaos magic. Many would applaud the sentiment expressed by Albert Wilmarth in Lovecraft's "The Whisperer in Darkness": "To shake off the maddening and wearying limitations of time and space and natural law—to be linked with the vast outside—to come close to the nighted and abysmal secrets of the infinite and the ultimate—surely such a things was worth the risk of one's life, soul, and sanity!"[13]

In his electronically circulated text "Kathulu Majik: Luvkrafting the Roles of Modern Uccultizm," Tyagi Nagasiva, writing under the name Haramullah, argues that most Western magic is ossified and dualistic, heavily weighted towards the forces of order, hierarchy, moralizing, and structured language. "Without the destabilizing force of Kaos, we would stagnate intellectually, psychologically and otherwise . . . Kathulu provides a necessary instability to combat the stolid and fixed methods of the structured 'Ordurs' . . . One may become balanced through exposure to Kathulu" (Tyagi's "mis-spellings" show the influence of Genesis P-Orridge's Temple ov Psychick Youth). Haramullah criticizes black magicians who simply reverse "Ordur" with "Kaos," rather than bringing this underlying polarity into balance (a dualistic error he also finds in Lovecraft). Showing strong Taoist and Buddhist influences, Haramullah calls instead for a "Midul Path" that magically navigates between structure and disintegration, will and void. "The idea that one may progress linearly along the MP [Midul Path] is mistaken. One becomes, one does not progress. One attunes, one does not forge. One allows, one does not make."

In the *Cincinnati Journal of Ceremonial Magic,* the anonymous author of "Return of the Elder Gods" presents a more evolutionary reason for Lovecraftian magic. The author accepts the scenario of an approaching world crisis brought on by the invasion of the Elder Gods—Qlipothic transdimensional entities who ruled protohumanity until they were banished by "the agent of the Intelligence," a Promethean figure who set humanity on its current course of evolution. We remain connected to these Elder Gods through the "Forgotten Ones," the primal forces of hunger, sex, and violence that linger in the subterranean levels of our being. Only by magically reabsorbing the Forgotten Ones and using the subsequent energy to bootstrap higher consciousness can we keep the portal sealed against the return of the Elder Gods. Though Lovecraft's name is never mentioned in the article, he is ever present, a skeptical materialist dreaming the dragons awake.

WRITING THE DREAM . . .

Within the mythos tales, one finds two dimensions—the normal human world and the infested Outside—and it's the ontological tension between them that powers Lovecraft's magick realism. Though Cthulhu and friends have material aspects, their reality is most horrible for what it says about the way the universe *is.* As the Lovecraft scholar Joshi notes, Lovecraft's narrators frequently go mad "not through any physical violence at the hands of supernatural entities but through the mere *realization* of the existence of such a race of gods and beings." [14] Faced with "realms whose mere existence stuns the brain," they experience severe cognitive dissonance—precisely the sorts of disorienting rupture sought by Chaos magicians.

The role-playing game *Call of Cthulhu* wonderfully expresses the violence of this Lovecraftian paradigm shift. In adventure games like *Dungeons & Dragons*, one of your character's most significant measures is its hit points—a number which determines the amount of physical punishment your character can take before it gets injured or dies. *Call of Cthulhu* augments this physical characteristic with the psychic category of sanity. Face-to-face encounters with Yog-Sothoth or the insects from Shaggai knock points off your Sanity, but so does your discovery of more information about the mythos—the more you find out from books or star charts, the more likely you are to wind up in the Arkham Asylum. Magic also comes with an ironic price, one that Lovecraftian magicians might well pay heed to. If you use any of the binding spells from *De Vermis Mysteriis* or the *Pnakotic Manuscripts*, you necessarily learn more about the mythos and thereby lose more sanity.

Lovecraft's scholarly heroes investigate the mythos as much through reading and thinking as through movements in physical space, and this psychological exploration draws the mind of the reader directly into the loop. Usually, readers suspect the dark truth of the tale while the narrator still clings to a quotidian attitude—a technique that subtly forces the reader to identify with the Outside rather than with the conventional world view of the protagonist. Magically, the blindness of Lovecraft's heroes corresponds to a crucial element of occult theory developed by Austin Osman Spare: that magic occurs over and against the conscious mind, that ordinary thinking must be silenced, distracted, or thoroughly deranged for the chthonic will to express itself.[15]

In order to invade our plane, Lovecraft's entities need a portal, an interface between the worlds, and Lovecraft emphasizes two: books and dreams. In "Dreams of the Witch-House," "The Shadow out of Time" and "The Shadow over Innsmouth," dreams infect their hosts with a virulence that resembles the more overt psychic possessions that occur in "The Haunter in the Dark" and *The Case of Charles Dexter Ward*. Like the monsters themselves, Lovecraft's dreams are autonomous forces breaking through from Outside and engendering their own reality. But these dreams also conjure up a more literal "outside:" the strange dream life of Lovecraft himself, a life that (as the informed fan knows) directly inspired some of the tales.[16] By seeding his texts with his own nightmares, Lovecraft creates a autobiographical homology between himself and his protagonists. The stories themselves start to dream, which means that the reader too lies right in the path of the infection.

Lovecraft reproduces himself in his tales in a number of ways—the first-person protagonists reflect aspects of his own reclusive and bookish lifestyle; the epistolary form of the "The Whisperer in Darkness" echoes his own commitment to regular correspondence; character names are lifted from friends; and the New England landscape is his own. This psychic self-reflection partially explains why Lovecraft fans usually become fascinated with the man himself, a gaunt and solitary recluse who socialized through the mail, yearned for the eighteenth century, and adopted the crabby outlook and mannerisms of an old man. Lovecraft's life, and certainly his voluminous personal correspondence, form part of his myth.

Lovecraft thus solidifies his virtual reality by adding autobiographical elements to his world of creatures, books, and maps. He also constructs a documentary texture by thickening his tales with manuscripts, newspaper clippings, scholarly citations, diary entries, letters, and bibliographies that list fake books alongside real classics. All this produces the sense that beyond each individual tale lies a metafictional world that hovers on the edge of our own, a world that, like the monsters themselves, is constantly trying to break through and actualize itself. And thanks to mythos storytellers, role-playing games, and dark-side magicians, it has.

. . . AND DREAMING THE BOOK

In "The Shadow out of Time," Lovecraft makes explicit one of the fantastic equations that drives his magick realism: the equivalence of dreams and books. For five years, the narrator, an economics professor named Nathaniel Wingate Peaslee, is taken over by a mysterious "secondary personality." After recovering his original identity, Peaslee is beset by powerful dreams in which he finds himself in a strange city, inhabiting a huge tentacle-sprouting conical body, writing down the history of modern Western world in a book. In the climax of the tale, Peaslee journeys to the Australian desert to explore ancient ruins buried beneath the sands. There he discovers a book written in English, in his own handwriting: the very same volume he had produced inside his monstrous dream body.

Though we learn very little of their contents, Lovecraft's diabolical grimoires are so infectious that even glancing at their ominous sigils proves dangerous. As with their dreams, these texts obsess Lovecraft's bookish protagonists to the point that the volumes, in Christopher Frayling's phrase, "vampirize the reader." Their titles alone are magic spells, the hallucinatory incantations of an eccentric antiquarian: the *Pnakotic Manuscripts*, the *Ilarnet Papyri*, the *R'lyeh Text*, the *Seven Cryptical Books of Hsan*. Lovecraft's friends contributed *De Vermis Mysteriis* and von Junzt's *Unaussprechlichen Kulten*, and Lovecraft named the author of his *Cultes des Goules*, the Comte d'Erlette, after his young fan August Derleth. Hovering over all these grim tomes is the dreaded and forbidden *Necronomicon*, a book of blasphemous invocations to speed the return of the Old Ones. Lovecraft's supreme intertextual fetish, the *Necronomicon* stands as one of the few mythical books in literature that have absorbed so much imaginative attention that they've entered published reality.

If books owe their life not to their individual contents but to the larger webwork of reference and citation within which they are woven, than the dread *Necronomicon* clearly has a life of its own. Besides literary studies, the *Necronomicon* has generated numerous pseudo-scholarly analyses, including significant appendixes in the *Encyclopedia Cthulhiana* and Lovecraft's own "History of the *Necronomicon*." A number of FAQs can be found on the Internet, where a mild flame war periodically erupts between magicians, horror fans, and mythology experts over the reality of the book. The undead entity referred to in the *Necronomicon*'s famous couplet—"That is not dead which can eternal lie,/And with strange eons even death may die"—may be nothing more or less than the text itself, always lurking in the margins as we read the real.

Lovecraft's brief "History" was apparently inspired by the first

Necronomicon hoax: a review of an edition of the dreaded tome submitted to Massachusetts's *Branford Review* in 1934. Decades later, index cards for the book started popping up in university library catalogs. It's perhaps the principle expression of Lovecraft's magick realism that all these ghostly signifiers finally manifested the signified itself. In 1973, a small-press edition of *Al Azif* (the *Necronomicon*'s Arabic name) appeared, consisting of eight pages of simulated Syrian script repeated 24 times. Four years later, the Satanists at New York's Magickal Childe published a *Necronomicon* by Simon, a grab bag that contains far more Sumerian myth than Lovecraft (though portions were "purposely left out" for the "safety of the reader"). George Hay's *Necronomicon: The Book of Dead Names*, also a literary child of the '70s, is the most complex, intriguing, and Lovecraftian of the lot. In the spirit of the master's pseudoscholarship, Hay nests the fabulated invocations of Yog-Sothoth and Cthulhu amongst a set of analytic, literary, and historical essays.

Though magicians with strong imaginations have claimed that even the Simon book works wonders, the pseudohistories of the various *Necronomicons* are more compelling than the actual texts. Lovecraft himself provided the bare bones: the manuscript was penned in 730 ACE by a poet, the mad Arab Abdul Alhazred, and named after the nocturnal sounds of insects. It was subsequently translated by Theodorus Philetas into Greek, by Olaus Wormius into Latin, and by John Dee into English. Lovecraft lists various libraries and private collections where fragments of the volume reside, and gives us a knowing wink by noting that the fantasy writer R.W. Chambers is said to have derived the monstrous and suppressed book found in his novel *The King in Yellow* from rumors of the *Necronomicon* (Lovecraft himself claimed to have gotten his inspiration from Chambers).

All of the *Necronomicon*'s subsequent pseudohistories weave the book in and out of actual occult history, with John Dee playing a particularly conspicuous role. According to Colin Wilson, joining the fun, the version of the text published in the Hay *Necronomicon* was encrypted in Dee's Enochian cipher-text *Liber Logaeth*. Colin Low's *Necronomicon* FAQ claims that Dee discovered the book at the court of King Rudolph

II's court in Prague, and that it was under its influence that Dee and his scryer Edward Kelly achieved their most powerful astral encounters. Never published, Dee's translation became part of celebrated collection of Elias Ashmole housed at the British Library. Here Crowley read it, freely borrowing passages for *The Book of the Law*, and ultimately passing on some of its contents indirectly to Lovecraft through Sophia Greene. Crowley's role in Low's tall tale is appropriate, for Crowley certainly knew the magical power of hoax and history.

The *Necronomicon* is not the first fiction to generate real magical activity within this potent twilight zone between philology and fantasy. In the early 1600s, a series of anonymous Rosicrucian manifestos claimed to issue from a secret brotherhood of Christian Hermeticists who had deemed it time to come above ground. Many readers immediately wanted to join up, though it is unlikely that such a group existed at the time. But the hoax focused esoteric desire and inspired an explosion of actual Rosicrucian groups. Though one of the two suspected authors of the manifestos, Johann Valentin Andreae, never came clean, he made veiled references to Rosicrucianism as an "ingenious game which a masked person might like to play upon the literary scene, especially in an age infatuated with everything unusual."[17] Like the Rosicrucian manifestos or Blavatsky's *Book of Dzyan*, Lovecraft's *Necronomicon* is the occult equivalent of Orson Welles's radio broadcast of the *War of the Worlds*. As Lovecraft himself wrote, "No weird story can truly produce terror unless it is devised with all the care and verisimilitude of an actual hoax."[18]

Perhaps the history of the occult itself is nothing but such a confabulation, its lies wedded to its genealogies, its timeless truths fabricated by creative visionaries, madmen, and pranksters. In his novel *Foucault's Pendulum*, Umberto Eco suggests that esoteric truth is nothing more than a semiotic conspiracy theory born of an endlessly rehashed and self-referential literature—precisely the sort of intertextual fabric that Lovecraft understood so well. For those who need to ground their profound states of consciousness in objective correlatives, this is a damning indictment of tradition. But as Chaos magicians remind us, magic is nothing more than subjective experience interacting with an internally consistent matrix of signs and affects. In the absence of orthodoxy, all we have is the dynamic tantra of text and perception, of reading and dream. These days the Great Work may be nothing more or less than an ingenious game, fabricating itself without closure or rest, weaving itself out of the resplendent void where Azathoth writhes on his Mandelbrot throne.

1995

Notes

[1] "The Haunter of the Dark," *The Best of H.P. Lovecraft: Bloodcurdling Tales of Horror and the Macabre* (New York: Ballantine, 1963), 220.

[2] "The anomalous is neither an individual nor a species; it has only affects, it has neither familiar or subjectified feelings, nor specific or significant characteristics. Human tenderness is as foreign to it as human classifications. Lovecraft applies the term 'Outsider' to this thing or entity, the Thing, which arrives and passes at the edge, which is linear yet multiple, 'teeming, seething, swelling, foaming, spreading like an infectious disease, this nameless horror.'" Gilles Deleuze and Felix Guattari, *A Thousand Plateaus* (Minnesota: University of Minnesota Press), 244–5.

[3] "The Haunter of the Dark," *Best of . . .*, 202.

[4] One of these notable exceptions is *The Starry Wisdom* (London: Creation Books, 1994), D.M. Mitchell's British collection of mythos tales and art.

[5] Fritz Leiber, Jr., "A Literary Copernicus," in S.T. Joshi, et al., *H.P. Lovecraft: Four Decades of Criticism* (Athens, Ohio: Ohio University Press, 1980), 51.

[6] S.T. Joshi, *H.P. Lovecraft* (Mercer Island, Wash.: Starmbat House, 1982), 58.

[7] "The Silver Key," *Best of . . .*, 53.

[8] See Nadia Choucha's *Surrealism and the Occult* (Vermont: Destiny Books, 1991), 51–74.

[9] "The Call of Cthulhu," *Best of . . .*, 83.

[10] Colin Wilson, "Introduction," in George Hay, ed., *The Necronomicon: The book of Dead Names* (London: Corgi, 1978), 35.

[11] Anton LaVey, *The Satanic Rituals* (New York: Avon, 1972).

[12] Private e-mail correspondence.

[13] "The Whisperer in Darkness," op. cit. *Best of . . .*, 162.

[14] Joshi, 32.

[15] Following the logic of the Freudian slip, Spare workings such as sigil magic must be "forgotten" in order for their encoded intention to "break through" into reality.

[16] August Derleth collected Lovecraft's letters about his dreams in *Dreams and Fancies* (Suak City, Wis.: Arkham House, 1962).

[17] Roland Edighoffer, "Rosicrucianism," in Antoine Faivre and Jacob Needleman, eds., *Modern Esoteric Spirituality* (New York: Crossroads, 1992), 198.

[18] Quoted in S.T. Joshi, "Afterword," in H.P. Lovecraft, *The History of the Necronomicon* (West Warmick, R.I.: Necronomicon Press, 1980), 9.

TRICKSTER AT THE CROSSROADS

The gods of the Fon and Yoruba peoples of West Africa stand as some of the most vital and evocative beings ever to make their way through the souls of human beings. These *orisha* are profoundly living gods, constellations of images and forces that actively permeate the psychic lives of their devotees. On the simplest level they are alive because they are worshiped: to this day, the orisha are prayed to, invoked, and ritually charged by many millions of people in both Africa and the Americas. They are long-lived as well; unlike, say, the host of contemporary Neopagan deities like Brigid and Thor, which have essentially been reconstructed from the inquisitional ashes of history, the orisha have been sustained by countless generations of worshipers with little interruption.

The orisha are also alive in the most fundamental way that we know—the way we ourselves experience life. Though West African tradition does posit a central creator god, he/she is generally quite distant, which means that the orisha are, like us, left in a world they did not create—a world of nature and culture, of war, rivers, stars, and marketplaces. So though they possess godlike powers, the orisha are not transcendent beings; rather, they are idiosyncratic personalities thoroughly bound up with ritual, practice, and the sort of exchanges that define human community. They eat, drink, fib, and sleep with each other's mates, and are ritually "fed" with animal blood, food, and gifts. During these ceremonies the gods frequently possess the human bodies of some devotees, and their subsequent behavior reflects, in addition to whatever boons they may grant, the full range of human hungers, from sexuality to humor to intoxication.

Depending on your view of religious ritual, this can be consternating, even bracing stuff. Even sympathetic polytheists sometimes feel aversion; as one Neopagan I know put it, "Why be interested in these grotesque and parasitic deities?" You could answer that these deities are not so much grotesque as rich with character, not so much parasitic as deeply and reciprocally bound up with the daily lives of their devotees. More importantly, they also serve as a window onto the unique metaphysical universe of West Africa and the black traditions that have shaped the New World. The almost "instinctive" sense of recoil many of us feel when confronted with West Africa's more intense religious practices is itself a lingering afterimage of colonialism and its own narratives of savagery. The fact that modern people tend to hold simplistic images of precolonialist Africa—for example, imagining rustic villages where there were cosmopolitan city-states replete with bureaucrats, poets, and sewer systems—is only one indication of the lingering tendency to see Africa as the repository of the primitive, and therefore in need of "development." Looking toward Africa, the first thing the West encounters is its own dark mirror.

The images of West African spirituality that come most forcefully to mind in Western culture are images of ritual possession. Though still very much a performance, possession by the orisha is also a rather visceral fact, one that often seems to be triggered by particular drum patterns struck within the complex webs of polyrhythmic drumming that underlie these rituals. Haitians call these often jarring, rhythmically "dissonant" patterns *cassés* (or "breaks," a term used in a similar musical sense in hip-hop). Possession may result from the cognitive dissonance of the cassé, as the alien cross-beat enters from another dimension and shakes up the rhythms of the everyday dance. At this point, the possessed person (usually a dancer; in Haitian parlance, the "horse" who is to be ridden) shakes, falls to the ground, rolls his or her eyes, perhaps froths at the mouth, and speaks in different voices. Once the incoming orisha is recognized by his or her words or mannerisms, the dancer is taken to a ritual room and costumed appropriately, and then proceeds to prophesy, harangue, ask for food or booze.

I have been amazed by some vodoun rites I have seen in Haiti and Brooklyn, but even from photographs and film it is clear from the eyes of the possessed that a qualitatively different order of consciousness has momentarily annexed the everyday self. Whatever spiritual realm is accessed through these performances, it seems to be strengthened by interfacing with the "lower" traits of ordinary human personalities. Possession by the orisha thus concretizes spirit and ties it to the cycle of human ancestors and the rhythms of procreation, family, and social exchange. So too does blood sacrifice—the feeding of the orisha that so disturbs many observers—affirm the material dimension of spirit. After all, it is we humans who keep the gods who animate the spiritual world alive, and this spiritual feedback loop depends upon a process of mutual contract and exchange. Molly Ahye, a scholar of Trinidadian dance as well as an orisha worshiper, speaks about how one "must have the blood, which is a life force, which spirit lives on. You think that spirit doesn't need sustenance, but spirit needs sustenance." (Ahye admitted, however, that she did not kill animals herself.)

Even if we cannot accept possession or animal sacrifice as legitimate spiritual practices, we err in seeing the orisha as evidence of simple animism, or superstition, or folk culture elevated to the level of gods. The orisha are highly evolved and intelligent archetypal patterns, and they work out metaphysical problems that lie at the heart of life. They compose a living and evolving network of forms and forces that, from certain angles anyway, resonates deeply with Western esoteric lore and the "perennial tradition."

Proof positive of this resonance lies in the Yoruba deity Eshu-

Elegbara (or Eshu for short), the uncanny and sophisticated trickster who demanded of me this essay (a very similar figure, Legba, exists among the Fon in neighboring Benin). More than a well-hung culture hero (though he's that too), Eshu is a divine mediator of fate and information, a keen linguist, a crafty metaphysician who rules the network that binds humans and gods. Eshu is a trickster not just because he fools people and creates chaos, but more profoundly because he escapes the very codes that he establishes. He gives the world the divination system of Ifa, but does not rule over its poetic prophecies, because he is always flowing through the cracks of fate. Eshu expresses the spiritual principle of *connection*, the copulation or *conjunctio* between being and world, and the pandemonium and chicanery of this exchange. That he is a "street god" with stratagems and feral lusts only shows that in the West African tradition, spiritual principles are most actualized when they're brought into the fabric of daily life, of the recognizably human network of money and sex, power and information.

THE HERMETIC LINGUIST

Like the Attic god Hermes, Eshu is a divine messenger, and relays information between the gods and between humans and the gods. A small, very dark man, he walks with a large staff, often sucking on a pipe, candies, or his fingers. He the "roadmaker." He "sets the affairs of the earth in order . . . is so swift that he can be the messenger for many . . . [and] can circle the earth in an instant."[1] Eshu's caprice, quickness, and agility of body and mind are all characteristics he shares with Hermes, perhaps reflecting some abiding archetype of communication and exchange.

Because Eshu is the messenger, the lord of the liminal, he is always the first to be invoked in any orisha ritual. For the Fon, the primacy of Legba, their version of Eshu, comes about through his linguistic facility. In the beginning of things, Mawu, the female aspect of Mawu-Lisa, the androgynous high god of the Fon, gives her seven children different realms to rule—earth, sea, animals—and provides them with a language separate from her own. But she allows Legba, her youngest and most spoiled child, to remain with her and to relay messages to her children.

> So Legba knows all the languages known to his brothers, and he knows the language Mawu speaks, too. Legba is Mawu's linguist. If one of the brothers wishes to speak, he must give the message to Legba, for none knows any longer how to address himself to Mawu-Lisa. That is why Legba is everywhere.[2]

As a hermetic linguist, Legba knows the cosmic language as well as the tongue of the earth. This is why humans must ritually acknowledge him before all other gods. According to the religions of Abraham, God's information no longer flows directly; the era of prophecy is closed, and we are left with scripture and the babble of interpretation. Legba embodies the hope and the peril of a more open spiritual channel: hope, because he allows us to speak with the gods and for them to speak with us; and peril, because he plays games with the messages he carries, games that keep us continually aware that the network of exchange he oversees is never purely transparent. His nickname is *Aflakete,* which means "I have tricked you."[3]

In many tales, Legba simultaneously causes and solves a power play among the orisha, and he does so by playing with the circuits of communication. One story takes place against the backdrop of the ongoing conflict between Sagbata, the lord of earth, and his brother Hevioso, the lord of sky, who considers himself the superior of the two. Legba lies to Mawu, proclaiming that there is no water in the sky. This allows Hevioso to cut off the rain, causing a terrible draught. Then Legba goes to Sagbata and tells him to build a huge fire on earth, which he does. Mawu becomes afraid that the flames will consume everything, even heaven, and she orders Hevioso to make it rain, which reduces his status but also tentatively reconciles the brothers. In the tales of the Yoruba, Eshu similarly manipulates relationships defined by envy and power by dispensing just the right amount of data—not the whole story, but just enough to make the plot unfold. At one point, Shango the thunder god asks him, "Why don't you speak straightforwardly?" "I never do," Eshu responds. "I like to make people think." [4]

Perhaps the most famous Yoruba story about Eshu concerns two farmers who work on adjacent fields. The two friends swear undying fidelity to one another but neglect to acknowledge Eshu in their vow. So one day Eshu appears, and takes a stroll between their two plots of land, wearing a cap that is black on one side and red (or white) on the other. As he saunters along the dividing line, he chats with both men. Afterwards, the two farmers discuss the man with the cap, and fall to violent quarreling about the color of his hat, calling each other blind and crazy. The neighbors gather around, and then Eshu arrives to stop the fight. The friends explain their disagreement, and Eshu shows them the two-sided hat, and chastises them for not putting him first in their doings. The multi-perspectival lesson of the tale is penetrating. But just as interesting is where the story structurally locates the god. Moving along the liminal seam between two different world views, Eshu confuses communication, reveals the ambiguity of knowledge, and plays games with perspective. This is why his shrines are found both at crossroads and at the market, for he is master of the crossed purposes that define networks of exchange and circuits of desire. In a characteristic example, Eshu uses his magician's skills to craft serpents that bite people on the way to the market, where he then sells them the cure.[5]

The Fon have a wonderful way of imagining Legba's mastery of converging and contradictory forces. Mawu tells the gods that whoever can come before her and simultaneously play a gong, a bell, a drum, and a flute, while also dancing to the music, would be chief of the gods. All the macho gods attempt and fail, but Legba succeeds, demonstrating not only his agility, but also his ability to maintain a balance between contrary forms and forces (and incidentally providing a window into the metaphysical dimension of West African polyrhythm). Legba dances not only to the beat of a different drummer, but to the beats of many different drummers at the same time.

As Robert Pelton writes in his excellent book, *The Trickster in West Africa,* the Fon are "dazzled by [Legba's] metaphysically fancy footwork just because they know that the pathways of new order that he opens always skirt the edges of chaos."[6] The creator of plots, the player of many instruments, the trickster Legba always risks unleashing a Pandora's box of powers. But it is only in risking such chaos that novelty is continually reborn, allowing the community to interact dynamically rather than submit to some rigid structure. The potential for this dynamic chaos is the metaphysical heart of the trickster. There is a Yoruba prayer that goes:

> [Eshu], do not undo me,
> Do not falsify the words of my mouth,
> Do not misguide the movements of my feet,
> You who translate yesterday's words
> Into novel utterances,
> Do not undo me,
> I bear you sacrifice.[7]

Eshu can transform the past into "novel utterances" because he knows that the ambiguity and multiplicity of perspectives that define the world can change the fixed into the free. New connections always create the potential for a new world. Eshu/Legba puts creative chaos in the heart of tradition, of "yesterday's words," and takes advantage of the zones of novelty that emerge. As Pelton states, this god "finds in all biological, social, and metaphysical walls doorways into a larger universe."[8]

Of all the lines that Legba transgresses, the most visible ones are erotic. A small and spry young fellow, he has a ravishing sexual appetite, and when Mawu punishes him for some transgression by commanding that his penis remain always erect, Legba smiles and immediately begins groping the nearest female. In another episode, after tricking many suitors out of deflowering the daughter of a king, he has sex with the woman himself. The happy king proclaims that Legba may sleep with any woman he chooses, and names him the intermediary between this world and the next. "And that is why Legba everywhere dances in the manner of a man copulating."[9]

Sexuality expresses the trickster's need to go beyond boundaries, to create new order through the partial collapse of previous barriers. More profoundly, copulation is the most fully embodied of *connections*, Legba's pet project everywhere. Legba puts sex in the heart of spirituality, not as transcendent tantra, but as the more immanent principle of direct communication. Of course, Legba's sexual appetite can cause just as much trouble as his propensity to tinker with data, as the following song shows:

> We are singing for the sake of Eshu
> He used his penis to make a bridge
> Penis broke in two!
> Travelers fell into the river.[10]

Eshu makes us recognize the fundamental relation between sex and the evolving, continually reconnecting cosmos. As Pelton writes, "He is a living copula, and his phallus symbolizes his being, the limen marking the real distinction between outside and inside, and the wild and the ordered."[11]

GARBLING THE BOOK OF FATE

Among the Yoruba, Eshu casts a darker, more malevolent shadow than Legba. Though he still delights in contradictions, and to a lesser extent sex, Eshu also deliberately stirs up confusion and violent conflict. Robert Farris Thompson relates one particularly twisted tale that involves Eshu-Yangi, the father of all Eshu. (Like most orisha, Eshu exists in a numberless multiplicity of individual aspects.) Eshu's mother offers him a bounty of fish and fowl. Eshu eats it all, and, not sated, eats his mother as well. But Eshu's father—in this tale Orunmila, the god of divination—is prepared for his cannibalistic son when he comes after papa with jaws agape. Orunmila hacks Eshu into bits that are scattered like the corpse of Osiris across the earth, where they become individual shards of laterite. After pursuing Eshu through the heavens, Orunmila catches the god, who promises him that all the stones will become the representatives of Eshu's spirit. All Orunmila has to do is consult the stones, and they will do his mystic bidding. After granting the world access to him through the laterite fragments, Eshu also coughs up his mother.

In this weird tale of cosmic give-and-take, Eshu demonstrates both his generosity and his caprice. The Yoruba declare Eshu the god who has access to *ashé,* which literally means "so be it," and is considered to be a morally neutral power of creation given by the supreme being. Eshu first receives ashé when the gods journey to the supreme being to find out who among them is the most powerful. Each brings a huge sacrifice, carrying it on his or her head. But Eshu consults the oracle before he goes, and finds that all he needs to bring is a bright red feather set upright on his forehead. When the supreme being sees this sign he grants Eshu the power of ashé, because Eshu had shown his unwillingness to carry unnecessary burdens, as well as his agility with information. (To this day, Eshu figurines often have a large phallic plume or nail attached to the head.) As Thompson says, Eshu teaches us that one must "cultivate the art of recognizing significant communications . . . or else the lessons of the crossroads—the point where doors open or close, where persons have to make decisions that may forever effect their lives—will be lost."[12]

Such moments of crisis, of turbulent communication, are oracular opportunities, and it is appropriate that Eshu has a subtle and complex relationship with the Yoruba system of divination, Ifa. The procedures of Ifa are eerily similar to those of the *I Ching.* The *babalawo,* or diviner, quickly passes sixteen palm nuts between his hands; depending on how many he winds up with, he draws either a broken or solid line in powder. He (and the babalawo is always a he) draws two groups of four lines each to create one of 256 possible patterns, or *odu.* He then recites from memory various verses associated with that odu, and he and his client will settle on those verses that seem relevant. Like the kabbalistic Tree of Life, Ifa is described as having "roads," "pathways," or "courses"—resonant exchanges of images and meanings that are obviously Eshu's bag.[13] For the Fon, whose system of Fa divination is very similar to Ifa, Fa is considered to be destiny itself: the pattern of the day, the individual, and the cosmos. Each person has an individual Fa, just as each person has an individual Legba. Because Legba is the only god who knows the "alphabet of Mawu," he is "sent to Mawu to bring to each individual his Fa, for it is necessary that a man should know the writing which Mawu has used to create him."[14]

Sometime before Ifa existed, a Yoruba myth goes, the human race lost its will to live and stopped sacrificing to the gods. The gods became hungry, so Eshu decided to give humans something that would restore their enthusiasm. Passing a palm tree, he met some monkeys who gave him sixteen palm nuts and told him to go around the world so that he might hear "sixteen sayings in each of the sixteen places." After traveling this circuit, Eshu gave this knowledge to men through Ifa, the "sixteen places" being the sixteen primary odu and the sixteen palm nuts. This tale manifests the feedback loops that sustain humans and gods, a circuit ruled by Eshu, without whom the gods would go hungry. For even after he provides men with Ifa, Eshu continues to trick them into defying the gods so that they will then need to perform sacrifice in order to win back divine favor. But in addition to such tricks, Eshu remains a world-bridging mediator who integrates different points of view through learning and passing on information.

Legba's relationship with Fa, and Eshu's with Ifa, shows a subtle and lively understanding of divination and destiny. Eshu gives the world Ifa, and on the babalawo's divining tray, twin Eshu statues stare out at each other from either end (Hermes as well is linked to twins, the primal copy). But Eshu/Fa is not the master of the oracle. In one Fon tale, Fa, the god of divination and fate, sneaks into Legba's home and sleeps with his wife, who later tells Legba she did it because his own penis wasn't big enough. Taking up the challenge, Legba eats an enormous amount of food and swears to have sex with his wife until she tires. As he makes love to her, in front of a crowd, he calls out "Gudufu, the path of my destiny, is large—large like a large penis."[15] Legba then makes Fa remain in the house, while Legba takes his wife and hits the road, vowing that he will always be first, and will always be ready to fuck.

As Pelton writes, "Fa keeps a certain dominion over destiny, or inner space, but Legba's elasticity gives him mastery over destiny's paths . . . Legba can roam as he chooses, going in and out to bring men to their destiny, but never ceasing to widen the path for them."[16] By comprehending the whole network of destiny, Eshu can make his escape, slipping through the cracks of fate. This is why Eshu's odu is the seventeenth pattern, the first one outside the core sixteen.[17]

Freedom is always tied to the fate revealed by oracles, if only for the simple fact that oracles must always be *interpreted*, their messages decoded. As Eshu makes abundantly clear, such interpretations are always ambiguous and never purely transparent. The literary critic Henry Louis Gates, Jr., whose book *The Signifying Monkey* uses Eshu to establish a model of African-American textual analysis, says that at the crossroads "there is no direct access, or contact, with truth or meaning, because [Eshu] governs understanding."[18] And Eshu is a tricky governor, whose pathways of understanding are always splattered with mud.

NEW WORDLY WISDOM

The orisha survived the cultural holocaust that brought Africans to the New World, though their character and activity inevitably changed as the condition of their devotees changed. Mixed together, cut off from traditional structures, hemmed in by Christianity and the whip, New World Africans developed the world's most vibrant form of syncretism, as Catholic saints, indigenous deities, and the orisha blended into one another, even as the lore and metaphysics of West Africa became disguised in song, drum, and celebration. Eshu himself went through many changes, with different groups of African descendents extending his peculiarly multivalent being into a number of sometimes almost contradictory directions.

In Brazil, Exu—as his name is written in Portuguese—became a rather menacing being. In *condomble,* Brazil's most African tradition of orisha worship, Exu continues to rule over sexual intercourse and is still served before other gods are invoked. But this pride of place does not so much open up a divine communications channel as placate an irascible deity with a penchant for chaos and confusion. Eshu's traditional predilection for trickery and vengeance also made him an ideal orisha for restive slaves, who crafted him into a saint of revenge against their dominators. His more destructive aspects were intensified and multiplied to cover a range of nasty magical acts that might catalyze rebellion and spiritual revolt. In *umbanda,* the urban, highly eclectic fusion of condomble and nineteenth-century European spiritualism, Exu quite simply becomes the devil.

In Haiti, where the orisha are known as the loa and their worship known as vodoun, Legba went through other drastic changes. He remains lord of the crossroads, the *grand chemin* whose channel between earth and the gods is contained in the ritual house's peristyle, or *poteau-Legba*. The image of the crossroads is also apparent in Legba's *vévé* (a cosmic diagram, drawn with white flour, that represents the loa). But in Haiti, Legba has become an old man, a bent and crippled peasant with a cane. In her book *Divine Horsemen,* the American avant-garde filmmaker Maya Deren characterizes possessions by Legba as particularly terrible and twisted. In Haiti, then, Legba comes full circle, like the answer to the riddle of the sphinx, no longer the virile child of the morning but the impotent old man of evening. He remains the omniscient observer—as one Haitian informant tells Deren, "We do not see him, he sees us. All those who say the truth, he is there, he hears. All those who speak evil, he is there, he listens."[19] But his omniscience has become centered in the knowledge of death.

As in Brazil, Haiti's Legba is known as a powerful magician. One prayer goes "*Sondé miroir, O Legba,*" which means literally "to fathom the mirror" and figuratively "to uncover the secrets."[20] As with most Haitian loa, Legba has two main aspects: a Rada and a Petro, the Petro being meaner and more frightening. Legba's Petro aspect is called Carrefour, the crossroads, and he is lord of black magic, linked to Ghédé and Baron Samedi, other fearsome baddies of death and the grave. Legba's sacrifice is a white cock whose neck is twisted; Carrefour gets a black cock who is set on fire and allowed to run about in agony. While Legba's vévé emphasizes the four distinct cardinal points of the metaphysical axis, Carrefour's sigil encompasses all the wayward points—the chaos, if you will—that lie in between.

In Haiti and Cuba, Legba does not become the devil, but is syncretized with certain Catholic saints, particularly St. Anthony, St. Lazarus (who is old and walks with a cane), and occasionally St. Peter, the gate-keeper. These correspondences are not fixed in stone, but mutate as social and cultural reality changes. This ability to adapt shows the deeply pragmatic character of the orisha, for, as practical students of the mysteries recognize, the strongest magicians are revisionists, not classicists. But for all the West African trickster's different forms and aspects, some devotees of the orisha insist on his central unity. Molly Ahye, for example, insists there is no difference between Haiti's Legba and the Trinidadian/Brazilian Eshu:

> Eshu is Legba, Eshu-Elegbara. Legba is a contraction. Eshu is the connection, the spiritual connection between man and divinity . . . Eshu is a mirror of us. He embodies all the forces, positive and negative. Eshu is the one who guards the secrets. He has the power to manipulate man or to free man, because there is so much of man in him. You are linked to him by your humanness and he plays on that. And you are linked to him by your divine spirit and he tests that . . . How do you know you're good and righteous if you haven't passed through the fire? What is the force that will test you through that fire? Even if that thing has to bear your weight—infamous, evil, whatever—that is the thing that gives you the opportunity to test yourself. That is what Eshu does.[21]

Because the orisha are not frozen patterns of tradition, they are able to continually shape themselves to the world as it is for people now. Because they do not hold themselves in a separate space of the sacred, they can travel everywhere. The character of Papa La Bas in Ishmael Reed's *Mumbo Jumbo* is no less real a Legba than the ones you can read about in anthropology books, or the one that haunted Robert Johnson at that mythical crossroads in Mississippi. In his 1986 book *Count Zero*, science fiction writer William Gibson put the orisha in the heart of cyberspace, his computer-generated astral data plane, and the entities took root in that imaginal place far better than any hoary Egyptian deity or Irish fairy could have. Gibson, who tossed in the orisha when he was bored with his book and happened to open a *National Geographic* article on vodoun, told me in an interview that he felt "real lucky, because it seemed to me that the original African religious impulse really lends itself much more to a computer world than anything in Western religion. It almost seems as though those religions *are* dealing with artificial intelligence." Gibson also pointed out how similar vévés look to printed circuits.

While Gibson was talking about fiction, his words nonetheless reflect the contemporary relevance of the orisha, even for folks who are not willing to kill a cock with their bare hands. For Robert Pelton, Legba embodies Carl Jung's principle of synchronicity; for Henry Louis Gates, Jr., he is the ambivalent Logos. In our wired world, Eshu can also be seen as the spirit of the network, nomadic lord of the codes and protocols that tie movement and trade, image and perspective, data and sex. Of all the orisha, he perhaps speaks most forcefully to us today because he is about the very process that we engage in order to understand and recognize him: the tangled process of communication itself, ever sacred, ever vexed.

1991

Notes

[1] Robert Pelton, *The Trickster in West Africa: A Study of Mythic Irony and Sacred Delight* (Berkeley, CA: University of California Press, 1980), 136.

[2] Ibid, 73.

[3] Ibid, 72.

[4] Migene Gonzalez-Wippler, *Tales of the Orisha* (New York: Original Publications, 1985), 45.

[5] Pelton, 153.

[6] Ibid, 126.

[7] Henry Louis Gates, Jr., *The Signifying Monkey: A Theory of African-American Literary Criticism* (Oxford: Oxford University Press, 1988), 35.

[8] Pelton, 119.

[9] Ibid, 87.

[10] Ibid, 131.

[11] Ibid, 130.

[12] Robert Farris Thompson, *The Flash of the Spirit: African and Afro-American Art and Philosophy* (New York: Vintage Books, 1983), 19.

[13] Gates, 24.

[14] Ibid, 27.

[15] Pelton, 126.

[16] Ibid, 119.

[17] Gates, 38.

[18] Ibid, 41.

[19] Maya Deren, *Divine Horsemen: The Living Gods of Haiti* (New York: McPherson & Co., 1984), 98.

[20] Ibid, 34.

[21] Molly Ahye, private interview with Katherine Ramsey, February 7, 1990.

SNAKES & LADDERS

In an era when everything breaks down and everything comes together, spiritual explorers find themselves in a vast and tangled forest. Myths and metaphors, practices and words of wisdom form crisscrossing paths that multiply in all directions. In many ways, this eclectic and fragmentary zone defines our moment of religious experience. Perhaps the question is less which path you find yourself on—what religious philosophy or spiritual technology you're remaking yourself with—but how you move through the space itself. How do you engage its polymorphous shapes, the density of its data, the absence of traditional clues? With rigid, one-pointed determination? Loose eclecticism? Craziness?

In my own tentative drift, I've come to identify two contrasting modes of spiritual movement, two pervasive styles or religious impulses. On the one hand, there is the desire to establish an intense, deeply wedded connection with the imaginative matrix of the natural world; on the other, a desire to overcome desire, to ascend towards virtual light, to escape the demands of matter and wake up to a new order of knowledge and being.

The tension between these impulses takes many forms, replicating across many levels of scale: gnosis and nature, masculine and feminine, transcendence and immanence, evolution and eternal return, sky gods and chthonic spirits, monotheism and polytheism, unity and multiplicity, soul and body, spirit and soul. But though they certainly bleed into one another, and may ultimately meet in the bosom of the Ultimate, I distrust any easy attempt to shove them under one holistic roof. It's too simple to paper over their real differences by appealing to the supposed unity of mystical experience or the clichéd notion that various religious languages describe the same truth from different perspectives. What if the truth itself is multiple?

Nor can the dynamic tension between these modes simply be subsumed into a larger dialectic of spiritual progression. Such a view already aligns itself on the side of unity and hierarchy, imagining an abstract evolutionary drive towards ultimate oneness. As James Hillman writes, "the polytheistic alternative does not set up conflicting opposites between beast and Bethlehem, between chaos and unity; it permits the coexistence of the psychic fragments and gives them patterns in the imagination . . ."[1] The shaman does not climb a ladder of binary oppositions towards a glowing monad. The jungle does not grow dialectically.

Today, a rising tide of environmentalists, Neopagans, and traditional peoples from around the globe are calling on us, not to mitigate, but to reject the philosophical and spiritual paradigm of the West. They point out that monotheism's mythic episteme, and its underlying dualisms of body/soul and man/nature, have helped produce devastating effects on the earth and the human spirit. Even mainstream Christianity and Judaism are now wrestling with a Green Goddess unleashed in their folds.

At the same time, science edges closer to its gnostic promises of material transcendence—off-world space colonies, synthetic virtual realities, life extension, and the preservation of human consciousness in the deathless body of machines. Are such technologies symptoms of a deeply spiritual intuition, or of an arrogant and deadly rift with nature made long ago? Those who reject humanity's drive towards incorporeal light and instead attempt to embrace the ancient fertility gods and their collective web of life face another problem—do the angels of light, at least in their modern guise, become the new demons? For despite their punch, many eco-spiritual critiques often boil down into simplified attacks on Christianity and its ascetic undertow. I'd like to suggest instead that the impulse to transcend—the Neoplatonist's ascent through the spheres, the Gnostic's sudden awakening, the desert monk's rejection of the *élan vital*—is not simply a philosophical error or the mark of patriarchy, but is fired by an intensely lucid yearning for the highest of goals: *liberation*.

Wrestling with my own internal tension between these impulses led me to give two lectures at the New York Open Center, and what follows is culled from those talks. In some sense, I've written a speculative myth that intensifies the conflict between these modes in order to highlight their distinctions and cut through to the raw and frequently conflicting desires that characterize spirituality. Within societies, religions and individuals, these two modes are clearly deeply imbricated, and even seem to call forth each other. The Neoplatonism I criticize for its over-determined reliance on hierarchy nonetheless served to keep the gods and the ensouled earth alive during the Renaissance. And while Gnosticism expresses a desire to transcend the material world far more intensely that normative Christianity, my favorite image for nature—the ouroboros—is in fact a Gnostic symbol. Perhaps spirituality can synthesize what religion elsewhere drives asunder.

SNAKES AND LADDERS

My favorite analogy for my own somewhat schizophrenic spiritual explorations is the kid's game Snakes and Ladders (known more antiseptically as Chutes and Ladders). In the game, you begin at the bottom row of the board and advance square by square towards the top row. If you land on a square that contains the bottom rung of a ladder, you can climb straight up, skipping rows. If you land on a square that has the upper end of a snake on it, you have to slide back down.

Of course, "getting to the end" is already a component of the linear and transcendent drive towards a goal, and the game is in the ladder's camp from the get-go. The ladder is a human artifact, a tool defined by the right angles which we discover in their "pure" Platonic form in our minds rather than the sinewy forms of nature. The ladder describes a linear vector, and embodies a hierarchy of rungs. As with a pyramid, the "higher" heavenly powers rule over the lower powers of the earth. Laid on its side, the ladder describes an evolutionary movement through time, both the "great chain of being" that places man as the leader of the pack, and the millennial historical movement of spirit towards a teleological end that exceeds the order of nature.

But the serpent slips in and upsets this order. The snake is an endless curve, a living beast that hugs the horizontal folds of earth or coils into the ouroboros, the primary image of cyclicity and return. The snake doesn't step—it flows, and never in a straight line. Its wet tongue whispers of pagan mysteries, of chthonic and sexual powers, of the immanence of embodied spiritual experience. In one common Central American Christian icon, a snake coils at the base of a ladder set beside the crucified Christ. The snake is the "base"—the deepest instinctive life force, the beginning, the original sin. Hindu yogis make their bodies into pyramids and force the creature coiled at the base of their spines up the ladder of their chakras. But others let the serpent lead them, through confusion and resplendent darkness, deep into the cool crevices of earth.

NATURE VS. GNOSIS

You are an archaic nomad. You are deeply and inextricably embedded in the immanent matrix of natural rhythms, flows, and forces. The earth runs through you, through your food and your shit and the weather and the things you eat and your relationships with other bodies. There's not even any space you could inhabit that would let you think you were separate from this matrix, no inner sanctum, no clear and distinct Cartesian camera, no immortal soul. You live in a world without settlements, and where there are no settlements there are no walls.

It is impossible for us to know the mind of such a person, but perhaps something like the following is true. The earth is alive, imbued with a consciousness distributed through animals and plants and rocks and storms. Your budding imagination creates an interface between your awareness and these entities, a magical interface that manifests mutual relationships with these figures. You form alliances with animal spirits, which are both visionary images and actual creatures. You align yourself with Cougar and partake of courage and mystery; you become Coyote and take on craftiness. Perhaps at a particularly pregnant juncture in time, an actual coyote passes in front of you and the world becomes an omen. Nature gives you a sign, not of an abstract law but a moving message written on the wind.

Agriculture and the development of the urban state change everything in this myth I have sketched. The walls go up. Eventually monotheism appears, perhaps partly as a metaphysical resonance of the vertical organization of state-craft (the pinnacle of the pharaoh's pyramid), and partly as an inevitable expression of the synthetic and relational logic of the human mind. (The notion of a singular god is, perhaps, a necessary product of religious calculation.) Meanwhile, the virus of written text spreads, creating a psychic space for the intensification of rational and increasingly abstract thought that is graphically separated, through the man-handled glyphs of writing, from the living sensual semiotics of nature. This space pulls us inside and up, towards an increasingly interior and immaterial sense of the character and locus of truth—the Platonic world of transcendent concepts, the Logos. The body and matter correspondingly suffer as spiritual principles, becoming imperfect copies of abstract truths.

Gnosticism becomes the paradigmatic spiritual expression of the transcendent religious drive that characterizes late antiquity. The core Gnostic myth is that the creator god described in Genesis is not the true god, but an inferior and even deluded demiurge. This lower god commands a variety of rulers, or archons, and together they are responsible for running our miserable prison planet of a world. But though we are imprisoned in this "abortion of matter," humanity carries within itself the leftover sparks of the precosmic Pleroma that existed before the demiurge and his creation. Human beings are thus absolutely superior to the ecosystem—not stewards, but strangers in a strange land. Our body and the soul (or *psyche*) cloak this spiritual spark and must be tossed aside for us to rediscover our true being. The primary trope of Gnosticism is therefore not sin and redemption, but ignorance and gnosis, forgetting and memory. We don't need to expiate our crimes, but to discover and remember the way out of a false world created through no fault of our own. And this way out is *way out*—Gnostic texts crackle with a peculiar energy, an almost sci-fi sensibility of "alien gods" and supramundane universes of light. Though not the first cosmic dualists, the Gnostics may have been the first spiritual off-worlders.

In addition to fusing Neoplatonic thought and the rhetoric of freedom that characterizes the young Christianity, Gnosticism also presents a continuity with, rather than a rejection of, the intense spiritual experience found within urban pagan and even archaic shamanic traditions. Its rejection of the embodied cosmos is not merely intellectual, but reflects a lived spirituality of gnosis. But unlike earlier and rival Neoplatonic philosophies, Gnosticism also presents an extremely critical perspective on nature and the body, and thereby casts antiquity's overall religious drift away from embodied experience into extreme spiritual relief. While this world-denying trend will come to characterize normative Christianity to some degree—especially after the ex-Manichaean Augustine leaves his mark on it—the intensity of Gnosticism's desire to break out of this world may be unparalleled.

From the perspective of rural pagans, carrying on their ancient and varied practices of nature worship, Gnostic cosmology would have seemed revolutionary, if not insane. Ritually blending with the rhythms and forms of nature, the worshippers of the old gods embrace the deep groove of the seasons and draw sustenance from balancing with the forces of change. Of course, rituals attempt to control nature as well as honor it, but one of the most essential aims is to catch the *élan vital*, the bursting surge of spring. The Gnostic, in contrast, denies this spirit. The immanent life of the visible cosmos is a trap, and the Gnostic rejects it. Reflecting an intense critical sublimation and a profoundly unbalanced internal split, the Gnostic goes against the grain. The Gnostics were spiritual Prometheans; like the alchemists they later inspired, they dedicated themselves to an *opus contra naturam*.

FATE VS. FREEDOM

Here is another way to appreciate the situation. As a pagan embedded in nature, you are compelled to honor the powerful spirits that animate the environment that surrounds and in a sense defines you and the homogeneous cultural world you share with your fellows. The gods and nature spirits that you are bound to determine your sense of place in the cosmos and even your role in society. Frequently, through omen or dream or clan membership, these entities claim you. You have little choice in the matter. They are ultimately in control.

Astrology is our civilization's most animated expression of these ancient polytheistic relationships of necessity and fate. Reflecting an arguably evolutionary drift away from the immediate world of sensuous forms towards the literal heights of abstraction, the gods of astrology ascend and take up residence in the pinpoint mysteries that wander among the constellations of the fixed stars. The ouroboros slithers up into the zodiac, recreating on a cosmic scale the polytheistic networks that surround humanity and determine the life of the individual. You're born into a certain cosmic arrangement of planets, and that particular constellation of forces determines to a greater or lesser degree your personality, your role in society, and the shape of your life. If Saturn rules over your natal chart, to some degree you are his slave.

Then the Gnostics appear with their anti-astrological rants against the star-demons that rule the zodiac along with the rest of the visible cosmos. The wheel of the heavens becomes, in their view, a great machinery of dark fate controlled by lower powers. But they also offer an esoteric escape route: gnosis, which seems to combine the experience of direct mystical knowledge with useful information about the structure of reality. With Gnostic knowledge, one can escape the clutches of the archons upon death, or learn how to manipulate them through magic while alive. The star-demons no longer have total control.

Within a heavily astrological climate, this is a powerfully libertarian notion, one which Christianity to a degree shared. (In addition to breaking the bonds of the pagan gods, Jesus was said by Paul to replace the law which dominated the Pentateuch with a new dispensation of forgiveness and grace.) Embedded within Gnosticism's almost maniacal hostility to the ecosystem, then, is a passionate if somewhat paranoid cry for freedom, a refusal of servitude to the necessity of matter. Gnostics were, in essence, antinomian—against the law. The Gnostic condemnation of the world was not simply schizoid asceticism, nor a histrionic form of *ressentiment*, Nietzsche's penetrating characterization of Christianity's "slave morality." Gnosticism also represents a particularly intense form of resistance to the powers that bind—in the self, in the body, in human society.

By imagining the world as a trap, Gnosticism creates a space to step back and critique the dominant situation, a space of visionary alienation that reveals the cracks in the surface of apparent reality. It's as if you were lazily strolling through an Edenic garden and suddenly discover that there are surveillance cameras hidden in the flowers and that the blue sky is actually a painted dome. The distrust of nature and matter grows from the distrust of the body of perception. The Gnostic chooses to wake up rather than deepen the dream, and the dream is a world without end.

THE CORPORATION OF HEAVEN AND THE CARNIVAL OF EARTH

Once, during a weekend course on the Kabbalah taught by Warren Kenton, the group was led through a guided visualization of holy Jerusalem. As we moved through the city, Kenton was also symbolically leading us through the ten sephirot on the Tree of Life, one of the most powerful "ladders" of esoteric thought and experience. We began outside the walls of the city, with the trees and shepherds, the "simple people" of Malkuth. Climbing through the city, we eventually passed a barracks that housed the soldiers who protected the city, and that corresponded to Geburah, or Severity.

Immediately, my imagination coughed up unbidden images of Israeli troops firing at Palestinian kids armed with handfuls of rocks. At that moment, I could no longer travel through Kenton's symbolically holistic Jerusalem, because I realized that the desire to literalize that symbolism partly inspires or at least justifies the intolerance of many reactionary and fundamentalist Israelis. The sparkling city of our imagination was splattered with the mud of history.

Most students of Kabbalah are probably too sophisticated to attempt to submit the relative world we actually live in to the often idealized cartography of the spiritual imagination. After all, the messy multiplicity of Malkuth needs to be embraced as thoroughly as the crown of Kether—in fact, the Jewish tradition presents a particularly robust and charitable record regarding sexuality and the body. Nonetheless, the codes that issue from the ineffable flux of mystical tradition—symbols, myths, metaphysical principles—become part and parcel of that same relative world. Like any other language, spiritual language leaks and drifts into other domains. As it solidifies into history, spirituality becomes ideology, often with very specific social and political results. Arguably, the Christian belief that man is master of the earth has helped put a torch to the very planet man is supposed to steward.

Formed into political ideologies, spiritual hierarchies can be rather pernicious. Such hierarchies often begin with the idea that reality originates from a supreme monad, which immediately creates the challenge of how to relate this singular godhead with our lived world of multiplicity and change. Instead of an immanent or pantheistic metaphysics, in which that intense unity is folded immediately into the world, spiritual hierarchies like the Tree of Life work on the cosmogenic principle of emanation. The godhead emanates increasingly "coarser" gradations of reality, which form a descending ladder of lower and lower planes. It's the spiritual equivalent of trickle-down economics. The coarsest plane is the material earth, and the task of the aspirant is to arduously climb back up the ladder. The principle of immanence—the Kabbalist's Shekinah, the Christian's Logos—is, with some notable exceptions, subservient to the supreme principle.

One of the primary architects of the metaphysical ladder was the Christian theologian Pseudo-Dionysius the Areopagite. In *The Celestial Hierarchy* and *The Divine Names,* he helped establish the familiar Neoplatonic cosmic cartography within medieval Christian cosmology. In this picture, the cosmos becomes a series of spheres that surround the earth like an onion skin. In the celestial imagination of Pseudo-Dionysius, God rules the supreme sphere, while much of the work is performed by various ministering angels in descending degrees of power: thrones, dominions, principalities, etc. Below the angelic orders lie the astrological powers that rule the visible cosmos, and below them the elemental forces of earthly nature.

As hermetic cartographies of spiritual and psychological forces, the Tree of Life and Pseudo-Dionysius's celestial hierarchy are powerful and profound. But if you hold that the hermetic axiom of "as above, so below" applies to political structures as well, then these maps could easily be construed as depicting a highly authoritarian political structure that invests absolute power in a supreme sovereign. This is indeed how medieval royalty fit itself into the divine scheme. Lesser beings must take their assigned place in the social hierarchy, just as the elementals of nature are imagined as slaves or demons to be bound. But for all its visionary punch, the politics implied by this hierarchical model is one that only the most reactionary among us could stomach. Indeed, it is precisely the attraction to this notion of divine hierarchy that explains the strong right-wing current that animates certain areas of esotericism, especially in Europe.

But what happens when parliamentary and democratic forms in turn displace the divine rule of kings? The kingdom of heaven becomes a corporation. Reading through popular spiritualist and Christian accounts of the higher planes from the late nineteenth century until today, one increasingly finds the comparison of the spirit world to a business, with God the president and various angels and astral souls his employees. As we reincarnate, we work our way up the corporate ladder. Besides maintaining a top-down power structure, now shifted from kingship to corporate capitalism, this transposition keeps the earth low beneath our feet, a degraded if not willfully exploited realm with no voice.

Here the radical character of some contemporary Neopagan perspectives become clearer. The Neopagan, at least in my speculative myth, takes a self-conscious stand against this vast metaphysical architecture. I hate corporations, she says. I hate working for the man. Spirituality is not a business, and my allegiance is to the "lowest" rung: earth. I do not want to lord over nature, but immerse myself in its tides and rhythms, form alliances with its elemental powers rather than enslave them. I look forward to physical reincarnation—I have no desire to leave the Wheel. What others see as a trap, I embrace as a mysterious celebration that knits beauty and love with suffering and death. I acknowledge my own Promethean urges, but I recognize that Prometheus is only one of many gods with claims on my being.

In the place of a static, top-down corporation, the Neopagan imagination conjures a carnival, a horizontal zone of becoming, a loose gathering in the field. The carnival swirls with energy and chaotic erotic connections. One feral group holds a hand-fasting over here, while some wanderers are selling stuff over there, and behind the distant bushes you expect people are making love. Through the dust, faces emerge and disappear, some wearing animal masks. People become beasts while the gods become human. There are no devils, just tricksters and their traps.

The carnival creates its own hierarchies of course, but they tend to be nested hierarchies, folded within the fractal properties of the field itself. Inner circles form and compete with other inner circles, wizard wars with witch. But the flavor has changed—rather than fixed forms, these dynamic relationships are self-emergent properties. The center is always decentered. As a formally polytheistic space, the carnival fragments and distributes the power that the ladder concentrated into one supreme point. Nature speaks again, in a thousand networked tongues.

In addition, there is no desire to leave the field. The carnival embodies immanence, the spiritual intensity of in-your-face multiplicity. There is nowhere to go. James Hillman uses precisely the image of "peaks and vales" to distinguish between the drive towards spiritual transcendence (peak experience, detachment, unity) and the rich fragmentary and animistic world of the soul and the polytheistic imagination.[2] From the Neopagan perspective, the chilly peaks in the background do not call as heartily as they do to solitary climbers with their urge to transcend the fray. As one Druid I know put it, "People are always saying how all paths lead to the same mountain top. But why climb the mountain in the first place, when you can explore the valleys?" That's the snake hissing in your ear.

BUDDHAS AND CUCUMBERS

Despite Gnosticism's many complex echoes in modern thought and experience, one might be tempted simply to reject the Gnostic impulse as an alienating pathology. Instead, I'd like to suggest evidence for a more embodied Gnosticism, a subtle rapprochement between snakes and ladders that can be found within the most historically robust Gnostic movement: Manichaeism. Lasting for over a millennium and spreading at one time from North Africa to China, Manichaeism is probably the most important dead world religion. On paper, the Manichaeans were radical dualists, adapting the Zoroastrian notion of two co-eternal principles: light and darkness, good and evil, spirit and *hyle* (matter). At the origin of things, these forces fought a series of primal battles, during which the evil archons swallowed some of the Light and imprisoned it in matter. Unlike many Gnostics, the Manichaeans believed the supreme light was not restricted to the human spirit, but was scattered all about, and circulated through plants, animals, and minerals. Thoroughly intermixed, nature itself thus awaits redemption.

Two central Manichaean figures for this redemption are the sun and the moon, the "ships of light" that the Manichaeans worshipped as avatars of the supreme spark. As the moon waxed, the Manichaeans imagined the orb drawing up particles of light from the earth, a storehouse that would then be transferred to the sun as the moon waned. The sun then returned this divine substance to the Kingdom of Light—a notion that perhaps explains Gurdjieff's curious claim that in our unenlightened state we are "food for the moon." So while the Manichaeans shared with other Gnostics a hatred of astrological fate and the sinister spheres of the archons, they nonetheless imagined a counterforce inscribed within nature, a cosmic purification-machine embodied in the two primary heavenly bodies.

In his classic book *The Gnostic Religion*, Hans Jonas emphasizes the Manichaeans' dreary pessimism, which for him was exemplified in their visionary notion that the world around us was built from the corpses of demons. The later scholar Ioan Couliano argues that this judgment is overly hasty. Couliano points out that while the substance of the earth is demonic to the Manichaean, it is nonetheless crafted by a demiurge of light—the Living Spirit. In any case, Couliano notes, "the theory of the double nature of humanity and cosmos can lead to various attitudes, including the perfectly optimistic one according to which the world reveals itself every day as an epiphany of the Kingdom of Light."[3] In this view, the alienated eye of gnosis expands to encompass the whole of nature, a shimmering fabric of immanence and release.

An even more nuanced picture emerges if we examine the world of Manichaean ethics. The Manichaean community was divided between the Elect and the Hearers, or lay community. On the surface, the Elect sound a lot like devoted hippies—they didn't accumulate wealth, didn't work much, abhorred violence, believed in reincarnation, and prayed to the sun and moon. They were not only vegetarians, but vegans, and believed that by consuming foods filled with light—like cucumbers and melons—they were freeing its imprisoned spark.[4] The Elect followed strict chastity, but Augustine reported that they consumed semen (apparently filled with light) as their Eucharist, which needless to say complicates this non-erotic picture. Perhaps some Manichaeans objected less to pleasure than to procreation, which delivers more souls into bondage. Turning orthodox Christian morality on its head, the Hearers were encouraged to avoid conception, not copulation.

Of course, most modern hippies would find the dualistic, world-denying vision these crunchy ascetic practices rested upon highly objectionable. But is Couliano right? Was there a quietist optimism in the Manichaean relationship with the natural world? We find an echo of this in St. Augustine's snide descriptions of his former brothers in faith: "They believe that the herbs and the trees are alive, and the life that is in them is endowed with sensibility and able to suffer when hurt. This is why no-one can sever or pluck anything without inflicting suffering upon it."[5] In a book on Augustine, the French historian Prosper Alfaric further elaborates on this natural ethics:

> Before passing over into plants and trees, the divine substance abducted by the demons lies all over the ground. It is also spread in the air and even in the depth of the earth. Even stones have the faculty for feeling and thinking. Thus a perfect Manichaean would try to live at peace with the whole of Nature. He knows that everything in it leads to the triumph of the good. Therefore he will refrain from upsetting its harmony; will not plow, for he could not do with torturing God's limbs.[6]

If we read this passage not as an indication of the Manichaean's underlying cosmology but as an immediate outlook on the natural world, we sense a deep respect for the webwork of life rather than the loathing and contempt for matter one might suspect from such a "Gnostic" sensibility.

This almost fanatical sensitivity to sentient life in all its forms reminds us less of Christians berating the sins of the flesh than of the Jains, who so fear harming life that the most extreme among them cover their mouths with cloth so as not to inhale insects. In contrast with normative Christianity, which sets man up as the exclusively ensouled ruler of creation, and which thereby demonized the spirits of nature, Manichaeans bring a strong flavor of Eastern panpsychism to their dualism. For the Manichaean, the light is scattered everywhere, and thus the essence of nature, of goats and melons and mountains, is co-substantial with our own. Even the mud is complex, base matter flecked with gold.

Mahayana Buddhism also resonates with Manichaeism, not only in its ascetic ethics but in its emphasis on intense and lucid insight. For the Buddhist, as for the Manichaean, we are locked into a life of suffering. Desire, the passionate *élan vital* that courses through living beings, is the productive force that binds us to suffering. Since desire is ultimately founded, not upon sin, but upon ignorance, release from bondage—and the endless cycle of reincarnation—occurs through a kind of gnosis, a total lucid understanding of the nature of reality. Though Manichaeism's belief in an eternal soul marks one of many radical points of divergence, both systems could be said to privilege intuitive knowledge and direct perception over devotion and belief. Yet for both Manichaeans and Mahayana Buddhists, this transcendent overcoming of the world is balanced with a practical commitment to free the "light" scattered throughout the body of nature, a global soteriology founded on balance and nonaggression.

Though direct historical influences are difficult to track in the nomadic byways of ancient history, religious historians have long sensed a tangled relationship between Manichaeism and Mahayana Buddhism. Mani himself included the Buddha as one of his precursors, and imagined himself as the future Buddha Maitreya. In the middle of the third century, the religious leader made his first missionary jaunt from his home in Babylon to northwest India, where he converted the Buddhist king of Turan. Jonas points out that if Mani cribbed much of his cosmology from Iranian religion, he borrowed his ethical and ascetic ideals from Buddhism. The monastic structures that surrounded the Elect, for example, resemble Buddhist religious communities far more than their Christian cousins.

In *Gnosis on the Silk Road,* which compiles fragments of Central Asian Manichaeism, Hans-Joachim Klimkeit proposes that as Manichaeism moved east, its classical pessimism "gave way to a more composed, tranquil, and cheerful attitude, such as we often find in Mahayana Buddhism."[6] Running the other direction, some scholars have found distinct Manichaean elements in Tibetan Vajrayana cosmology, while Klimkeit suggests that Mahayana texts concerning the "Western Paradise" of the Buddha Amitabha—the Buddha of Light central to the devotional Pure Land school—may be direct outgrowths of Manichaean myths about the cosmic Kingdom of Light. In the East, Mani himself was known as the "Buddha of Light."

The differences between Manichaeism and Buddhism clearly outweigh their similarities, but there remains a fundamental resonance between these two religions of gnosis. (In *Awakening of the West,* Stephen Batchelor argues that the Gnostic system of Basilides has even more doctrinal similarities to Buddhism than Mani's.) Why is this resonance important here? Because while Mahayana Buddhism shares Gnosticism's drive towards liberating knowledge and self-overcoming, its dynamic cultural forms—particularly in their Chinese and Japanese expressions—temper the off-world impulse of the transcendent with a gentle and even earthy respect for nature that seems far more accepting of the material plane than most Gnostic, Neoplatonic and Christian currents of the West. In creating a middle way between the intense world-denying asceticism of Hindu mendicants and an immanent embrace of nature and the polyvocal world, Buddhism presents a sort of radical escape from the pagan/monotheistic dualism that haunts the West's spiritual tradition. Buddhism could even be seen as a parallel world of transcendence, an alternate history of gnosis, one which views the prison of existence as arising, not from the material conditions imposed on us from without, but from the reified structures of ignorance built up from within. As such, the arrow of its liberation curves more than it ascends.

Perhaps this path of liberation begins with dissolving the idea that there is any essence to be liberated, Neoplatonic or otherwise. Such a view would not annul the tension between snakes and ladders, but would instead acknowledge their incommensurable characters: they speak to and from different aspects of an entity that is no longer an "individual soul" but a complex multiplicity of forces, habits, and voices. Such a view suggests a mutation of the Western spirit, one in which we cease to "follow a path" up the mountain and begin, instead, to travel through an almost fractal field of contradictory and constantly shifting possibilities, forces, perspectives, and practices. With each step we take, a thousand paths emerge, rippling through a vast, open-ended network. We pray, and the Egyptian beast-gods crash through the sacristy and build a Zen rock garden. We meditate, and the dissolving fragments of the ego coagulate into Rilke's terrifying and incandescent angel. We move like magicians through the mossy forest of symbols, without culmination or rest, evolving and returning simultaneously: worlds without end, proliferating in the arms of earth, ranging through a matrix of chaos and serenity that climbs toward the very light it already rides.

1994

Notes

[1] James Hillman, *A Blue Fire* (New York: HarperCollins, 1989), 44.
[2] Ibid, 114.
[3] Ioan Couliano, *The Tree of Gnosis* (New York: HarperCollins, 1992), 176.
[4] Ibid, 178.
[5] Ibid, 179.
[6] Hans-Joachim Klimkeit, *Gnosis on the Silk Road* (New York: HarperCollins, 1993), 22.

SHARDS OF THE DIAMOND MATRIX (A *LUDIBRIUM*)

In January of 1994, while attempting to scrounge up my first assignment for *Wired*, I visited a Tibetan Buddhist monastery located in the Indian state of Karnataka. Along with their usual tasks, the young monks at Sera Mey were inputting rare and crumbling woodblock sutras into cheap XT computers. Under the auspices of the Asian Classics Input Project, mountains of this digital dharma eventually found its way onto freely distributed CD-ROMs and the Internet.

One evening, after the monks served me a bowl of noodles and beef my vegetarian self choked down out of politeness, an older monk sidled up to the table. Furtively he reached into his maroon robes and handed me a thick, dog-eared notebook, wrapped in a pair of sweat socks. He made sure I secured the book in my satchel, but when I asked what was going on, he only smiled, bowed, and walked quickly from the dining hall.

I unwrapped the package late that night. The words "Open the Folds!!" were scrawled on the notebook cover, which gave off a faint odor of opium. The sticky, yellowing pages were covered with a minute, seemingly impenetrable scrawl. Like a printed circuit or a magical grimoire, the indecipherable density of these bug doodles *signified*. When I returned to the States, a microscope confirmed my suspicions: the scrawl was a text, written in English, and employing a curious variant of the arcane Chinese art of microscopic calligraphy.

The author himself turned out to be no less arcane, though in a manner far closer to home. His name was Lance Daybreak, and a subsequent call to a Southern California pop historian corroborated his claim to be one of the first surfers to hang around the Santa Monica pier in the late 1940s. All Daybreak's assertions about his stateside activities checked out. After getting his B.A. in archeology from UCLA in under two years, he did a long stint as a merchant seaman and treasure hunter. In 1965, he enrolled at Stanford, where he was working on a thesis that combined Maturana's cybernetics with Nagarjuna's second-century Madhyamika Buddhist philosophy in an attempt to solve some dizzying problems in data sets and computational linguistics. Socially, Daybreak covered all the fronts: he huffed it over the Bay Bridge for Students for a Democratic Society actions, designed psychedelic light shows for the Pranksters, and cranked out idiosyncratic code with the hackers at the Stanford AI Lab. In 1968, Daybreak either dropped out or was expelled. On July 20, 1969, the day Apollo 11 landed on the moon, the man left for Asia.

It's here that Daybreak's tale becomes pretty ludicrous. In the manuscript, he claims to have somehow eluded the Soviet authorities and entered East Turkestan. There, in the savage gullies of the Karakorum Mountains, a few hundred kilometers southwest of the Taklamakan Desert, on the southern fork of the ancient Silk Road, he "discovered" an unknown and isolated people—the ngHolos. Though the lay ngHolos had settled down into a sedentary life of subsistence farming, weaving, and hash-growing, the community's religious order of monks and nuns, known as the Virtuous Ones, remained nomadic. The Virtuous Ones wandered on foot or horseback through the "Folds:" the high passes, hidden valleys, and endless plateaus of their severe mountain surroundings. But Daybreak's descriptions also make it clear that for the Virtuous Ones, this bleak physical environment "unfolded" into an abstract, visionary realm, a constantly shifting locus of cosmic memory and oracular landscapes haunted by demons, "alien gods," and insectoid Buddhas. Daybreak repeatedly cites one of the ngHolo's countless slogans: *Here your eye does not follow the warp of the land. Here you follow the warp of your own eye.*

To judge from his tone, Daybreak does not seem to have gone insane or sunk into the mire of narcotic psychosis. I choose to read his text as I read Castaneda, with a mind not particularly concerned with anthropological accuracy I wouldn't really be able to judge anyway. In any case, from the fragments I've been able to decipher, the Virtuous Ones—or "Virtuals," as Daybreak sometimes calls them—are fascinating. Their radically eclectic and syncretic religious philosophy juggles elements from the various faiths that passed along the Silk Road—gnostic Manichaeism, Mahayana Buddhism, Mongolian shamanism, Catholicism, heretical Sufism, Taoism—without trying to tie them up into one grand system. As Daybreak writes, "The path is a network of paths."

Even more fascinating than the ngHolo's religious collages are their spiritual machines. In the early seventeenth century, a Jesuit named Francis Lumière brought the first clock to the region. Daybreak writes, "Having long since assimilated whatever Christian motifs that compelled them, the ngHolos found the man's uncompromising theology obnoxious and his clothes in poor taste. But they loved his machine." The lay community put great store in their bronze prayer wheels, whose constant revolution supposedly generated the compassionate energy that kept dreams alive and that cloaked the Virtuous Ones from wild animals and enemies during their mystic peregrinations. Inspired by Lumière's device and ngHolo beliefs about the cosmic implications of metallurgy, a Virtual nun named Aieda made the spiritual link between metals and mechanics. Along with the somewhat baffled Jesuit, she set about applying the clock's mechanism to the ngHolo prayer wheels. Their subsequent machine not only relieved the peasants of the daily chore of spinning the wheels, but it led within decades to a number of inventions, including irrigation pumps, automated pottery wheels, and a programmable loom used to weave the mystical patterns of the ngHolo's rugs (apparently, they never bothered making more clocks). Aieda believed that the punched cards used to program the looms—an incomplete Italian Tarocco (tarot) deck still venerated today—allowed the ngHolos to communicate with the "Metal-mind," the spiritual consciousness that lay asleep in all metals and was awakened through metallurgy.

After a yearlong nomadic meditation, during which she never stopped walking, Aieda "received" the knowledge of how to program open-ended and unpredictable combinatory sequences into the mechanical looms. The spontaneous patterns that appeared on subsequent rugs were read as auguries from the Metal-mind. Despite a tradition of symmetrical mandalic forms, the ngHolo rug patterns Daybreak reproduces from this period show a striking asymmetry, density, and self-similar fractal dimensionality.

Daybreak reports that the ngHolos were mythologically prepared for this development because of one of their quasi-Manichaean metallurgic myths. While the four elements familiar to the West—air, earth, fire, and water—were considered to emerge from the earth's eternally fertile womb, metals were believed to be the remains of the Alien God's semen, which had fallen upon earth following a celestial tantric rite. For the ngHolos, metals were not only sacred but contained the potential "seeds" for a powerful galactic consciousness. Through the slow process of metallurgy, these seeds would ripen into Metal-minds, which were imagined to be (or at least represented iconographically as) colossal grasshopper bodhisattvas. At the end of the world, these beings would shed the material substance of their green-grey bodies until only the metallic shine remained. Millions of these ghostly, angular light-bodies would then combine into a boundless and collective temple that would draw the Alien God back to earth.

Aieda interpreted the gears of Lumière's clock as the grasshopper's mandibles, and the random patterns from the loom as the first stirrings of the Metal-mind. Though a few traditionalists labeled her a heretic, Aieda's work transformed ngHolo spiritual life. The dense patterns emerging from the loom were magically mapped onto the semi-mythic landscape of the Folds, where they formed an immense and lucid matrix of consciousness known as the "Jewel-net." Daybreak calls this net "a symphony of interpenetrating mandalas, an immense and luminous enfolded architecture." The ngHolos came to believe that the Jewel-net maintained its coherence through the automated prayer wheels and the psychic intensity generated by the ngHolo's most dangerous and esoteric rites: equestrian tantra.

Daybreak estimates that by the eighteenth century, the Virtuous Ones lived an almost entirely psychic existence on the Jewel-net, their nomadism having shifted from the Karakorum Mountains to the more visionary and abstract plateaus of the Folds. Apparently, just as the myth had predicted, the Jewel-net was growing.

In the Tibetan regions to the south, the Nyingmapas and the shamanic Bon follow the *terma* tradition, which holds that the sage Padmasambhava hid hundreds of sacred texts in the earth (and the spirit realm), texts that would only be discovered centuries later by tuned-in lamas (the so-called *Tibetan Book of the Dead* is such a text). Many were encoded in mystical "Dakini" scripts. The ngHolos carried this tradition into the Jewel-net, where hundreds of thousands of encoded sacred texts were uncovered—or "unfolded"—from their visionary matrix: texts of theology, philosophy, history, iconography, sacred geography. Various spiritual beings co-operated to decode these "treasures." Using a collective form of the *ars memoria,* or memory palaces, picked up from Lumière or another Jesuit, the Virtuals then stored, swapped, and recombined their *termas* throughout the ever-expanding Jewel-net.

The overwhelming amount of this information, combined with the ngHolo's already intense eclecticism, resulted in radical spiritual anarchy. Reflecting the philosophical shift from transcendent renunciation to immanent becoming, the plateaus of the Folds were no longer considered to be "revealed" forms of spiritual reality, but as spaces created "on the wing" out of the infinite potential of the Jewel-net. Lineages broke down into splinter groups, impartial agnostic "librarians," iconoclastic magicians, and "anti-monks." As the Virtuous Ones continued to discover, interpret, and store an increasingly boundless supply of *termas,* they formed constantly shifting and precarious alliances, frequently struggling with rivals through endless debates or magical "pattern-wars."

By the time Daybreak arrived, most of these fierce power struggles had relaxed. The following comments, which "unfold" a number of the ngHolo's countless mnemonic slogans, describe the more balanced philosophy that developed after generations of nomadism in the Jewel-net. The slogans are in italics, and the text is all Daybreak's, except for a few of my explanations which appear in brackets. Much of Daybreak's text remains thoroughly obscure.

The eye is furrow, seed, and source.
The eye symbolizes attention. Everything follows from attention, and the awareness of attention is the beginning of awakening: "the cock-crow." The Jewel-net pre-exists the eye only as a field of potential. Attention cuts furrows into this field, preparing the ground for the objects we perceive—the seeds—to both appear and find their place. But this grid of furrows and seeds, of points and tangents, is not enough to produce "reality"—you need the "source," the energy of desire or fascination that operates "behind" the eye, to water the seeds. This eye of attention is like a spring which can choose its direction of flow, though over time this spontaneous power is reduced by habit. But awareness and control begin with this awake gaze, and it should be cultivated.

Since ngHolo society is evenly divided between agriculture and nomadism, they picture this reifying tendency in profoundly ambivalent terms. Our habits of perception and action are seen as ruts as much as furrows. In this sense, seeds are materialistic delusions that karmically grow into something larger and more demanding than they initially appear. *Sift the seeds,* they warn. Some Virtuals interpret Adam and Eve's expulsion from Eden into the toil of agriculture as a fall into the ruts of perception. *The rain that feeds the wild poppy falls from the sky,* they will say, indicating the "pure production" that is to be aimed for: a spontaneous growth of unpredictable objects generated from the ultimate field of emptiness.

We ourselves are nothing but seeds grown within furrows dug and watered by the attention of others. Assessing the value of this prepared plot of land that is our "given" world is of primary spiritual importance. The path towards the Jewel-net comes through preparing our own ground, for the furrows dug by the attention (our patterns of perception) in many way determine the seeds, or objects, that will appear. Because they farm on hillsides, ngHolo plots are rarely regular, but follow the various possible folds of the land. So we should carefully prepare the patterns of our attention, its mode of organization, its blend of curves and grids, randomness and order. For the ngHolos, the chaotic mandalas that issue from the loom of the Metal-mind are occult keys to these patterns. But the ngHolos also emphasize the supreme momentum of rootless flight, the nomadic spread of weeds and wild poppies rather than the conscious cultivation of philosophical or material ground. As a famous slogan puts it, *I become mushroom, without root, my dharma seeds scattered to the wind.*

The soul weaves Indra's net.

Following the *anatman* doctrines of Buddhism, the Virtuals insist that any fixed notion of self, even the Universal Self, is an illusion. The Virtuals do not deny the conventional self, but rather fill it with space and emptiness. They call this "weaving the net." Like a net, the conventional self or ego is something we toss into the infinite potential of reality in order to "catch" our desires. If the net is too thick and tightly wound, it will retain everything, for there is no void to escape into, and everything will become very heavy and egocentric. If the net is too loose and weakly bound, it will not function—larger catches will break its threads, and the smaller will escape.

The path is a plateau.

For the ngHolos, the notion of a spiritual "path" is a misnomer, for spiritual reality is an endlessly proliferating manifold. The path is a network of paths, a plateau. One can not "follow" a network, but must constantly probe it. Each footprint is a node, which constantly re-produces a number of possible directions. Arrival and departure are fused. As such, immediate and fragmentary spiritual tactics—including these slogans—are prized more than grand strategic methods that attempt to lay out a well-organized hierarchy of stages towards gnosis. Many Virtual Masters achieved fame not for their diligence in pursuing one of the ngHolo's countless philosophical cults, but for the specific topology of the plateaus they created as they moved through different and frequently antagonistic fields of thought and experience.

Webs mar the net.
The Virtuous Ones contrast the image of the suppleness of the open net with the centralized and sticky organization of the web. In a web, the self becomes a spider, a solidified, grasping ego which sits at the center and captures everything for itself. Because great power over others can be generated through webs, black magicians worshipped the spider of their own egos. The greatest ngHolo necromancers would clandestinely seed webs in the Jewel-net in order to "catch" the eye of other adepts, who would slowly become bound in an immense pattern they believed to be a new revelation. These webs would capture the victims in a paranoid spell. Many such victims went mad or become so convinced of having discovered the ultimate pattern that they would be ostracized from the collective. Jewel-net healers would often attempt to free such individuals by binding them in "devotional webs," patterns of compassionate paranoia that "kill the spider."

The horseman is poised as he flies through the night.
Found on many prayer wheels, saddles and shrines, this slogan contains both an exoteric and esoteric meaning. Esoterically, it refers to the astounding Virtual art of high-speed equestrian tantric sex. Exoterically, it refers to the quality of balance needed to properly navigate the Jewel-net: the subtle contrast between the knowledge you accumulate and your beginner's mind before the

new. Given the encyclopedic density of the net, the Virtuals obviously put great emphasis on the proper gathering, organizing, and storage of *termas*. But as the masters say, *The greater your store, the slower your flight*. The greatest net nomads are as naive as they are wise, know when to jettison information, and avoid the hoarding of knowledge for its own sake. The "web" here also symbolizes the spider-nests that grow around stored or hidden containers. By compassionately sharing this wealth, you unbind yourself from the sticky burdens of knowledge.

Crack the dawn!
As in the English phrase, ngHolo's Indo-Chinese dialect contains the image of the dawn as a "crack" or "break." The peasants believe this crack is real—that a day literally ossifies over its twenty-four-hour period, ultimately trapping the earth inside the shell of night. The shell is then ruptured by the rising sun. The Virtuals play with this image to emphasize both the violent and nurturing aspects of "always waking up." On the one hand, perpetual gnosis constantly rends the dreamlike illusion—or more exactly, the tentative construction—of whatever plateau you are on. On the other hand, such gnosis pervades the mind with the empty but pregnant possibility of the glowing morning sky.

Some compare perpetual gnosis to a chick breaking through an endless series of nested eggs. While this image of gnosis as a movement through a cosmic collection of Chinese boxes may remind Westerners of the "existential" interpretation of Sisyphus, the Virtuals saw it as the supreme affirmation of perpetual nomadism. *Crack the dawn!* not only continually grounds the lucidity of gnosis in the present moment, but it also cuts against the mind's tendency to make gnosis a goal. Even cosmic knowledge must be rent if it devolves into a web. The nomad knows that there is no ultimate escape, for liberation is achieved only in the act of flight.

1994

INNER SPACE

MEDITATING IN SENSURROUND

It would be nice to begin the journey with who we are. But "who we are" is a house of mirrors, a tangled knot, a great and terrible Oz that in the final analysis may consist of nothing more than, well, nothing. The self, I am afraid, may be more of an onion than a fruit, and "who we are" is the skin we shed.

So instead we start, as the Yankee Tibetan Pema Chodron suggests, from *where* we are—which is another way of saying where we've been. It is no accident that so much spiritual writing these days is autobiographical and confessional. When it comes to spirituality, that amorphous and easily misheard inner call, we have come to trust experience, however mundane and confused, more than belief systems or philosophical reflection. Practice, along with the mutations in subjectivity that practice brings, is our primary tool. But this tool warps the hand that holds it, and that warp is our story.

For my generation, born in the 1960s, the turn towards practice and personal experience in matters of the spirit is part of our heritage, not just as Americans, who have always fetishized exploration and knowhow, but as kids who ride the spiritual wake of the baby boomers. In their desire to crack open the nut of spirit and eat the meat within, the '60s generation raided the world storehouse of mystical techniques. They *experimented* with spirit, along with drugs, sex, food, and unconventional social structures, and their protocols and inconclusive results still dominate the spiritual scene. We came of age as they gradually turned away from the heady dreams of Enlightenment, chemically induced or otherwise, and moved towards everyday responsibility, sobriety, and the practices that support a mindful but ordinary life. Our own turn towards autobiography reflects this legacy as well, but it also expresses, I hope, a tiny bit of spiritual wisdom often lost in the absurdities and revolutionary excesses of the counterculture: that we are not just children of the moment, but of history, and especially of the biological and social forces that shape and constrain our bodies, our perceptions, and the still infinite potential that lies shrouded within the hooded self.

But again, we start with where we are, or rather where we have been, which in this particular case means a tent in the mountains of Southern California. The portable alarm clock chirped to life at 3:30 a.m., finding me in an all-too-familiar state: disoriented and in the dark. Tugging on loose black pants and yanking a long-sleeve pullover over an Aphex Twin T-shirt, I staggered out of my tent into a night filled with stars and satellites. It took a moment before I recalled my exact coordinates: east of Los Angeles, in the San Bernadino mountains, on the grounds of the Zen Mountain Monastery. It was deep summer, in the middle of 1995, and I had just driven down from San Francisco for sesshin, a week-long silent retreat consisting largely of interminable hours of zazen. Barely half an hour after rising, with a blast of coffee in my gut, I was at it again: sitting with my legs scissored in the half-lotus position, eyes hazily gazing at a blank wall, my mind gradually settling into the breath that filled and fled my belly like the air in a bellows.

A week later I would hurtle down the mountain into the heart of Los Angeles to attend SIGGRAPH, a huge industry convention devoted to the latest advances in computer graphics: video games, animation, web technologies, virtual reality. But I wasn't thinking about any of that at the Mountain Center—in fact, I was trying not to think about much at all. The monastery's strict regimen gave me a rare opportunity to tune out the details, distractions, and seductive chimeras of our yammering information age, the glut of signals and noise that I, like so many folks today, navigate for bread and butter—and sometimes, it must be admitted, for a sense of self as well.

For people habituated to media, its abrupt and total absence can be both refreshing and alarming. Cult "deprogrammers" (notice the technological metaphor) warn that authoritarian religious groups severely restrict or eliminate access to information from the outside world in order to inculcate their world view in new recruits. While a number of sects have certainly abused such tactics, the deeper implication of these warnings is that today's barrage of media is healthy and normal, and that the stream of images, ads and information that saturate our world is not *already* infested with vivid and manipulative seductions, with cargo cults of consumerism, greed, and celebrity worship.

In any case, I felt a brief media fast would do no harm. In fact, I hoped it would allow me to do some de-programming of my own. Our ordinary stream of consciousness flows from deeply ingrained habits: cultural, biological, karmic. Practice partly consists of creating the space for these tics and knots to gently deconstruct themselves, until the whole constricted sense of "I" begins to loosen like an old sweater.

But sitting there hour after hour, sensing my body settle into a relaxed immobility and my brain trance out on its own babble, all I encountered was a tumultuous buzz of restless chatter—what sages have dubbed the "monkey mind," but which I rapidly came to think of as "TV mind." I was amazed how much media clogged the pipes: Led Zeppelin songs, *Simpsons* episodes, Wallace Stevens poems I read in college, the most recent reports from the latest distant war. Though I occasionally channel-surfed into moments of pregnant stillness, I spent far more time realizing what anyone who feels lonely or anxious and instinctively flips on the television knows: media is much easier to process than a moment of unvarnished experience.

A number of channels were showing "The Erik Davis Story," though most of the episodes appeared to be reruns. I weathered collegiate video porn and scratchy 8 mm films of embarrassing childhood flubs, high-production fantasies of future triumphs and tests of the Emergency Anxiety System. But as the tatters of autobiography flapped by, they also begged the inevitable question: well, how did I get here?

As a kid growing up in Del Mar, an upwardly mobile suburban Southern California beach-town, I was exposed to about as much traditional spirituality as you can string on a pine tree. I was a child of *Gilligan's Island*, Bugs Bunny, *The Hobbit*, and the sandy arroyos and red-rock cliffs of my hometown, wild places where my friends and I created fantastic playgrounds of elves and superheroes on the way home from school.

When I hit teendom in 1980, my fondness for such reveries bloomed into a fondness for drugs, especially LSD, pot, and psilocybin mushrooms. My friends and I stoked the dying embers of the California counterculture. We read Carlos Castaneda and *Be Here Now*, traveled to Dead shows, took psychedelics seriously, and meditated at the local Siddha Yoga joint. I was a huge reader, and became particularly fascinated by religion and the occult. Like the Lovecraft stories and science-fiction classics I also devoured, the "metaphysics" section of the mall bookstores offered up coherent but astoundingly imaginative worlds that somehow mirrored, mocked, and resolved the tensions of the rather disappointing one I greeted everyday. Because I was basically raised a heathen (I learned the Gospel from a scratchy copy of *Jesus Christ Superstar*), I had no sour taste of dogma in my mouth; I found atheism boring and accepted the appealing if somewhat fuzzy notion that all paths led to God. I met Hare Krishnas, yoga freaks, witches, *I Ching* Taoists and mystical Catholic teens wielding Ouija boards; I bonded with heavy-metal Satanists and born-again Christian surfers.

I had many dreams, trips, and experiences that bordered on the fantastic and occult, but it's pretty easy to write them off today as a morass of bubbling hormones, naivete, and a drug-induced eruption of what psychologists call the "primary processes" of the psyche. In any case, the inevitable loss of that adolescent magic was hastened by the Ivy League college professors who initiated me into the deeply skeptical traditions of critical theory, deconstruction, and other post-everything razzmatazz. I was taught that neither science nor common sense nor Enlightenment categories of knowledge were fixed in stone; I grew to believe that all claims about reality took their place in an ambiguous and shifting network of language games, historical constructions, and political power grabs.

Though it took me many years to wed my younger seeking self with the East Coast intellectual I was coming to be, the postmodern house of mirrors also confirmed my already strong suspicion that reality can only be glimpsed through a kaleidoscope of overlapping and even contradictory points of view—an "aperspectival" sensibility first nurtured by psychedelics and the motley spectacle of California's spiritual culture. And so I came to see the world as a carnival of hybrids, of people and places and things woven from nucleic acids and epiphanies, money and mind, sex and technologies. Though I found traditional religious claims as suspicious as any absolute truths, I understood that people's gods, myths, and everyday spiritual practices were irreducible strands in the webwork of the real.

After college, I found myself a freelance writer, covering the popular culture of the day—rock music, television, digital media. Like the religious historian R. Laurence Moore, who once wrote that he followed religion the way others followed baseball, I continued to track the spiritual and religious dimensions of our world, and I did so with the same enthusiasm and curious fascination I brought to the colorful subcultures that populate our age. Unlike religious traditionalists who bemoan rap stars and the horrors of heavy metal, I found that many of mass culture's fandoms, images, and electric rituals distinctly echoed the more populist and imaginative expressions of religious activity in earlier ages. And so I followed those echoes: *Star Trek* fans who held Neopagan rituals; Elvis devotees who found in the King the solace they no longer felt in Jesus; computer games that raided the occult; freaks who turned raves or Dead shows into psychedelic Eleusinian Mysteries.

And the spirit never stopped tugging inside me, but exactly what that spirit was became more and more difficult to explain. The cultural trends I tracked spoke to spiritual needs unsatisfied by the secular technoscientific world of late capitalism, but they hardly touched my own aches. What called me was something more intuited than described, more experienced than codified, more wagered than known.

Books fed it, but those wonderful word-machines weren't enough, and most spiritual groups I checked out seemed plagued with the mystical equivalent of office politics. I grew to suspect paths that depended on powerful teachers or an unleashed imagination, for those strategies often seemed to play off, in a different key, the same obsession with fantasy and celebrity that undergirds the so-called "society of the spectacle."

Like a lot of over-educated people, I became attracted to Buddhism for the simple reason that it seemed to emphasize practice over belief. In other words, I could follow the bare-bones recipe of following the breath with the experimental attitude one approaches any intriguing technology—or drug, for that matter. The first Zen priest I met was a crazed Texan with a bad back who described himself as a "Zen failure." As we talked, the topic turned to UFOs, and he showed me a videotape of Darryl Anka channeling an intriguing and rather amusing extraterrestrial being named Bashar. Six months later I met a monk at a Tibetan monastery in the Indian state of Karnataka, a diamond-eyed American man who had been practicing solidly in the Gelugpa tradition for twenty years. We talked about Philip K. Dick and William Gibson, and he showed off the laptop he used to prepare for the intense philosophical debates his monastery was hosting that month, an event he likened to a Buddhist Olympics. Returning to the States, I hooked up with my first serious meditation teacher, a Zen lesbian who taught multimedia at New York University. Then I met Taizan Maizumi Roshi, a diminutive Japanese monk who, rumor has it, may have partly inspired the *Star Wars* character Yoda. Definitely my kind of path.

So that's how I wound up staring at a wall on a mountain above San Berdoo, with a warm belly, aching knees, and an internal monologue that oscillated between a relaxed embrace of the passing present and a feverish spew of memes. As the days passed, I no longer paid much attention to the internal play-by-play, and my inner sportscaster gradually faded like the sound of a transistor radio carried away down the beach. Cresting into one particular heartbeat one particular afternoon, I felt myself expand and dissolve. There was no longer a world "out there" that sent me information that I processed "in here." Events simply occurred within a shimmering and bountiful field of lazy and luxurious becoming. A stomach rumble, a bird call, a flash of intense warmth in a knee, a warm breeze—they were like notes in an atmospheric symphony, organically related but freed from the linear rule of melody or the steady beat of clock time.

Kindergarten satoris like this disappear faster than skywriting. But my experience that day helped me realize that meditation, which many outsiders see as an ascetic disengagement from reality or at best a kind of relaxation exercise, can actually bloom into an awareness of the world far more crisp and, dare I say, information-rich than our usual murky and multitasking consciousness can allow. Though I don't believe that my zazen did a damn thing for the kids in Bosnia or the stressed ecosystems that fringe LA, I began to see that sitting practice can not only affirm the "binding" with things and beings that lies at the core of religion, but can train and nurture one of the most vital and highly prized commodities of our time: attention.

This lesson really hit home when I descended from the mountain a few days later. I still felt a serene balance, as if a gently whirling gyroscope was centered in my belly. But from the moment I slouched into the SIGGRAPH convention, it was clear that the center was not going to hold. At least 35,000 people had traveled to the downtown heart of LA's glittering strip-mall void to attend the event: company reps and computer geeks, Hollywood schmoozers and goateed digital hipsters, and hundreds of civilians who coughed up big bucks just to ogle the tech. And there was lots of tech to ogle: hundreds of games, software packages, virtual reality systems, media art projects, hardware platforms, Web technologies, and loads of digital eye-candy. Add that to panel discussions on everything from artificial life to feminist critiques of the Cartesian coordinate system, and mere anarchy was loosed upon my mind.

For a wide-angle cultural observer like myself, conferences like SIGGRAPH provide convenient one-stop shopping for signs of the zeitgeist. In my sensitized state of mind, SIGGRAPH's frenetic hype, mind-bending machines and garish color schemes began to take on the apocalyptic momentum and incandescent hubris of the information age itself. It was as if my newly hatched subtle body was loosed in some bad electronic purgatory, cacophonous and claustrophobic.

Like modern airport terminals or malls, the LA Convention Center is one of those abstract, weightless structures that belong in orbit. The poorly ventilated cavern serving as the main showroom floor was devoid of windows, because the game here—like the game at the Zen Mountain Monastery—was attention. Bruce Sterling said that attention is the money of the information age, the one genuinely scarce resource in the false infinity of the Internet. Both on and offline, the marketing engines of late capitalism have turned the capture of that attention into a science of psychological tease that rivals the fascist propagandists and religious mesmerists of earlier ages. Advertisements saturate the social field, as tag lines and slogans infect our speech and manufactured images organize our unconscious perceptions of the world.

Hucksters and salesmen have been catching people's eyes in the dusty din of the marketplace for millennia, of course. But at SIGGRAPH I began to feel like the machines themselves were attempting to lock onto my central nervous system and draw it in like a Star Wars tractor beam. And perhaps the best way for a machine to get your attention is to swallow your senses whole—in other words, virtual reality. Like the digital paint programs that specialize in simulating human flesh, virtual reality promises to translate our very bodies into the weightless condition of life inside the media. The old dream of angel flight, of rainbow bodies and astral doubles, has been electromagnified into the virtual avatar.

The first VR machine I test-drove at SIGGRAPH was a simulated hang-glider flight that used a full-body sling to provide a sense of floating as you navigated the twists and turns of narrow red-rock canyon projected on the screen before your eyes. As with some other VR experiences that have quickened my blood, the hang glider triggered a bit of the quicksilver serenity I've felt in lucid dreams. It's an odd and somewhat disturbing experience to have your most intimate forays into the otherworlds of the psyche recalled by an arcade game on a showroom floor, but there you have it. Moments like this have led me to take the connection between media technology and the archetypal imagination seriously. In this sense, SIGGRAPH was a savage temple of the electronic image, its booths and exhibits shrines for a cacophony of cults, whose terminal screens offer magical gateways into the surreal and tacky landscapes of the digital unconscious.

"See the Unbelievable! Witness the Unthinkable in 3D!" the garish sign proclaimed. It was a Straylight "virtual theater," and featured a dozen blank-faced folks reclining on chairs that occasionally shook, each person outfitted with a bulky head-mounted display that projected a computer-animated 3D video into their eyeballs. These folks looked like zombies in a liquid-crystal opium den, though I had to remind myself that, after all, I had just spent a week staring at a wall.

The video that so absorbed their attention was an intense, hallucinogenic spin on one of the most potent and infectious mythologies of the modern West: the extraterrestrial encounter. The video's creator was Steve Speer, a brash and innovative computer animator who mixes scatological satire with archetypal splendor—his "Carl Jung's Dream" brilliantly fuses images of cathedrals and Norse gods with golden feces and giant worm-like penises. In this piece, a little kid gets sucked into an alternative dimension by a crew of diminutive, almond-eyed gray aliens.

Strapping on a head-mounted display, I found myself somewhat underwhelmed with the ride, mostly because the point-of-view kept switching between first- and third-person perspectives—jarring cuts that ruined VR's goal of psychic immersion. But when it came to the primal scene of UFO abduction lore, the piece became all too compelling. "I" lay on a surgical table in a flying saucer, and a group of impassive Grays leaned over me with buzzing surgical drills in their spidery hands. I shivered as their tools descended toward me, even though I do not usually fear psychic surgery at the hands of cartoons.

Perhaps what spooked me was the sense that this VR "experience" symbolized the secret dream of contemporary media: to invade and rewrite consciousness itself. It drove home how insane technological culture has become. Unmoored from folkways, grasping after figments, addicted to the novelty and tyrannical demands of our hyperactive society, we drift in overdrive. Amidst all the distracting noise and fury, the hoary old questions of the human condition—Who are we? Why are we here? How do we face others? How do we face the grave?—sound distant and muffled, like fuzzy conundrums we have learned to set aside for more compulsive and profitable queries. Unless we open up clearings within the space-time of our lives, unless we take media fasts and dare to wander off the grid, such questions may never arise in all their implacable awe.

And so we try to recover our attention, and draw it back towards embodied experience, towards real earth and the mindful now. We hear a lot about ordinary enlightenment today, about embracing our own equivalent of chopping wood and carrying water. This desire for authenticity, for reality and the natural, is also part of our popular culture, packaged and marketed in New Age catalogs and the shelves of beauty salons and health food chain stores. The fact is, we don't really live in a world of chopping wood and carrying water anymore. The processes that we call, variously, globalization, the information age, postmodernism, and the biotech revolution are now the backdrop of seeking, and they perhaps need to be drawn into the foreground. The fact that you can buy CDs of Siberian shamans or score a paperback copy of secret Dzogchen manuals by aiming your Web browser at Amazon.com is only a trivial symptom of a far more tumultuous transformation in the world spirit.

Some fear that the relentless growth of global capitalism will dash whatever hopes we have of creating a sustainable future on the surface of this bleeding and tottering globe. Others fear that the new world order will lead to insidious forms of media surveillance and social control. And even if we dodge this multinational *1984*, we still have to face *Brave New World*, and its specter of rampant genetic engineering, happy pills, and an entertainment culture of soulless simulations. So how does one embrace spiritual practice in a world of digital capitalism, commodified DNA, psychopharmacology, and a steady stream of information about a planet falling apart at the seams? Though nostalgic and even "reactionary" sentiments have their place in a world intoxicated by novelty, I do not believe that a romantic retreat into old religious myths or Luddite primitivism is the answer. Though pockets of the gone world persist, there are no "traditions" that have not been marked by the peculiar dynamics of our time—not Tibetan Buddhism, not esoteric Christianity, not Native ways.

Slowly, tentatively, a "network spirituality" suggests itself from the midst of yearning and confusion, a multi-faceted path that might humanely and intelligently navigate the technological house of mirrors without losing the resonance of ancient ways or the ability to slice through the venality and delusion that court human life. Against the specter of new and renewed fundamentalism, freethinking seekers both inside and outside the world's religious traditions are trying to cut and paste a wealth of teachings, techniques, images, and rites into a path grounded enough to walk upon. The mix-and-match spirituality derided by traditionalists is only the surface of a far more supple and dynamic synthesis in the making, one that demands a form of being we have only begun to intuit: open-ended and integral, embodied and viridian-green. This path is a matrix of paths, with no map provided at the onset, and no collective goal beyond the tenacity and grace of our step.

Such a networked path opens up an ecumenical space far more radical than New Age fantasies of global unity or the bland interfaith chats between liberal monotheists. We log onto this emerging Indranet when we accept that we will not transcend the sometimes agonizing tension between the world's various structures of belief and practice. Nor will we simply overcome more contemporary conflicts between faith and skepticism, the stones and the stories, the mundane absurdity of everyday life and the incandescence of the absolute. Instead, these tensions and conflicts become dynamic, calling us to face the Other with an openness that does not seek to assimilate them to our point of view. By replacing the need for a common ground with an acceptance and even celebration of our common groundlessness, network spirituality might creatively integrate these tensions while also learning when to let the gaps and ruptures alone. These are the spaces in which we simply breathe.

2002

THE PAISLEY GATE
Tantric Psychedelia

I first visited Green Gulch Farms on a sunny Sunday in the fall of 1995. A group of students were sitting beneath the alien rows of eucalyptus trees, talking casually with Tenshin Reb Anderson, then abbot of the San Francisco Zen Center. Jerry Garcia had recently died, and at one point in the conversation, a blond, fortysomething woman asked Anderson, in all seriousness, whether Garcia was a bodhisattva.

Myself, I would have failed this particular Marin County koan. But not Anderson, who answered the question promptly and without condescension. He first described the Buddhist idea of protectors: beings who can be said to encircle and guard the dharma without being entirely within the fold. Presumably, Anderson was taking inspiration from the *dharmapalas* of Tibetan Buddhism, especially the *lokapalas*: ferocious local spirits who swore allegiance to the Buddha-way only after being magically subjugated by the tantric missionary and wizard Padmasambhava. Some of these shamanic entities are even said to not fully accept the Buddha's teaching; though integrated within Tibetan Buddhism, they retain an intense liminality, or "in-betweenness." And as the recent Tibetan culture wars over the protector spirit Dorje Shugden makes clear, one monk's manifestation of Manjushri can be another monk's blood-thirsty demon.

In any case, Anderson's response was brilliant. Without castigating whatever visionary and communal ecstasy Deadheads managed to extract from their loopy scene, Anderson established an open border between Garcia and the dharma, at once separating the two while acknowledging their connection—a connection that, in the Bay Area anyway, is as local as a lokapala. But though American Zen and the Grateful Dead have both served as major attractions in northern California's spiritual carnival, the abbot also needed to draw the line. On the far side of this line lay drugs, because drugs, Anderson made clear, were definitely not the Buddha way.

Anderson did not name the drugs, which was just as well, as the day was growing short and the Dead's curriculum vitae is long. Garcia's appetite for heroin and freebase was at times prodigious, and few would make an argument for the enlightening nature of these substances. But in the larger context of the Grateful Dead experience, "drugs" means psychedelics—the LSD, peyote, mushrooms, and other compounds that transformed the Dead's cowboy jazz into occasions for Dionysian romps in the electric bardo. In Anderson's analogy, then, psychedelics correspond to the unassimilable shamanic elements of Tibetan folk magic, to those pre-Buddhist beliefs and practices, Bon-po or not, that remain outside the circle of dharma they nonetheless helped shape.

Leaving the Grateful Dead aside, I'd like to suggest that the overlap between American psychedelic culture and American Buddhism is roughly analogous to the liminal zone inhabited by the less sublime dharmapalas. The analogy works both historically and, if you will, institutionally. On top of providing an imaginative slant on the significant historical links between American Buddhism and psychedelics in the 1960s and '70s, the tantric tension between local demons and dharma protectors also helps us understand how some contemporary American Buddhists grapple with the controversial, even heretical specter of psychedelic spirituality. When Tibetan Buddhists engaged the fierce and sorcerous entities of the pre-Buddhist mindscape, they faced the same sort of problem that greets American Buddhists attempting to account for the convulsively magic molecules in their midst: how to simultaneously honor and vanquish, integrate and control.

The grizzled bearded visage of "Maha Jerry" tells us something right off the bat: the question of psychedelics and American Buddhism remains intimately bound up with the collective spiritual narrative of a particular generation of Americans. Though American Buddhism sprouted from seeds planted long before the emergence of "the '60s," the dharma rode to relative prominence on the same countercultural wave of mind-expansion that thrust Timothy Leary into the limelight. Indeed, if there had been no Pranksters, no acid tests, no "instant nirvana," it is hard to imagine that places like Green Gulch would exist at all. Buddhism in

America first hit its stride in the context of countercultural spirituality, and it is simply impossible to understand countercultural spirituality without taking psychedelics into account. Indeed, such understanding is probably impossible without taking psychedelics, period.

The legitimacy of psychedelic spirituality is a vexing question, especially given the ideas of authenticity and illusion that play such a pivotal role in the spiritual assessment of drugs. Anthropologically speaking, though, it's hard not to see the question of legitimacy as anything other than a mechanism of cultural power through which religious institutions and lineages define and police their borders. As we now know, psychedelic substances, not to mention other psychoactive drugs, have played a profound role in the history of the human spirit. We may never know what materials composed the soma praised in the Vedas or the punch that gave the Eleusinian Mysteries their mystical zap, but its a pretty safe bet that something more than watery oatmeal was being quaffed. Psychoactive plants are even more fundamentally linked to those ancient indigenous practices rather loosely described as "shamanism." The religious culture of pre-Buddhist Tibet, for example, was part of a huge shamanic complex that stretched throughout Eurasia and included, in its more northern stretches at least, the ritual use of the psychedelic mushroom *Amanita muscaria*.

In any case, psychoactive drugs must be featured prominently in any catalog of what Mircea Eliade called humanity's "technologies of ecstasy"—a tool-kit of altered states production that includes dancing, drumming, fasting, fucking, and physical ordeal. But in the 1960s, in a culture that had swept its mystical and ecstatic traditions under the moldering carpet of mainline Christianity, there was little to no context for the experiences such technologies helped produce. While one can certainly explore psychedelic space as a "modernist," looking to art and science for models, some people found that only mystical language and occult images could frame their chemical illuminations. Many Westerners turned, in particular, to Eastern religion, partly because the Orient has long been an imaginal zone where Westerners scamper when they want to escape the prison of scientific materialism. The "Eastern

turn" also makes phenomenological sense. LSD could send serpentine energy shooting up your spine, or thrust you into apocalyptic mandalas, or vibrate the world into an energetic void. At the same time, drugs could also unveil the simple, immanent "Zen" of the ordinary world: a leaf, a breeze, or, as in Aldous Huxley's famous mescaline tale from *The Doors of Perception*, a fold in one's trousers.

Drugs and dharma were themselves only a few of the ingredients in a heretical countercultural stew that included free love, astrology, street protests, long hair, anarchism, electric guitars, an active press, Carlos Castaneda, and Hindu iconography. From the perspective of serious Western Buddhists with Eastern teachers, not to mention the roshis and lamas who themselves arrived in the 1960s and '70s in order to found institutions, the freak scene must have seemed, in its eclectic mania, almost as wild and fierce as Tibet seemed to the Indian missionaries of the eighth century. In a sense, the counterculture was America's own fractured shamanism, seething with untamed energies and magical phantasms. By taking root within this intensely vibrant culture, the Western dharma was able to make the transition from a marginal pursuit of intellectuals and cultural mavericks to the influential if constrained mass phenomenon it is today. While those roots may have been inebriant-free, the soil they found was psychedelic, and its peculiar nutrients fundamentally shaped the blooms to come.

For one thing, Buddhism owed many of its recruits to the widespread fascination with altered states of consciousness—a fascination that was largely sparked, if not fueled, by drugs. Simply put, psychedelics gave people a taste for the excitement, power, anxiety, insight, and joy of tweaking their perceptions. On an even more basic level, drugs also encouraged people to explore their own immediate experience, and to recognize that heaven and hell were functions of their own minds. Many Westerners were drawn to Buddhism because it too offered a "hands on" dimension lacking in Christianity, one that also loosely accorded with the modern "scientific" temperament that drugs, in their own way, subtly reinforced. This democratic turn towards direct experience became one of the hallmarks of countercultural spirituality, just as it became a hallmark of American Buddhism. The notion that samadhi was available to all, that everyone possessed something like the Buddha-mind, was emphasized by the universal action of the Sandoz molecule. "Have you ever been experienced?" Hendrix asked. If not, why not?

Once blown, many Western minds were far more likely to put up with alien rituals and grueling disciplines that promised even deeper and subtler experiences. The notion of *practice*—perhaps the richest and most multivalent term in American Buddhism—is crucial here. One basic meaning of practice is technique: one does not believe, one acts. (Or, perhaps more accurately, "action happens.") In other words, one adopts a technique, an internalized technology or a psycho-behavioral recipe, and explores the results. Though the act of swallowing a sugar cube is a pretty rinky-dink operation compared to the rigor and depth of zazen or hatha yoga, psychedelics did teach people that altered states, even refined ones, could be accessed through technologies of perception.

Indeed, LSD was only one device in the counterculture's ever-expanding occult tool kit, which included divination systems like tarot cards and the *I Ching*, biofeedback devices and flotation tanks, as well as a variety of internal and physical disciplines: breathwork, t'ai chi, massage, pranayama, veganism, Kriya yoga. Given the unprecedented technological experience of the baby boom generation, it's not surprising that they developed the conviction that technique, in some form, was integral to the process of transformation and insight. Whether the technology was external or internal was less important—was an acid test, with its feedback systems, light shows, and communal chemistry, inside or out? LSD helped insure that the Eliadean metaphor of spiritual practices as "inner technologies" would find its way into the lexicon of countercultural spirituality, so much so that it continues to appear in the writings of a serious Buddhist scholar like Robert Thurman.

The problem with the metaphor of technology is that technologies often encourage a dualistic viewpoint, while mature practice erodes the perception that there is a doer using a tool to pursue a goal. This was an important lesson for American Buddhists during the freak years, when the goals were cosmic. In those idealistic times, there was a veritable obsession with the achievement of enlightenment experiences—an obsession that may have owed much of its ferocity to expectations first laid down by drugs. Over the decades, the emphasis has shifted away from such fierce pursuits, and many teachers go out of their way to deflate the excitement surrounding powerful meditation experiences. Indeed, I suspect that the hostility that some contemporary Buddhists express towards psychedelics conceals an anxiety that their practice remains tainted, on some level, with the desire to get high. But this is an understandable desire—it's hard to say how many people would continue the practice over the years if they didn't occasionally "get the goods," whether on the pillow or on the drugs.

But psychedelics don't just get people high. Like literal acid, they work to empty, on both individual and social levels, the apparently solid substance of conventional reality—so-called common sense. Regardless of the otherworldly visions drugs can bestow, the deeper psychedelic message concerned the relativity of thought and perception—a "philosophical" insight that drugs reveal directly through the operation of your own nervous system. Unfortunately, as Nietzsche saw with a prophet's eye, relativity is only a stone's throw away from nihilism. Strong psychedelics gave people a glimpse of emptiness, but while the void can be glittering at its peak, it can feel like a bottomless pit the morning after. The ease with which so many psychedelic users sank into cynicism, mental instability, and addiction to more insidious drugs shows that psychedelics themselves do nothing to build the contexts of meaning and spiritual aspiration necessary to prevent such ecstatic technologies from becoming hollow and even destructive mechanisms. Some of the new religious movements of the 1970s—like the long-haired Jesus Movement—reacted against the druggy void with a new fundamentalism. But the dharma—whose full-frontal embrace of sunyata is coupled with a compassionate rejection of nihilism—seemed unusually poised to answer the problems posed by a stark psychedelic confrontation with the ultimate relativity and provisional nature of all phenomenal experience.

So how do we express and characterize the relationship between psychedelics and dharma practice? The conventional answer, offered by many once-tripping Buddhists, is that drugs "open the door." Without much work or knowledge on the part of the user, psychedelics can crack open consensus reality, expand identity beyond the confines of the conventional self, induce ego-death, and unveil the connection between mind and the totality of the real. However "inauthentic" these experiences may be judged to be, many people respond to them by turning to Eastern practice in order to extend, comprehend, and deepen their insights. Once their practice has stabilized and opened up, many of these people abandon drugs as needless or even harmful distractions. In this view, spiritual practice becomes something like the lift-off of Apollo 11. Drugs point you towards the moon of enlightenment, and somewhat violently thrust you away from the gravity of consensus reality. Having done so, they can then be abandoned like the early stages of a rocket. Or as Alan Watts quipped about psychedelics, "If you get the message, hang up the phone."

But what happens when serious practitioners continue to follow what poet Dale Pendell calls "the poison path"? What happens when you open the door and don't shut it tightly behind you? Here is where the real controversy begins. No one's logging any numbers, but I suspect that a healthy chunk of self-identified practicing American Buddhists keep at least occasional dates with the writhing, world-rending void lurking in the heart of psychedelic hyperspace. But I also suspect that, if asked to pass judgment on such activities, most dharma teachers would deliver a fat thumbs down. Indeed, psychedelic spirituality may well be the only real heresy in American Buddhism (except, maybe, for voting Republican). Heresy, though, is a Western concept, the stuff of witch burnings and gnostic cults. And though serious psychedelic culture certainly has its gnostic aspects, in the context of American Buddhism, it is perhaps best described as a kind of tantra—a crude and scandalous one for sure, but homegrown at least, arising from our "native" tradition of countercultural craziness.

Given the generally cheesy spectacle of American neo-tantric sexology, I want to emphasize that I am not claiming that psychedelics have much of anything to do with authentic Asian tantra, an immensely rich and complex tradition about which I have only a scattering of book learning. Nonetheless, in the spirit of productive analogies rather than proclamations of metaphysical truth, I'd like to suggest a number of intriguing parallels. The most obvious one is secrecy. Despite their crucial role in the propagation of American Buddhism, psychedelics are basically not the stuff of dharma talks, Shambhala books, or *Tricycle* articles. Discussions occur within the context of *sangha* and teacher-student relationships, but only selectively and probably not very often at all. One reason for this secrecy derives from another similarity: as with the *panca-tattva* practices of "left-handed" tantric adepts—who, among other things, ritually consume booze, fish, and meat—the materials of psychedelic Buddhism are socially unsanctioned. They are, literally, "against the law." In fact, the condemnation that surrounds psychedelics may actually lend them some of their esoteric power, just as the negative social mores surrounding the consumption of animal flesh and alcohol contribute a certain antinomian buzz to the feistier tantric practices.

The connection between psychedelics and tantra goes beyond social practices, into the heart of esoteric perception. This material is difficult to describe, but one could say for starters that psychedelics usher the bodymind into a magical zone that unfolds between the consensual sensory world and the worlds depicted in the different languages of dream, art, and high-octane metaphysics. Within this "bardo logic," memories, ideas, and images multiply and pulse like hieroglyphic sigils, suggesting patterns of association and hidden resonances that voyagers often take—or mistake—for revelations. But the real object of revelation is the mind itself—not simply as a source of meaning, or linguistic categories, but as an organic machine of perception, a machine that can be tweaked. Simply put, psychedelics present the imagination. And by "imagination" I don't simply mean the source of our hazy daydreams or visionary flights, but the synthetic power that Kant posited as the generally unconscious mechanism through which our basic conceptual faculties construct the world of space-time.

The status of the imagination in Buddhism is, to put it mildly, ambivalent. On the one hand, the imagination is often treated as a synonym for *avidya*—it is the imagination that mistakes the rope of reality for the frightening (or seductive) serpent. The very literary form of the earliest Buddhist texts—their dryness, repetition, and lack of flavor—argues that the desiccation of the imagination was a goal of practice. On the other hand, many Mahayana sutras are brimming with the fantastic: galaxies of bodhisattvas, infinite garlands of wish-fulfilling gems, clouds of spheres of light the color of the curl of hair between the Buddha's eyebrows. All this can seem very familiar. Indeed, I have not come across a canonical religious text that can approach the psychedelic majesty of the *Avatamsaka Sutra,* whose infinite details and ceaseless lists captures both the adamantine excess and the fractal multiplicity of deep psychedelia.

What is the literary function of such apparently "imaginative" materials? Are they glimpses of *sambhogakaya*, seductive folk material, depictions of literal powers, allegories of wisdom? Whatever its function in sutra, however, the work of the esoteric imagination in tantra is central, even on the most literal level of visualization. For the generation stages of tantra, during which deities and their associated mandalas are constructed with the inner eye, the merely individual imagination is used as a gateway, an engine to tame and train for the powerful perceptions of tantric reality. Through diligence, conduct, and ritual, the imagination itself is alchemically transformed, and the completion stages actualize, according to traditional accounts, what had only previously been imagined. Psychedelics are generally too chaotic and willful for this kind of controlled work; nonetheless, serious psychonauts will often encounter feelings, images, and pocket universes with an intensely tantric flavor. And why not? If one buys into tantric accounts of the subtle body, with its nadis and chakras and winds, then it is not too tough to imagine that, just as physical practices like Hatha yoga, mantra, and Tummo can stir up the energies of transformed perception, so might swarms of molecules swimming in the neural bath of the brain. Certainly it is the case that psychonauts who also practice yoga, t'ai chi, and visualization often find their work reshaping the phenomenology of their trips.

Even if drugs trigger actual changes in the esoteric bodymind, they may be quite harmful, even demonic—a fear immortalized in the notorious folkloric claim that drugs somehow put "holes in your astral body."

As David Gordon White makes clear, however, medieval tantrics were not above ingesting alchemical elixirs, even as renegade sadhus ingest hashish and Jimson weed today. It is hard to imagine that if LSD, peyote, or DMT existed in ancient India, these substances would not have been used by at least some folks who conceived of their path as tantra. Despite the thoroughly integrated example of Vajrayana in Tibet, the religious temperament of tantra suggests that a percentage of its practitioners will almost inevitably stray towards heterodoxy; its extreme wings will adapt extreme technologies, dangerous or not. Representatives of orthodoxy may argue that such activities represents degenerate tantra, and they may well be right. But technology is about nothing if it is not about speed, and tantra is the lightning path, appropriate for a time of waning dharma. Perhaps psychedelics are the greased lightning appropriate for an even more degenerate West, where only the philosophy of Malcolm X makes sense: by any means necessary.

2002

DIAMOND SOLITAIRE

In 1997, I had a bona-fide, Grade A, no-shit "mystical" experience—or at least something that felt a hell of a lot like a mystical experience. The deal went down, absurdly enough, during a month-long retreat at a Zen center in northern California; even more absurdly, it happened while I was washing a bunch of beets in the garden. I had come to the center to recover and reorient after the agony of finishing the final draft of *Techgnosis*. I was pretty wrung out. During work period one afternoon, I found myself alone in a shady corner field, rinsing a pile of freshly unearthed beets in a free-standing outside basin. I stood there, in the cool but sunny air, washing big clumps of moist, fragrant mud from the red roots. I hadn't had any alcohol or drugs in weeks.

What happened next is tough to describe, and I think I need to lay down a bit of background first. One idea you'll find in esoteric psychology (and elsewhere) is the notion that there is a vital difference between the content of consciousness—sensations, feelings, perceptions, thoughts, etc.—and the Witness that perceives or, better, witnesses these feelings and perceptions. On the surface, the Witness might seem to be needlessly "dualistic"—a redeployment of the Cartesian split between mind and body that everybody is always bitching about. But its still kind of true, and meditation, to say nothing of rigorous self-observation, helps clarify the Witness by loosening identification with the thoughts, feelings, and perceptions that enmesh our being without entirely defining it.

So I'm rinsing the beets, minding my own business, vaguely enjoying the cool water washing away the moist and pungent mud, when my "I" suddenly rockets like a sci-fi space elevator into the highest, most barren and serene realms of Witness consciousness. I became the *watcher of the watcher of the watcher of the watcher of the watcher of the watcher . . .* , a bootstrapping eensy-weensy spider of observer and observation that shed layers of identification as it flip-flopped up the water spout into ever more rarified levels of subjectivity, until there was little left. The analogy that arose most forcefully a few moments later, when I was able to reflect again, was of some seafarer's spyglass rapidly being drawn open, an action which extends the reach of the eye even as it, in some sense, increases the distance between the eye and the surface medium where the world inscribes its traces. My eye, my I, was now peering into my experience from Olympian climes.

It's tough to describe what this new "I" felt like without leaning on mystic rhetoric, which I really don't want to do because it sounds like bullshit, and my experience was anything but bullshit, at least to me. One thing is for sure: there was nothing particularly human in it. It felt like a being, but it had no attributes I can really name other than awareness and perception. It felt like diamond, like hard serenity, a clear and crystalline meta-mind that was both individual and, in some ungrokkable, transpersonal way, collective. And ever so slightly amused.

There was a soft but implacably unemotional quality as well, a passionless intelligence I will take the risk of characterizing as "angelic." I am thinking here of the angels in Wim Wenders's *Wings of Desire*, who gaze with equanimity upon struggling humanity, like long-suffering but interested cosmic shrinks. My experience may also reflect what Thelemite and other Solomonic magicians mean—if they mean anything concrete at all—when they describe the goal of ritual magic as the "knowledge and conversation of the Holy Guardian Angel."

Even as I arrived at this adamantine peak, I also rolled downhill, attending to the situation at hand: washing beets in a dappled field on a cool but sunny afternoon. The spacious crystalline entity my mind had become now hovered in infinite approximation to the dude I normally am, watching hands that were no longer exactly "mine" continue to rinse the roots. At that moment I understood, with an unshakable clarity, two things: that the causal, billiard-ball flow of the world proceeds absolutely lawfully, and that I suffer because the bright shards of witnessing angelstuff that lie at the root of my being get caught up in attempting to push and pull this procession, to cling and resist and identify.

The word *lawful* seemed to appear in my mind as the experience unfolded, but it may have popped up shortly thereafter. It's a funny word. I never use it favorably, for one thing, having a typical lefty countercultural prejudice against "the law"—either religious stricture or the cops or conservative ideals of absolutism and obedience. But that is how I saw our little slice of space-time. As *lawful*.

Later, as I puzzled over this somewhat odd word, I recalled that one of the meanings of *dharma* is law. Maybe not law in the sense of the law of karma or the four noble truths or the five amazing thises or the six sobering thats, but just *the way things are*. And for those brief moments, the way things are was not causing me the slightest bit of tension or pain, unlike, I could see, pretty much the rest of the time, when the double-binds of agency, choice, and desire set me at cross purposes to the flow.

In the final movement of the experience, I looked up from my hands in the basin towards a row of pine trees and eucalyptus that fringed the edge of the field. This was the universe: the wind moving slowly through the branches. I remember being startled, even at the time, that everything still moved. Despite the extraordinary otherness of my perception, time seemed to mosey along at its usual pace.

Except not so usual, because everything was light and surface and dancing, like sunlight reflecting on an inland sea, like mist in the morning, like Vegas (or the playa) at night. The wind, the leaves, the dappled light, the eucalyptus scent—it all vibrated with a consistency and dynamic togetherness I can only compare to a symphony, and like music it seemed to be fundamentally incorporeal, diaphanous, all void of substance, of that inertial stuff that gravity drags down. It was marvelous, beautiful, bittersweet, and just the way things are.

Then, about maybe thirty seconds after it had begun, the cosmic boomerang was back. I slipped on the heavy duds of good ol' anxious and horny me, finished up with the beets, and shuffled back to the zendo for the next period of sitting, more dazed than confused.

Nothing even remotely similar has happened to me in the years since, though I sometimes get a gnostic whiff of the angel hovering over my shoulder. I could try to say more about the experience, about how it changed and, mostly, did not change me, but this little tale will have to do. I'll say this though: even if what happened to me was a neural hiccup, I still know, in the way we know the mad unions of love, that we carry something cosmic within us, that the self is a doorway to another Self, and that death might swallow us in glory after all.

2007

THE BAD SHAMAN AND THE FROG

The man we called the Bad Shaman held forth on many obscurities lurking in our planet's natural pharmacopeia, but few he praised so highly or so often as the venom obtained from Phylomedusa bicolor, a tree frog found throughout the Amazon basin. Used principally by Panoan-speaking Indian men in preparation for hunting, the venom was initially brought to the knowledge of the experimental underground by the intrepid *High Times* explorer-head Peter Gorman. Though neither psychedelic nor particularly pleasurable in its effects, the venom was, according to the Bad Shaman, definitely *the shit.*

However, one could not always trust the Bad Shaman on such matters—he was the Bad Shaman, after all, *el brujo malo,* a New Jersey halfbreed known for pranks and a prodigious appetite for insects (he once described the taste of a wasp as "Brie on a Triscuit"). So it was with a mixture of excitement and trepidation that Pie, the Bear, and I all gathered at the Bad Shaman's high mountain home that early winter afternoon. Live phylomedusa greeted us in the Southwestern-style foyer—spindly green Gollums that, so far, had not responded to the Bad Shaman's variously comic attempts to coax venom from their skins. The batch we sampled came straight from the jungle, a dark resinous goo with the consistency of Vaseline.

The procedure was simple, albeit odd: using smoldering incense sticks, we removed a few layers of skin from our upper arms, leaving a cluster of small round patches of exposed flesh. (Warned it would leave a scar, I etched the lower half of the Kabbalistic Tree of Life). The Bad Shaman then swabbed on a dab of the goo on the pink skin, and bade us to sit down on his plush couch and prepare ourselves for an intense and potentially nauseating rush. Our host indicated that it was OK to puke on his tile floor, which had already received many a purge.

Within moments I felt a full volume niacin rush, a blood-pounding vasodilation in the throat and lower head. My throat felt scratchy and hot as the venom raced through my body, shooting tiny bolts of electricity along my arms and descending somewhat ominously to my gut. My body was definitely freaking out, but I maintained a cool mindfulness in the midst of the moderately high flesh panic, as I extracted whatever pleasure can be gained from raw intensity. Wooze hit my gut, though I did not loose my cookies. A host of lightning strikes and hot flashes continued to charge through my system, but in five minutes or so, the blast was basically over. The three of us lingered on the couch for a while longer, sipping Reed's Ginger Brew and allowing the last cloudbursts of the neural storm to trail off.

The froggy rocket-ride was weird, and valuable for its novelty alone. I could also sense that at higher doses one would slip into that death rehearsal rag that compels so many envelope-pushing psychonauts. But I was not prepared for the thoroughly excellent if subtle payoff the venom had in store for me over the next few days: a persistently "up" level of energy and mood, but without the edginess of stimulants or the dopey, somewhat plastic cast of Big Pharma mood elevators. Our encounter with the frog venom was only the beginning of a long weekend bacchanal, but even recreational compounds with heavy body loads left me feeling spry and chipper the morning after.

The Bad Shaman, whose upper arm looked like the cratered afterzone of a teenage acne scourge, loaded us up a day later, allowing me to finish my Kabbalistic tattoo. Though the Bad Shaman promised that the rewards depended on the heaviness of the dose, I still took a moderate amount. But the Bad Shaman blew out the stops for Hatboy, a particularly hard-headed member of our crew. After getting lathered up, he was reduced to a quivering, sweating wreck. The only payoff, he later said, was the immense relief that he did not, in fact, die. The Bad Shaman only smiled. "Maybe you didn't get enough."

2001

PSYCHONAUT

Say you're a buttoned-down organic-chemistry jockey at Merck. One day you tweak a molecule ripped off from a Peruvian native medicine, and you wind up with a powerfully psychoactive compound. Instead of squelching anxiety, instilling a reliable boner, or giving your young mind that magic amphetamine edge, the drug helps you touch the hem of God—or at least something a lot like the hem of God. At times it hurtles you into a blazing hieroglyphic phantasmagoria more sublime and gorgeously bizarre than anything on the demo reels of Hollywood FX shops. On other occasions it leads you to the lip of a fundamental insight into the dance of form and emptiness. And though later attempts to communicate your insight founder on the shoals of coherence, the experience still leaves you centered and convinced that ordinary life is fed by deeper springs.

Now, you think you'd zero in on this molecule, not only as a potential vector into the enigma of consciousness but as the basis for some really interesting commercial drugs. In other words, you'd be psyched. Right?

No way! It's common knowledge that such molecules have been recognized and consumed by people for millennia, but have been effectively banished from the scientific mindscape of the West. Despite their mighty psycho-spiritual effects, the potential insight they might provide into the mind, and the largely non-addictive behaviors they elicit, psychedelic drugs like LSD, psilocybin, mescaline, ketamine, and DMT have been crudely lumped into the same legal and sociocultural categories as speedballs and crank. And one result of this social policy is a withering of the research strategies that a rational civilization is supposed to bring to bear on the conundrums it confronts.

Despite the continued ferocity of the "war on drugs" and the largely foolish ideas about psychoactive substances it pushes, the last decade has seen a small renaissance in psychedelic research, both above and underground. On the official stage, advocacy groups like MAPS (Rick Doblin's Multidisciplinary Association for Psychedelic Studies) and the

Heffter Reseach Institute (headed up by Dave Nichols), as well as individual researchers like Rick Strassman and the UK's Karl Jansen, have done their homework, balancing loopy subjective accounts with the dry, methodical language of protocols, pharmacology, and action studies. Hopefully, these modest research reports are laying the groundwork for a resumption of the kind of official in-depth psychological studies squelched over thirty years ago.

Meanwhile, in the far margins of legality, small crews of brave, compulsive, and sometimes wacked individuals continue to compile and share fact, anecdote, and lore about exotic and newfangled psychoactives and the even more exotic combinations they allow. Think of these psychonauts as hobbyists of neural R&D. They like to plunge as far as any hippie into the bejeweled halls of hyperspace, but they also bring an almost geeky spirit of investigation to their exploits. They know their chemistry, and understand that the envelope of psychedelic pharmacology is pushed by recombining existing molecular Tinkertoys. They also take this recombinant logic a step further by mixing and matching different drugs from an ever-widening pharmacopoeia in order to craft new highs.

Even Burning Man veterans may not have heard of many of the esoteric compounds that float around the scene: AMT, 5-MEO-DMT, 2C-T-2, 2C-T-7, 5-MEO-DIPT, 4-Acetoxy-DiPT, DPT, DOB, 2-CB. With a few exceptions, these white powders have largely resisted being branded with cool names. Some have been known for decades, others are relatively new; a few have been scheduled, but many have so far been overlooked by the Feds and remain uncontrolled. However, because the vast majority of these substances are chemically similar to illegal drugs, people gobbling them technically can be snagged under the Federal Analogue Act, which allows individuals to be prosecuted for recreational use of drugs that are "substantially similar" to scheduled drugs. But this rarely seems to happen, especially given the obscurity of many of these drugs and the difficulties involved in proving "substantial" similarity.

It's impossible to say how many grams of these compounds are being synthesized and consumed annually, but there's probably morsels of intrigue all over Europe and America. Though some demand complex procedures and elusive precursors to synthesize, the lion's share can be cooked up by most anyone with undergrad training in chemistry and access to a lab. There's really nothing to stop curious amateur organic chemists from brewing up a small batch of AMT or 2-CB in a weekend to share with a small circle of friends, and anecdotal evidence indicates that many do. Some of these modern alchemists even exploit the gray-market status of these compounds by marketing them for nonhuman "research purposes" over the Internet.

The back-room circulation of these drugs has engendered a loose-knit and rather hermetic psychedelic scene devoted less to partying or cosmic communion than to a kind of weird science, where the purple haze is filtered through a knowledge and embrace of methyl groups, monoamine oxidase inhibitors, and the value of keeping your eye on the clock. The godfather of this particular psychedelic style is Sasha Shulgin, a cheery, eccentric Bay Area chemist best known for the rediscovery of MDMA, aka ecstasy. With his wife, Ann, he wrote *PiHKAL* and *TiHKAL*, two phone-book-size tomes devoted, respectively, to phenethylamines and tryptamines, the two pillars of psychedelic pharmacology. Though Shulgin once had a license to study scheduled drugs, an irritated DEA responded to the publication of *PiHKAL* by swooping down on Shulgin's grubby lab and slapping him with 51 violations they then effectively swapped for his license. In reaction, Shulgin simply continued to devote himself to the art of recombination that characterizes the synthesis of novel molecules. "Once they schedule something, I throw away my samples and continue my research in another direction," he says.

The creator of 2C-B and 2C-T-7, two drugs popular among psychonauts, Shulgin has described, synthesized, and analyzed scores of substances whose potential for thrills and profit remain untapped. Many of the hundreds of compounds described in *PiHKAL* and *TiHKAL* are duds; others are actively unfun. 2C-B, on the other hand, has gained quite a following for its electric visuals and mescaline-like effects, while the more esoteric 2C-T-7 can unleash a hyperactive barrage of 3-D psychedelic imagery that can take some users to the edge of delirium. Dosage, of course, matters greatly, but dosages are by nature provisional in this scene—a psychonaut recently died after snorting an ungodly amount of 2C-T-7. Still, even at the right amounts, it could turn out that nothing in the Shulgin universe will ever match the depth of LSD, mushrooms, or DMT. But the genie is out of the bottle. "I find postings about compounds that are slipped away in little corners of my books," says Shulgin. "And all of a sudden they are commercially available and people are talking about them. The seeds are all in there."

To no one's surprise, the weird scientists have embraced the Internet, which hosts the gossamer strands of data and debate necessary to support a shadowy and fragmented community that needs to stay informed. Sites like the Vaults of Erowid and the Lycaeum provide loads of information on dosage, chemistry, legal status, effects, and, perhaps most importantly, experiential feedback. The problem is that such public information also runs the risk of killing the scene, especially when kids get into the act. "The more people know about what's going on, the more likely somebody is to come in and try to squash it," explains Scotto, one of the more balls-out contributors to Erowid's growing vault of reports. At the same time, the persistent curiosity of psychonauts and the endless potential for pharmacological novelty may have created a perpetually expanding zone of gray-market psychedelia. "Humans are going to keep inventing these things faster than the government's going to make them illegal," says Scotto, pointing out that the efflorescence of esoteric synthetic compounds mocks the "logic" of the war on drugs. "Are we going to reach the point where I can be imprisoned for doing twenty milligrams of 4-acetoxy diisopropyltryptamine in my bathtub, when nobody even knows what that fucking is? What kind of culture is that?"

I'll tell you what kind of culture that is: a posthuman one.

This might seem like a tall claim. After all, if you take a random slice of human history, you can pretty much bank on the existence of some popular and dependable pharmacological route toward altered states of consciousness, whether through snuff, brews, bark, or herbs. What makes the coming drug culture posthuman is the historically novel conjunction of our exploding knowledge of psycho-pharmacology, the growing dominance of reductionist accounts of the mind, and a consumer culture increasingly focused on what some have called the "experience economy."

According to the drug researcher Earth, who runs the Vaults of Erowid with his also pseudonymous partner Fire, we ain't seen nothin' yet. "In the next fifty years, virtually everyone in developed countries will be faced with daily decisions about their psychoactive drug use," he says. He argues that the number of psychoactive chemicals in our midst is about to explode, the work not so much of underground drug designers as of pharmaceutical companies. "Imagine a thousand caffeine replacements," says Earth. "Myriad amphetamines, though less fun than ones today. Or, like Viagra, a coming class of pseudo-medicinal recreational drugs."

The signs of this emerging culture are around us. Just ask subway and train riders across the land what time it is, and they'll tell you: "It's Prilosec time!" The garish $50-million direct-to-consumer ad campaign for the "little purple pill" is a remarkable indication of the shift toward a mainstream embrace of psychoactive enhancement. Though you can't generally tell from the ads, the drug itself is indicated for nothing more interesting than heartburn. But the marketing machine presents Prilosec as a lifestyle drug, a kind of luxurious soma, floating against azure skies. Look at the connotations: the "little pill" is a microdot, the color a purple haze, and the image of the witchy New Age blonde exulting before the clock an ambiguous symbol of the slice of eternity that the greatest psychoactives promise—Eliot's "intersection of the timeless with time," hovering over hasty commuters.

Ordinary drugs can promise such magic in part because we have so thoroughly adopted the notion that our subjective experience is largely, if not exclusively, a product of the activity of neural tissue. It's a nineteenth-century idea, of course, but now we have twenty-first-century tools to back it up, not to mention a twenty-first-century identity crisis for marketeers to exploit. The thing is, if you push this reductionist paradigm far enough, then we are always on drugs. In other words, once you start aligning the subcomponents of selfhood with different rafts of neurotransmitters, you are already on the way toward reconceiving your experience as the product of a tumultuous cocktail of chemical triggers. When you hit the treadmill or string a full-spectrum light above your desk in order to ward off depression, not to mention pop a Prozac, you are in some sense treating your own neural juices as internal drugs whose flows you want to regulate. And this makes perfect sense. After all, the brain already makes its own equivalent of opium, cocaine, and psychedelics.

So we're all druggies now. The problem is that we also live at a time when the official lies and obfuscations about psychoactives, which are necessary to justify the drug war and the multibillion-dollar industries it breeds, have the additional effect of eroding the personal responsibility necessary to weigh costs and benefits and make choices about how we dose ourselves. "Prohibition has broken people's ability to manage their own psychoactive use," says Earth. "We've created a culture that can't choose." Instead, we are offered a simpleminded and historically insupportable view of "bad" psychoactive drugs as malefic invaders whose presence in human brains and human societies is somehow aberrant. At the same time, people are being encouraged to take socially approved psychoactives (or, in the case of Ritalin, to force them on their children). Rather than calling a spade a spade, however, the medical-industrial establishment coats these pills in "objective" rhetoric that elides the irreducibly subjective dimension of the drug encounter. From industry's perspective, psychoactives are presented not as avenues for modifying your own subjectivity, giving you the opportunity to explore pleasure or insight or calm, but as technical solutions to "syndromes" within the fixed machinery of the bodymind.

The paradox of psychedelics—which is partly a source of their continued subversive power, despite the fact that pop culture has already become so thoroughly trippy—is that they simultaneously materialize and spiritualize the problem of drugs and consciousness. On the surface level, they seem to support a reductive model, especially against traditional religious accounts of subjectivity. That is, psychedelics seem to prove that some of the most exalted states of the human spirit—cosmic communion, profound aesthetic appreciation for nature, the integration of self and other, the perception of primary pattern, the visionary eruption of archetypal phantasms, the illumination of memory—can be triggered with a pill or a plant. But from the inside, so to speak, these very same states often seem to unambiguously support a profoundly spiritual, or at least consciousness-centered point of view, over and against a mere biological reductionism. In other words, they bring us to the edge of a spiritual materialism.

Even if you discount this subjective "evidence" as untrustworthy (a perfectly acceptable move in my book), the profound reflexivity of psychedelic drugs still makes itself known through the famed role that "set and setting" play in the phenomenology of the trip. Forty years ago, long before he went sci-fi, Timothy Leary was already talking about the programmability of psychedelic experience, arguing that the individual's frame of mind and the surrounding mise-en-scène contribute substantially to the experience—a point that most later researchers only further underline. This acknowledgment profoundly changes the model of mind that emerges from the drug, because the attempt to purely mechanize the molecule—to see it as producing a small range of dependable perceptions and behaviors—founders on the enormous role that both culture and the psyche play in shaping the trip.

The dominant drug paradigm, in the rhetoric of drug warriors and industry pushers alike, depends on a very literalist model that ascribes agency to the drug itself. Psychoactive drugs challenge this scheme, functioning more like keys that open doors that you walk through. "The psychedelic drug doesn't do anything," says Shulgin. "The drug allows you to do something." At the same time, of course, the drug definitely has its own say in the matter of what gets done. But the act of introducing the thing to your synapses, and hence your life, is more like initiating a relationship than simply jacking into cyberspace through a video-game deck. Many psychedelic users naturally think of drugs as allies—even approaching traditional organic drugs like mushrooms and ayahuasca as if they were ensouled by ancient spirits. Many of these more explicitly "shamanic" trippers in turn denigrate synthetic, lab-produced compounds as soulless industrial chemicals.

But as the weird scientists point out, this is just mainstream literalism in reverse. The point is not the material; it's the dialogic relationship, the loop of meaning, that ties together mind and molecule. Indeed, much of the appeal of novel chemicals is that they deliver one to zones that have yet to be mapped by cultural consensus, underground or not. "I start with bottles that have no personality at all," says Shulgin. "You make a white crystal solid that you don't know and it doesn't know you. And so you begin to meet each other." In some sense, this structure of relationship, which is open to discovery and communication, applies to all psychoactives, even the most mainstream. Like all relationships, they can go terribly, terribly wrong; like most, they are mixed bags. And yet, to experience yourself as a mind arising from a brain means that you are already constantly in relation with neurochemistry. And in the years to come, when the expanding range of molecular modification may wrap our hands ever tighter around the tiller of the self, it might serve us well to keep in touch with the mind that moves through realms far outside that anxious simian serotonin buzz we experience as ordinary reality.

2000

AYA *AVATAR*

In paradoxical and altogether predictable terms, James Cameron's dazzling *Avatar* sets a blue man group of mystically attuned forest dwellers against the aggressive and heartless exploitation that characterizes the military-industrial-media complex, with its virtual interfaces, biotech chimeras, and cyborg war machines. The paradox, of course, is that an avatar of this technological complex is responsible for delivering Cameron's visions to us in the first place. To wit: before a recent screening of the film at the Metreon IMAX theater in San Francisco, we hapless begoggled ones were barraged with military ads, along with a triumphant techno-fetishist breakdown on the Imax gear that would soon transport us to the planet Pandora almost as thoroughly as the handicapped jarhead Jake jacks into his avatar body—a body that is, in reality, generated by computer, and so not quite reality after all. The message of all these nested media prostheses is clear: we are imaginatively handicapped, and need a commanding apparatus of virtuality to achieve fusion with the bygone but utterly concocted world of wisdom and myth represented by the Na'vi and their world.

But those are behind-the-scenes ironies, and like most people, I just gave into the ride. With its floating Roger Deanscapes and hallucinogenic flora, the manifest world of *Avatar* instead spoke another truth about our era's visionary consciousness: that the jungle pantheism that now pervades the psychoactive counterculture has gone thoroughly mainstream. Of course, noble savage narratives of ecological balance and shamanic wisdom have been haunting the Rousseau-mapped outback of the western mind for centuries. That said, *Avatar* represents some important twists in that basic tale. The most important of these is that the Na'vi's nearly telepathic understanding of their environment is grounded in more than ritual, plant-lore, and that earnest sobriety that afflicts Hollywood Indians everywhere. Their enviable at-oneness with things is also grounded in an actual organic communications network. Those fibrous, animated, and vaguely repulsive pony-tail tentacles not only allow the Na'vi to form direct control links with animals but also, through the optical filaments of the "Tree of Souls," to swap data with both ancestors and the Eywa, the biological spirit of the planet Pandora.

Eywa resonates with Erda, of course; Pandora is a dream of our own Earth. Occultists also have pointed out the name's eerie consonance with Aiwass, the disincarnate and—in sketches—alien-looking being that Aleister Crowley claimed dictated *The Book of the Law*, the central text of Crowley's revealed religion of Thelema. In any case, contact with Eywa is clearly a visionary operation, one perhaps best seen as ayahuasca lite. For while *Avatar* features nothing like the South American shaman songs and stupendous aya visuals that litter the otherwise very bad 2004 Western released here as *Renegade*, Cameron's film does suggest that the bitter jungle brew, and the spirit of ecological wisdom now attached to it, is having a trickle-down effect. After all, as online ads for ayahuasca retreats almost immediately noted, the *Banisteriopsis caapi* vine that gives ayahuasca its name (though not its most hallucinogenic alkaloids) is also known as the "Vine of Souls"—an echo of the Na'vi's Tree of Souls. And at one point in the film, when Sigourney Weaver characterizes the Tree's powers through a neurological discourse of electrical connection, the corporate tool Parker asks what she's been "smoking"—a backhanded way of acknowledging how much *Avatar*'s visionary take on jungle unity is grounded in psychoactive consciousness.

After all, beyond a thriving and in many ways damaging ayahuasca tourist market largely centered in Brazil and Peru, clandestine aya circles manned by South American shamans and all manner of Euro-American facilitators are now well established throughout the West. Among the professional creative classes who make up a sizable portion of West Coast seekers—after spirit and thrills alike—ayahuasca could almost be said to be mainstream. So it no longer matters whether Cameron or his animators have themselves drunk the tea; its active compounds are already swimming in the cultural water supply. Indeed, whether you are talking form (ground-breaking 3D animation) or content (cyber-hippie wet-dream decor), Cameron's visual and technological rhetoric is impossible to disentangle from hallucinogenic experience.

OK, maybe I am the one smoking something. But if there is an aya–*Avatar* connection, it would at least explain the most crucial way in which the film differs from conventional noble savage mysticism. Rather than ground the Na'vi's grooviness in their folklore, spiritual purity, or access to supernatural powers, the film instead argues for a direct and material communications link with plant consciousness. This means that Eywa (aka Aya) is not a religious fiction that has to be believed—she can be experienced through corporeal fusion. After temporarily plugging into the Tree of Souls, Weaver's chain-smoking left-brain doctor character happily confirms Eywa's existence even as she dies. She is smiling, no longer needing to explain or posit.

Like the Vine of Souls now wending its way through the psychedelic fringes of the developed world, the Tree of Souls becomes a kind of bio-mystical media, a visionary communications matrix that uplinks the souls of the dead and the network mind of the ecosphere itself. In the end, though, it is tough to say what the real object of enchantment is: the possibility of a biological interface with the plant mind of the planet, or the technological communications networks that already circulate our hopes and fears, our desires and fantasies, our Hollywood blockbusters and ayahuasca vacation packages. Indeed, if anything, *Avatar* suggests that eco-futuristic dreams are now indistinguishable from the visionary potential of media technology itself, a technology that must disguise its own poisoned environmental footprint through a continual invocation of holistic phantasms.

2010

TERENCE MCKENNA'S LAST TRIP

In May 1999, the psychedelic bard Terence McKenna returned to his jungle hideaway on Hawaii's Big Island after six weeks on the road. He was relieved to be home. Since claiming the mantle of tripster king from Timothy Leary, McKenna has earned his keep as a stand-up shaman on the lecture circuit, regaling groups of psychonauts, seekers, and boho intellectuals with tales of mushrooms, machine consciousness, and the approaching end of history. Weird stuff, and wonderfully told. But the teller was getting tired of the routine. A recluse at heart, McKenna wanted nothing more than to surf the web, read, polish up some manuscripts, and enjoy the mellow pace of Hawaii with his new girlfriend, Christy Silness, a kind young woman he had met the year before at an ethnobotanical conference in the Yucatán.

Soon after McKenna arrived home, he was hit with ferocious headaches. He'd long suffered from migraines, but nothing in his fifty-two years could match the ice picks now skewering his skull. On May 22, after dragging himself to the john to vomit, McKenna's mind exploded. Hallucinations cut in like shards of glass; taste and smell were bent out of shape; and he was swallowed up in a labyrinth that, as he later put it, "somehow partook of last week's dreams, next week's fears, and a small restaurant in Dublin." Then his blood pressure dropped and he collapsed, the victim of a brain seizure.

When McKenna came to, he was flat on his back, staring at the ceiling as his extremely agitated girlfriend called 911. Then he swooned again. In addition to being much younger than McKenna, Silness is also much shorter, but somehow she managed to load his lanky, 6'2" frame into their truck and drive down the mountain to meet an ambulance. To keep McKenna awake, she coaxed him into reciting a Robert Service poem his grandfather used to chant, "The Cremation of Sam McGee." But then a grand mal hit, and McKenna was out cold.

The ambulance guys knew McKenna's rep and were convinced he had OD'd. But a CAT scan in Kona revealed the presence of a walnut-sized tumor buried deep in McKenna's right frontal cortex. The growth was diagnosed as a glioblastoma multiforme (GBM), the most malignant of brain tumors. To McKenna's amazement, his doctor described the thing as a "fruiting body" that sent "mycelia" throughout the surrounding tissue—mycological lingo straight out of *The Magic Mushroom Grower's Guide* that McKenna had published in 1975 with his brother, Dennis, now an ethnobotanist. The rest was less amusing. Without treatment, McKenna would die within a month. With treatment, the prognosis was six months. "No one escapes," said the doctor.

McKenna was facing something that no shaman's rattle or peyote button was going to cure. With barely time to breathe, he had to choose between chemotherapy, radiation treatment, and the gamma knife—a machine that could blast the tumor with two hundred converging beams of cobalt radiation. At the same time, friends and comrades were stalking more ethereal treatments. On the Big Island, Hali Makua, a Grand Kahuna of Polynesia, hiked up the side of the Mauna Loa volcano to meditate on McKenna. He was illuminated with a handful of Hawaiian power words, words that he later phoned in to his ailing friend. From the wilds of Nevada, paranormal radio jock Art Bell went on the air and asked his thirteen million listeners to participate in "great experiment no. 8." At 2 pm Pacific time on Sunday, May 30, Bell's listeners sent McKenna a mass blast of good vibrations. "It's not something I really believe in," says McKenna. "But I am much more sympathetic to the idea of a huge morphogenetic field affecting your health than the idea that one inspired healer could do it."

Even after he went under the gamma knife, McKenna couldn't quite believe what was happening to him. "There are only about a thousand of these GBMs a year, so it's a rare disease. I never won anything before—why now?"

Like everybody else, McKenna suspected a lifetime of exotic drug use may have been to blame. "So what about it?" he asked his doctors. "You wanna hammer on me about that?" They assured him there was no causal link.

"So what about thirty-five years of daily dope smoking?" he asked. They pointed to studies suggesting that cannabis may actually shrink tumors.

"Listen," McKenna told them, "if cannabis shrinks tumors, we would not be having this conversation."

Word of McKenna's condition spread like taser fire through the list-servs that are the backbone of the psychedelic community. The suddenness of his illness freaked folks out. "It was almost like the night when

Howard Cosell came on *Monday Night Football* and said John Lennon had been shot," says Jordan Gruber, an attorney who works at NASA and the founder of Enlightenment.com, a web site devoted to spiritual psychology. "It was a similar sort of terrible shock to the nervous system." Within thirty-six hours of his seizure, fourteen hundred messages had poured into McKenna's e-mail box. A typical missive: "I love you for who you are and are becoming and all of what you have meant to so much of humanity." Over the next week, almost a thousand e-mails came in each day.

This flood of digital well-wishing is testament to McKenna's stature in the world of psychedelics, a largely underground realm that includes the ravers, old hippies, and New Agers one might expect, but also a surprising number of people who live basically straight lives, especially when compared with the users of the '60s. McKenna serves as this hidden world's most visible "altered statesman." He has written five books—two with his brother—and has developed a worldwide following. Brainy, eloquent, and hilarious, McKenna applies his Irish gift of the gab to making a simple case: going through life without trying psychedelics is like going through life without having sex. For McKenna, mushrooms and DMT do more than force up the resonant remains of last night's dream; they uncover the programming language of mind and cosmos.

"The psychedelic experience is not the equivalent of a dust bunny under your psychic bed," says McKenna. "It's a product of the fractal laws that govern the world at an informational level. There is no deeper truth."

McKenna is the most loved psychedelic barnstormer since Timothy Leary, the self-appointed guru of LSD who died in 1996 amid a flurry of digital hype about online euthanasia and his plans—which he scrapped—to undergo cryonic preservation. Like McKenna, Leary was an intellectual entertainer, a carny barker hawking tickets to the molecular mind show. McKenna calls it "the harlequin role," a role he plays almost willingly. At the same time, McKenna is a far mellower man than Leary. "I don't seek to live forever," he says, "and I don't want the removal of my head to become a net event."

Leary spent the late '60s attempting to gather a hippie army under the battle cry of "Turn on, tune in, drop out." Taking his advice, McKenna dropped out and headed to India, where he bought Mahayana art and smuggled hashish until a stateside bust forced him into hiding in the wilds of Indonesia. In 1971, he and his brother went to the Amazon to hunt for ayahuasca, a legendary shamanic brew. But when they arrived at the Colombian village of La Chorera that spring, what they found were fields blanketed with *Stropharia cubensis*, aka magic mushrooms.

In some ways, it was a turning point in American psychedelic culture. Back home, Leary's LSD shock troops had already disintegrated into harder drugs and bad vibes, and Leary himself was hiding out abroad after escaping from an American jail. Serious heads knew all about psilocybin mushroom from Gordon Wasson's famous June 10, 1957 *Life* magazine article, but no one in the US was eating much *S. cubensis* in the early '70s because no one had figured out how to cultivate it. After returning from South America, the McKenna brothers discovered a reliable method. While they were not the only heads to crack the shroom code in this era, they did publish their results. Magic mushrooms were now on the underground menu.

McKenna farmed shrooms into the 1980s. He could turn out seventy pounds of them every six weeks, like clockwork. The trade financed the middle-class existence of a relatively settled man. Then a good friend of his, an acid chemist, got busted. "They fucked him so terrifyingly that I saw I couldn't do this anymore. I had to work something else out." What McKenna worked out was "Terence McKenna," a charismatic talking head he marketed, slowly but successfully, to the cultural early adopters.

McKenna got his fifteen minutes of fame when four of his books came out in rapid succession. His 1991 collection of essays, *The Archaic Revival*, is particularly influential, especially among ravers and other alternative tribes attracted to the idea that new technologies and ancient pagan rites point toward the same ecstatic truths. *Food of the Gods*, published in 1992, aims directly at scholars. In it, McKenna lays out an unorthodox case that psychedelics helped kick-start human consciousness and culture, giving our mushroom-munching ancestors a leg up on rivals by enhancing their visual and linguistic capacities. Though anthropologists ignored his arguments, the time was right for McKenna's visions. He was tempted with movie deals, was featured in magazines, and toured like a madman. He hobnobbed with Silicon Valley hotshots like interface gurus Brenda Laurel and Jaron Lanier and performed at raves with techno groups like the Shamen. Timothy Leary called him "the Timothy Leary of the 1990s."

McKenna also was a popularizer of virtual reality and the Internet, arguing as early as 1990 that VR would be a boon to psychedelicists and businesspeople alike. But unlike Leary, who planned to use the net as a stage for his final media prank, McKenna realized that the Internet would be the place where psychedelic culture could flourish on its own. "Psychedelics were always about information," McKenna observes. "Their very existence was forbidden knowledge at one point. You had to be Aldous Huxley to even know about them." To his great satisfaction, McKenna has lived to see the psychedelic underground self-organize online on sites like Erowid and the Lycaeum. But to McKenna the net is more than an information source. He is also convinced that it is hosting an unprecedented dialogue between individual human beings and the totality of human knowledge.

"The Internet is an oracle for anyone in trouble," McKenna explains, using his illness as an example. "Within ten minutes I can be poring through reams of control studies, medical data, and personal reports. If anything, my cancer has made me even more enthusiastic about the idea that through information, people can take control of and guide their own lives."

Unfortunately, by last October, five months after the initial diagnosis and treatment, he needed a lot more than information. Despite the radiation therapy, the tumor was spreading. McKenna traveled to the medical center at the University of California, San Francisco, where a team of specialists surgically removed the bulk of the tumor. They then soaked the cavity with p53, a genetically altered adenovirus meant to scramble the hyperactive self-replication subroutines of the remaining tissue's DNA. Gene therapy is highly experimental; as Silness put it, McKenna became "a full-on guinea pig."

At first, the doctors at UCSF were extremely pleased with the results, and for four months the tumor cooled its heels while McKenna recuperated in Hawaii. But in February, an MRI revealed that it had returned with ferocity, spreading so thoroughly throughout McKenna's brain that it was deemed inoperable. He retreated to a friend's house in Marin County, and his family began to gather. By the time you read this, Terence McKenna will have died.

It is the end of 1999, and I am visiting McKenna at his jungle home during his recovery from brain surgery. He lives a mile or so up a rutted road that winds through a gorgeous subtropical rain forest an hour south of the Kona airport. His house—a modernist origami structure topped with a massive antenna dish and a small astronomy dome—rises from the green slopes of Mauna Loa like something out of the video game Myst. There's a small garden and a lotus pond, and the structure is surrounded by a riot of vegetation, thick with purple flowers and mysterious vines.

McKenna has owned land on this mountainside since the 1970s, but didn't start building the house until 1993. Every morning, I ascend a spiral staircase decorated with blue LEDs to get to the study. It's here that McKenna spends the majority of his time during my visit, either staring into his Mac or sitting cross-legged on the floor before a small Oriental carpet, surrounded by books, smoking paraphernalia, and twigs of sage he occasionally lights up and wafts through the air. With his widely set and heavy-lidded eyes, McKenna looks like a seasoned nomad merchant.

Silness has shorn McKenna's usually full head of hair down to gray stubble, and the upper right side of his forehead is gently swollen and graced with a Frankensteinian scar. Though he is desperately ill, his spirits are as alive as ever: gracious and funny, brilliant and biting. But he tires quickly, and seems intensely energized only when the prospect of chocolate cookies or ice cream arises. He is also very skinny, having lost a lot of muscle in his thighs, and he moves painfully slowly when he moves at all.

McKenna and Silness have hosted a regular stream of visitors and well-wishers over the last months, but the scene is definitely not Learyland. They are living life as close to normal as possible—which is how McKenna prefers it. "There are various options when you are faced with a terminal disease," he says in his unforgettable voice, a charming nasal singsong. "One is cure-chasing, where you head off to Shanghai or Brazil or the Dominican Republic to be with these great maestros who can save you. The other thing is to do what you always wanted to do. So that means head to Cape Canaveral to see a shuttle launch, on to sunrise over the pyramids, on to a month in the Grand Hôtel de Paris. I wasn't too keen on that, either. My tendency was just to twist another bomber and think about it all."

There's a lot to think about in McKenna's lair. An altar lies on top of a cabinet over which hangs a frightening old Tibetan tangka. With McKenna at my side, the altar's objects become icons in a computer game. Click and a story emerges. Click on the tangka and get a tale of art-dealing in Nepal. Click on the carved Mayan stones and hear about a smoking god who will arrive far in the future. Click on an earthen bowl and wind up in the stone age. "Back then," he says, tapping the vessel, "this was advanced technology."

Gamers know that the most interesting objects usually lie near the obvious ones, and indeed, the real prizes here lurk inside the narrow cabinet drawers. Butterflies. Click on these hummingbird-sized beauties and you'll be transported back thirty years to the remote islands of Indonesia, where McKenna dodged snakes and earthquakes in order to capture prize specimens for the butterfly otaku of Japan.

The most prominent features of the room are the fourteen large bookcases that line the walls, stuffed with more than three thousand volumes: alchemy, natural history, Beat poetry, science fiction, Mayan codexes, symbolist art, hashish memoirs, systems theory, Indian erotica, computer manuals. Deeply attuned to the future of consciousness, McKenna remains a devoted Gutenberg man. "The majority of my fans could not conceive of this room," he says. "They would have no idea that a printhead could push so hard against electronic culture."

McKenna derives great pleasure from pushing the envelope of the human mind, but he is equally turned on by technology. On the one hand, the house, which was only finished last year, is completely off the grid, irrigated with rainwater collected in a large cistern up the hill, and powered by solar panels and a gas generator. There are no phone lines. At the same time, Ethernet connections are built in everywhere, even out on the deck. The computers in his office—a 7100 Power Mac, a dual-processor NT, a G3 PowerBook, and Silness's PC laptop—jack into cyberspace at two Mbps through the fifteen-hundred-pound high-gain dish on his roof. Using spread-spectrum radio technology, McKenna's dish swaps packets with a similar rig on the roof of CTI, his ISP, thirty miles north. The twenty-thousand-dollar system carries voice traffic as well. His plan was to eventually stream lectures over the net, thus eliminating the need to travel in order to "appear" at conferences and symposia.

McKenna normally spends four or five hours a day online, devouring sites, weeding through lists, exploring virtual worlds, corresponding with strangers, tracking down stray facts. Sometimes he treats the net like a crystal ball, entering strange phrases into Google's search field just to see what comes up. "Without sounding too cliché, the Internet really is the birth of some kind of global mind," says McKenna. "That's what a god is. Somebody who knows more than you do about whatever you're dealing with."

As our society weaves itself ever more deeply into this colossal thinking machine, McKenna worries that we'll lose our grasp on the tiller. That's where psychedelics come in. "I don't think human beings can keep up with what they've set loose unless they augment themselves, chemically, mechanically, or otherwise," he says. "You can think of psychedelics as enzymes or catalysts for the production of mental structure—without them you can't understand what you are putting in place. Who would want to do machine architecture or write software without taking psychedelics at some point in the design process?"

It's a typical McKenna question: simultaneously outrageous and, in some twisty way, true. For obvious reasons, hard statistics on the extent of psychedelic use in the high-tech industry are tough to come by. But Rick Doblin, founder of the Multidisciplinary Association for Psychedelic Studies, will tell you that both MAPS and another psychedelic research outfit called the Heffter Research Institute have raised more than fifty percent of their funding from Silicon Valley heads. (See "Psychonaut" in this volume.)

"There's a sense," says Doblin, "that the creative chaos and visionary potential that people have gotten from some of their psychedelic experiences have played a role in their accomplishments in the computer industry." Steve Jobs is on record calling his first LSD experience "wonderful," while Mitch Kapor credits "recreational chemicals" with inspiring crucial programming insights. "Psychedelics have infiltrated the computer industry," says McKenna, "because psychedelic use is a response to the environment that's been found to actually work."

Psychedelics have certainly left their mark on computer graphics, virtual reality, and animation. From fractals to Kai's Power Tools to Hollywood f/x, digital imagery has often been inspired by the mutations in perception brought on by certain drugs. In the words of Mark Pesce, the co-creator of Virtual Reality Markup Language, "How often do you go to a web site and say, 'This is really trippy!'? Well, why? C'mon—it's because it was created by tripsters." McKenna learned about computer animation from his son, Finn, who studied at the San Francisco Academy of Art and now works in New Jersey. Together father and son would get high and go to museums to analyze the objects. "How would you CAD this? How would you get this Minoan vase, this Etruscan statue, up on the screen in 3-D? If you look at a seashell or a glass vase as a modeling problem, then everything is an animation."

Ultimately, McKenna wants something more than trippy images. He hopes that computer graphics will blossom into a universal lingo, a language of constantly morphing hieroglyphic information that he claims to have glimpsed on high doses of mushrooms. "There is something about the formal dynamics of information that we do not understand. Something about how we process language holds us back. That's why I encourage everybody to think about computer animation, and think about it in practical terms. Because out of that will come a visual language rich enough to support a new form of human communication."

In McKenna's mind we are not just conjuring a new virtual language. We are also, in good old shamanic style, conjuring the ineffable Other. McKenna argues that the images of aliens and flying saucers that spring up in numerous tripping reports are symbols of the transcendental technologies we are on the verge of creating. In other words, we are producing the alien ourselves, from the virtual world of networked information.

"Part of the myth of the alien," says McKenna, "is that you have to have a landing site. Well, I can imagine a landing site that's a web site. If you build a web site and then say to the world, 'Put your strangest stuff here, your best animation, your craziest graphics, your most impressive AI software,' very quickly something would arise that would be autonomous enough to probably stand your hair on end. You won't be able to tell whether you've got code, machine intelligence, or the real thing." McKenna thinks this is coming soon, within the next ten or twenty years.

McKenna ties all this into the Timewave, his kookiest notion. The Timewave is a strange fractal object McKenna pried out of the *I Ching*, the Chinese book of divination, back in the La Chorera days. He believes that it charts the degree of novelty active at any point in human history. The wave spikes in times of change, coinciding with the Black Death, the Enlightenment, and the birth of Mohammed. A computer program McKenna helped develop predicts the future as well, at least up until December 21, 2012, when novelty spikes to infinity and the Timewave stops cold. For McKenna, all of human history, with its flotsam and jetsam of books and temples and mechanized battlefields, is actually a backward ripple in time caused by this approaching apocalypse.

Coping with his own personal day of reckoning, McKenna spent much of 1999 sorting and answering fan e-mail. As he read on, he made an unexpected discovery. "It isn't really me they support," he says. "It's a statement they are making about something that has probably provided them more insight and more learning than anything else in their lives outside of sex and marriage and a few of the other major milestones. My real function for people was permission. Essentially what I existed for was to say, 'Go ahead, you'll live through it, get loaded, you don't have to be afraid.'"

To ensure that folks give psychedelics a proper shake, McKenna has always recommended what he famously calls "the heroic dose." Chew five grams of mushrooms, lie down in darkness and silence, and you'll realize "every man can be a Magellan in his own mind." There now exists a considerable community of people who have taken his advice. They are united in a belief that it's a trip worth taking, but endlessly divided on how, or whether, to tell the world about it.

Though most trippers are highly secretive about their activities, one part of the scene is starting to poke its nose above ground. The last decade has seen the first resurgence of official psychedelic research since the early '60s. Much of this work has been supported by MAPS, whose web site and journal is devoted to the dry, methodical language of protocols, statistics, and action studies. Though the National Institute on Drug Abuse continues to politicize the process with its war on drugs, the MAPS strategy has been surprisingly successful. "Now we can get FDA permission for various studies, and the regulatory system is pretty well open toward rigorously designed protocols," says Doblin. "The big limiting factor is the shortage of serious researchers and scientists willing to point their careers in this direction. There's still a lot of stigma attached to it."

Organizations like MAPS and the Heffter Institute emphasize the scientific and therapeutic side of the equation. "It's about as close as you can get to mainstream cultural values," says Doblin, who contrasts this approach with the hippies of the late '60s. "The idea then was that these substances were so liberating that we needed to create a countercultural movement, one inherently at odds with society. The fundamental distinction today is between those people who still have that view and those who recognize that we have to feed this stuff back into the major culture."

McKenna straddles this divide. He believes that psychedelics should be more fully integrated into society, through art, design, and pharmacology. But despite his love of science—he calls *Scientific American* the most psychedelic publication that crosses his desk—McKenna is ultimately a romantic, and romantics rarely shape mainstream values these days. Though he's no kook, talk of Timewaves and galactic mushroom teachers speaking a transcendental language may not be what the psychedelic movement needs as it gropes toward legitimacy. As Earth, who runs the Erowid web site, explains, "One of the primary criticisms of psychedelic users is that they're loopy as hell, and it can certainly be said that Terence McKenna's ideas are, at their best, controversial and, at their worst, confused and delusional."

Today, the psychedelic community has ripened to a point where it may no longer need a charismatic leader. In a sense, this was McKenna's goal. Because if Aldous Huxley was an aristocrat of psychedelics, and Leary was a populist demagogue, then McKenna is a crunchy libertarian. So it is perhaps fitting that, for the moment, McKenna is the last of his line, that no new harlequin hero waits in the wings. What does remain, however, is a network making sure that psychedelics remain an option, covert or otherwise.

"In the end, all McKenna is asking anyone to do is to become a shaman, to journey to the numinous, and draw their own conclusions," says Mark Pesce. Even if the invisible landscapes one discovers hold no more reality than dreams or virtual worlds, the trip itself forces a direct confrontation with just how weird life is. And how deeply, profoundly weird dying may prove to be as well.

Which means that McKenna is probably as prepared as anyone can be for the final journey into the dark. As he points out, "Taking shamanic drugs and spending your life studying esoteric philosophy is basically a meditation on death." McKenna calls death the black hole of biology. "Once you go over that event horizon, no messages can be passed back. It represents a limit case in the thermodynamics of information. You just can't hand messages back over that threshold. So get yourself pointed right, do not your mantras bungle, and that's about it. When you're actually dead, all bets are off. The best answer I've gotten yet is out of Don DeLillo's *Underworld,* where the nun discovers that when you die you become your web site."

Like many people staring unblinkingly into the black hole, McKenna has opened up a great deal in the months since his diagnosis. "Nothing lasts," he notes. "That's one thing I think you learn from life, psychedelics, or just paying attention. These Buddhists aren't kidding: you are here for a very brief moment, and you can sit on your thumbs and do whatever you want, but in fact the clock is ticking. What are you gonna do about it? Are you gonna blow it off, or be a hedonist? What are you gonna do with that? If most people took this situation seriously, a hell of a lot more would be done with more attention to quality and intent. Now I'm much more in tune with the Buddhist demand for compassion," he says. "The real dilemma is how to build a compassionate human civilization. If we betray our humanness in the pursuit of civilization, then the dialog has become mad."

In his heart, McKenna remains an optimist. "When I think about dying, the thing that surprises me is how much of the future I regard as history, but I don't want to miss it. I want to know how it all comes out. I would like to know how the universe came to be, if extraterrestrials exist, where biotech is going, where the Internet is going. Because this is it. We are on the brink of a posthuman existence. So what's it gonna look like? What's it gonna feel like?"

Facing his end, McKenna admits that he doesn't "have a lot riding on my vision of things." But his visions are precisely what make him such an inspiration to so many people. Every day we see another talking head clawing his way toward the role of visionary, trying to convince us that his speculations about the future are true. But real visionaries are more than just futurists. Their power lies less in prophecy than in giving us new perspectives on a constantly mutating world, perspectives that manage to be simultaneously timeless and new. Real visionaries are always dodgy characters, because they embrace strange, heretical, even dangerous ideas. Terence McKenna is a real visionary.

Note: Terence McKenna died in Marin County on April 3, 2000. His library and personal papers were destroyed in a fire on February 7, 2007. He is still missed.

2000

MAD SCIENCE

SAINT PHIL

When Philip K. Dick died after a stroke in 1982, he left behind almost forty science fiction novels, over a hundred short stories, a few remarkable essays, and the "Exegesis," a crazed document that attempted to interpret the divine intelligence that he claimed invaded his mind in 1974. Though Dick remains partially buried in the mildewed heap of yesterday's pop trash (best known as "the guy who wrote the book they based *Blade Runner* on"), his dedicated following has grown since his death. Some of his best books are out of print in the States, but a steady trickle of unpublished (and mostly non-sci-fi) work has been released in the last few years. Whether or not Dick hacked out the most brilliant American science fiction ever is debatable; that his work remains the most brilliantly fucked-up sci-fi is beyond doubt.

Though he uses generic devices like androids, spaceships, Martians, and moon colonies, Dick's worlds are usually bummers just around the corner, near-futures characterized by rampant overpopulation, surveillance, urban decay, repressive state apparatuses, ubiquitous ads, and invasive technology. As far back as the '50s, Dick saw the dark, paranoid side of McLuhan's global village. The animism that primitive humankind projected onto Nature was for him reborn in our technological environment, where ominous spiritual forces merged with the instruments of late capitalism. Dick's machines are black jokes rather than believable imaginings: the portable computerized psychiatrist, Dr.

Smile, in *The Three Stigmata of Palmer Eldritch*; the empathy machine in "The Little Black Box," which fuses the user's consciousness with a televised savior; *The Divine Invasion*'s holographic multicolored Bible.

Driven by what he called "divine discontent," Dick howled in his dystopic wilderness against the powers that be. His characters are ordinary schlemiels, bumbling Joes and Janes struggling with small moral dilemmas, poverty, politics, and psychic breakdowns in worlds where entropy reigns and communication breakdowns are inevitable. Unlike Pynchon—whose obsessions resemble his in many ways—Dick maintained little ironic distance from his characters, and his empathy for them and their hopeless struggles is palpable as well as odd. Not that Dick didn't undercut the pathos with comic gags. In *A Scanner Darkly*, Charles Freck tries to kill himself by consuming wine and a handful of reds: "However, he had been burned. The capsules were not barbiturates, as represented. They were some kind of kinky psychedelics . . . Well, he thought philosophically, this is the story of my life. Always ripped off . . . The next thing he knew, a creature from between dimensions was standing beside his bed looking down on him disapprovingly."

Dick's characters battle not only themselves, but also the second law of thermodynamics. Entropy is a major trope in sci-fi, but in Dick's hands it's a dark god. *Do Androids Dream of Electric Sheep?* features the semi-retarded Jack Isidore living

> alone in this deteriorating, blind building of a thousand uninhabited apartments, which like all its counterparts, fell, day by day, into greater entropic ruin. Eventually everything within the building would merge, would be faceless and identical . . . buried under the ubiquity of the dust. By then, naturally, he himself would be dead, another interesting event to anticipate as he stood here alone with the lungless, penetrating, masterful world-silence . . . Better, perhaps, to turn the TV back on.

This move towards the TV was characteristic, because Dick was obsessed with communications technology—radio, records, tapes, television, phones, computers—using it as a metaphor for the social web people build from their individual signals to keep entropy at bay. Technology only reinscribed for Dick the signals, noise, distortion, and overlapping frequencies that we are already simultaneously trapped in and estranged from.

He usually wrote in the subjective third person, jumping among the variable perspectives of the characters that made up his narratives. By switching viewpoints, Dick formalized and toyed with his contention that objective reality is both synthetic and fragile, a "hypothetical universalization of a multitude of subjective realities." Most of his tales contain false worlds, spurious environments simulated and controlled by nefarious powers using drugs, technology, and psychic power. In *The Three Stigmata of Palmer Eldritch*, the eponymous figure returns from space and markets Chew-Z, a drug which projects users into a world he controls. As Dick's creations discover off-kilter clues in their environment, their paranoia and sense of unreality grow, until their suspicions are not only fulfilled but often grossly exceeded. Dick was a narrative trickster, a master mindfucker. He pulled the whodunit inside out: Decoding small meaningful details doesn't put the picture together so much as rip it apart. By twisting the page-turning groove of pulp into a Möbius strip, Dick attempted to undermine the political, social, technological, and psychic structures of "reality." He wanted a pulp guerrilla ontology that deconstructed everyone's power trip—Nixon's, IBM's, God's, the author's.

Dick's fully fake world appeared in *Time out of Joint* (1959), which shivered with the Cold War. In it, Ragle Gumm spends his days drinking beer in '50s suburbia, supporting himself through his unusual skill at playing a newspaper puzzle called "Where Will the Little Green Man Be Next?" Strange slippages in normal reality occur—he finds a phone book with unfamiliar exchanges, picks up unlisted programs on his ham radio—and Gumm becomes increasingly paranoid, convinced his world is spurious. We eventually find out that it's 1996, the Earth is at war with lunar colonists, and the puzzle takes advantage of Gumm's uncanny ability to predict the next hostile bombing. It turns out that Gumm had become sympathetic with the colonists and refused to continue aiding Earth, so the military-industrial complex created the false environment and drugged him into useful forgetfulness.

Dick engaged the mutant logic of late capitalism and the technological simulacrum before Baudrillard knew a megabyte from a baguette, coming to the conclusion that only an antagonistic relationship with reality—even to the point of madness—is sane. In a world of crystal-clear transmission, Dick tuned to the static between channels, turned up the volume, and listened for hidden messages. His skepticism constitutes an increasingly fervent metaphysics. He was obsessed with the Gnostic concept of a demiurge, a false god who obscured the true world with illusory time and space. Part of the authorial fragmentation that pervades Dick's work arises because, though he clearly identified with his flailing characters and their metaphysical morality plays, he remained the trickster demiurge of his own narratives.

In *Valis*, Dick made the provocative statement that "the symbols of the divine show up in our world initially at the trash stratum." While the fragments of schizo vision scattered through Dick's work may not have been holy, he certainly got the trash part right. By almost every conventional standard of literary quality, Philip K. Dick was a hack. Most of his work is clunky, uneven, and occasionally awful. Having first published sci-fi in 1951, he never lost touch with the gaudy mechanics of earlier pulpsters like A.E. van Vogt. Though one develops an affection for his characters, their dialogue is sometimes forced and obvious. Both the science and the plots strain credulity. The hasty feel of many of his books is no accident. Driven by poverty, obsession, and frequently by amphetamines, he wrote like the madman he probably was. In 1965, he published four novels; two a year, plus numerous short stories, was his standard rate.

Dick's schizophrenic quality turns him into many authors: a poor man's Pynchon, an oracular postmodern, a rich product of the changing counterculture, a lunatic. As Thomas Disch said, he was a "science fiction writer's science fiction writer," respected in the sci-fi community even though his U.S. sales were mostly mediocre (he was much more popular in Britain and France). He's a particular favorite among scuzzy underground rock bands like Sonic Youth and the Reverb Motherfuckers, as well as scuzzy underground rock critics like Byron Coley. Diehards chronicle and compare his every word and deed, blurring the distinction between literary love and cult. And some academics of the leftist post-structuralist bent, most notably Fredric Jameson, love his political metafictions, his gaudy feel for the process of reification, his hack Kafka humor. On the other hand, Harold Bloom—an eternal advocate of imagination over reality—finds Dick vastly overrated; but that may be because, as anyone who's tried to make their way through Bloom's *Flight to Lucifer* knows, Dick can write Gnostic science fiction and Bloom can't.

Part of the appeal of Dick's oeuvre is that, despite its futuristic setting and outlandish events, it functions as autobiography. Most of the recent reissues of his novels feature his bearded visage on the cover, in part because his fans recognize that the real subject of his texts was his own frail, intense, and fragmented self. Because he didn't distance himself from his novels, they read as both Freudian confessions and Jungian dream journals. Dick himself had numerous wives and young girlfriends, and the relationships he described are invariably screwed up, sad affairs of misunderstandings, adulteries, and recriminations. But Dick's psychological obsessions go beyond the erotic and personal into the archetypal. Patterns and motifs reappear throughout his novels with the archaic and gaudy power of symbols: broken pots, the Black Iron Prison, policemen, toys, jewelry, books that are read randomly (based on the *I Ching*), miniature figures, simulacra. These two confessional aspects of Dick are well represented in *The Dark Haired Girl*, a collection of letters and dreams about the teenage girls he was obsessed with. One letter will sound depressingly naïve and pathetically sentimental; the next will describe some fascinating overloaded dream, followed by an equally strange interpretation of the symbolism involved.

Dick's most overblown reading of an event occurred in 1974, when the sight of a delivery woman's Christian fish necklace triggered his psychic contact with the "divine intelligence" he sometimes called VALIS, or Vast Active Living Intelligence System. Among other things, he communicated with a persecuted Christian living in ancient Rome, who warned him through a Beatles song that his son Christopher would die unless he was taken to a hospital. Dick also became convinced that the universe was a hologram and that VALIS was a camouflaged parasite that entered human beings through subliminal messages. The information lurked everywhere, especially in trashy artifacts of pop culture, so that in the end Dick must have believed himself to be less a writer than a pulp contagion, a pirate transmitter in a world jammed with increasingly vivid and increasingly delirious signals.

1989

DUB, SCRATCH, AND THE BLACK STAR

Lee Perry

Having abandoned the Jamaican tropics for the snowy peaks of Switzerland, the legendary reggae producer Lee Perry—aka Scratch, the Upsetter, the Super-Ape, Pipecock Jackson, Inspector Gadget, the Firmament Computer, and a cornucopia of other monikers and aliases—now makes his home in one of the quietest corners of Europe. It's an odd but somehow fitting environment for Perry—not because precision clocks and banks have much to do with the intense, spooky, and profoundly playful records he's known for, but because Lee Perry had always been something of a stranger in a strange land.

Though still capable of turning out brilliant tunes like "I Am a Madman" and "Secret Laboratory (Scientific Dancehall)," Perry's current output pales next to the pivotal music he made in the 1960s and '70s, especially the Rastafarian psychedelia he cooked up at the Black Ark, his recording studio in the mid-1970s. During that incredibly prolific period (he produced over a thousand sides in ten years), Perry fused his eccentric spiritual vision with powerful protest music, made some of the most surreal experiments with dub reggae, and sculpted the first (and arguably greatest) records by Bob Marley and the Wailers. Utilizing low-tech studio equipment with a brilliance and panache that continues to astound record producers and music fans today, Perry earned a place alongside Phil Spector and Brian Wilson as a visionary studio wizard who transformed pop music production into an art form all its own.

These days, it's Perry himself who is the work of art. He appears in public festooned with pendants, parts of machines, bits of tape, patches, buttons, and reflective mirrors. Everywhere he goes, it seems, he leaves a collage of scribbled notes, cryptic graffiti, scrap-metal idols, paintings of lions, and food. Responding to interviewers with a flurry of rhymes, riffs, and puns, Perry turns innocent questions into a cosmological launching pad, revealing what improv musician John Corbett describes as "a world of hidden connections and secret pacts," including multinational conspiracy theories, Old Testament prophecies, scatological rants, Rastafarian poetry, and incantations of the Jamaican folk witchcraft known as *obeah*. [1]

All this takes Perry to the edge of madness—at once his apparent mental instability and his intensely performative, almost shamanic, relationship with the chaos of creation. As Corbett points out, New World black culture has long linked the rhetoric of madness with excellence and innovation—musicians especially are praised for being *out of control, crazy, wild*. While Perry's hermetic language games and comic-book metaphysics certainly owe something to his daily intake of what one observer described as an "inordinate amount of high quality herb," his mischievous irony also shows all the signs of the trickster incarnate. Even his madness may be a trick. Some colleagues report that when it's time to talk business, Perry drops the loopy patois and cuts to the chase; the head of Heartbeat Records says that he "plays fool to catch wise."

Perry is also a kind of Caribbean techgnostic, deploying his almost supernatural imagination within the mechanical context of the modern recording studio. With its soundboards, mics, effects processors, and multiple-track tape manipulations, the studio is effectively a musical machine. However passionate and spontaneous pop songs may sound on the radio, the music itself is as much a product of engineering as of performance. Despite their crude equipment, reggae producers like Perry, King Tubby, and Bunny Lee became artists in their own right—especially when it came to dub, the instrumental offshoot of reggae, concocted entirely in the studio.

Modern Jamaican music begins with signals and machines. In the mid-1950s, when a diminutive Lee Perry first arrived in Kingston from the sticks, the popularity of mento—an upbeat and topical Afro-Caribbean music similar to Trinidadian calypso—was giving way to a rage for American rhythm & blues. At that time, powerful and increasingly independent U.S. radio stations were turning away from the old national networks towards an inexpensive and popular alternative: DJs playing records for local markets. For the first time, signals were beamed directly at African-American communities. When the weather was right, Jamaican kids churning through their radio dials would tune into Southern radio stations, and they went especially wild for the gritty, saucy sounds of New Orleans R&B.

From this enthusiasm sprang Jamaica's sound systems—mobile discos that would invade halls and auditoriums with high-wattage amplifiers, turntables, DJs, imported American vinyl, and massive speaker stacks. Besides transforming the invisible figure of the radio DJ into a performer, sound systems also gave their American grooves an unmistakable Jamaican twist by pumping up the bass. Amplifying their woofers to the max, sound systems transformed R&B's low end into a veritable force of nature—the kind of bass that does not just propel or anchor dancers but saturates their bones with near cosmic vibrations.

In the late 1950s, the sound systems were ruled by a host of colorful characters like Duke Reid, who lorded over his Treasure Isle dances with a cartridge belt, an enormous gilt crown, and a shotgun that he would occasionally brandish when the competition between sound systems boiled to a head. These fierce rivalries had an obviously economic edge, but their roots lay in the competitive performance traditions of many West African cultures. The fight over customers waged by sound system producers was also a style war, their fabricated alter egos, costumes, and elaborate verbal boasts taking on an almost ritualistic—yet constantly reinvented—dimension. Such style wars show up in various guises across the African diaspora, from the taunts and disses of rappers to the yearly carnival competitions of Trinidad and Brazil, when various roving bands try to top each other and woo the crowd with music, dance, and costume. As Lee Perry said, "Competition must be in the music to make it go."[2]

Jamaica's sound systems were unique in that this premodern, almost tribal competition was played out across the modern landscape of mechanically reproduced recordings. Rivalries were not so much a battle of the bands as a kind of technological and information warfare: who had the heaviest bass, who had the hottest records. In the 1950s, many DJs considered their imported sides exclusive, buying up all available copies of a new record or flying to the States to buy fresh discs. Spies would show up at rival sound system parties, peering at the record labels over the DJ's shoulder; in response, DJs would scratch off labels or stick on false ones.

Here was an environment where a character like Lee Perry could thrive. Rejected by Duke Reid, who was spooked by something in his eyes, Perry went to work for Clement "Sir Coxone" Dodd's rival Downbeat system, where he served as a talent scout, runner, gofer and occasional monkey-wrencher. Perry told an interviewer how he once put out the rumor that a certain fellow was selling really "dread sides." Duke Reid went and bought them all without listening to them first. "And they all old stuff, duds!" For such antics, Duke's men once stormed a Downbeat party and started punching people out, knocking Scratch unconscious.

With the decline of R&B in the U.S. market and Jamaica's independence from Britain in 1962, homegrown mutations begin to dominate sound systems. The most prominent was ska, a hopped-up, horn-driven and very danceable music whose intense offbeat punches one apocryphal story attributes to the interference patterns that sliced up radio signals from the States. Perry started churning out ska at Coxone's Studio One,

cutting edgy songs like "By Saint Peter" and "Chicken Scratch"—the latter earning Scratch his most lasting nickname.

Perry always had something of a persecution complex, and frequently turned on former friends and business partners. In part this reflects the cut-throat environment of the Jamaican record industry, where what British sociologist Dick Hebdige describes as "tough and wily" producers often acted like pirates. But with Perry—who once knowingly sold thousands of copies of Bob Marley and the Wailers' *Soul Revolution II* with the wrong record inside—one can also see the mischievous and occasionally malicious hand of the trickster. Perry certainly incorporated personal attacks into his mad persona: a number of Perry songs badmouth former associates or mumble threats concerning obeah men, while the 1985 cut "Judgment inna Babylon" accused the head of Island records of literally being a vampire. After splitting acrimoniously from two top studios, Perry started up his own Upsetter Studios in 1968, and soon released a tune attacking his former boss Joe Gibbs. Anticipating today's sampling craze, "People Funny Boy" included a crying baby in the mix in order to show how upset Perry was. But "People Funny Boy" also slowed down and reshuffled the usual rock steady rhythm, a bass-heavy groove that by the late 1960s had replaced the more simplistic beats of ska. In doing so, Perry helped engineer the beat that would come to dominate Jamaican music in the 1970s: reggae.

Though reggae recalls the relaxed rhythms of the old secular mento music, it has a meditative sustenance that some compare to religious church music or the Nyabhingi drumming of Rastafarian gatherings. Perry claims he just wanted to top his rivals with a new sound that had a "rebel bass" and a "waxy beat—like you stepping in glue." But the inspiration he cites was a Pocomania revivalist church he passed one night after drinking some beer:

> [I] hear the people inside a wail. And me catch the vibration and say, "Boy! Let's make a sound fe catch the vibration of the people!" Them was in the spirit and them tune me spiritually. That's where the thing comes from, 'cos them Poco people getting sweet! [3]

Pocomania was one of a number of independent revivalist churches that sprang up during Jamaica's Great Awakening in the 1860s—churches that exuberantly fused African and Protestant performance styles, images, and traditions. Pocomania leaned to the African side of things, its Pentecostal-style services owing an obvious debt to African possession ceremonies. Worshippers would dance counterclockwise to powerful drums while breathing deeply; this "trumping" would sometimes brings on possession—the little madness that lent the church its name.

So at the root of the reggae we have a little Lee Perry madness, a tale of catching vibrations and tuning into spiritual trance. But Perry played a far more direct role in developing the religious dimension of reggae when he began writing and recording songs with Bob Marley and the Wailers. The Wailers were a talented Studio One group known for sweet vocals, American soul covers, and a rebel stance. As residents of Trenchtown, Kingston's most notorious slum, the Wailers were associated with Jamaica's rude boys—tough, poor, and restless urban kids who flouted authority (and sometimes the law). By the late 1960s, Marley and the Wailers were also turning toward Rastafari, a rebellious counterculture that wove together Black Pride, an "Ethiopian" reworking of Biblical tenets, and a prophetic opposition to Babylon—the Rastafarian archetype of the modern nation-state, with its police, economic injustice, and corrosive lifestyles. Perry collaborated with the future superstar on some of his earliest and most powerful songs, tunes that mixed sharp social commentary ("a hungry mob is an angry mob") with an ardent yearning for Jah.

Since the trappings of Rastafari have been packaged by the international reggae market and embraced—often superficially—by legions of white college kids, punks, and hippies, we should scratch a bit beneath the surface of this vital New World religion. Like America's Black Muslims, the roots of Rastafari lie with the ethnoreligious world view sculpted by the Jamaican reformer Marcus Garvey. Founding the Universal Negro Improvement Association in 1914, Garvey attempted to uplift and unite New World Africans by emphasizing the superiority of the black man and the glories of African civilization. Anticipating the Afrocentricity of today, Garvey preached the love of a black deity, a God of Ethiopia. He also called for repatriation to the motherland, even founding a shipping and transportation company called the Black Star Line with the intention of transplanting New World blacks to Liberia.

But Garvey never visited Africa, and his vision of Ethiopia had more to do with the visceral power of the religious imagination than with the concrete geopolitical realities of an African continent struggling with the ravages of European colonization. By Garvey's time, Black Christian churches had already embraced the Biblical Ethiopia as a potent allegorical image of spiritual fulfillment, the millennial Zion that offered both a redemptive future and a glorious origin. Though Garvey's call for repatriation offered black folks an apparently concrete solution to the nightmare of abduction and slavery, the Africa he offered was a landscape of religious desire—a virtual world.

When Garvey quit Jamaica for the United States, he reportedly left his followers with this potent prophecy: "Look to Africa for the crowning of a Black King; he shall be the Redeemer." In 1930, when Haile Selassie—aka Ras Tafari—was installed as King of Ethiopia, Garvey's Jamaican followers believed they had found their living god, and Rastafari was born. Ethiopia has been Judeo-Christian longer than most nations on the earth, and Selassie's bloodline was supposed to stretch back to King Solomon, his official titles—like King of Kings and Lion of the Tribe of Judah—drawn directly from Biblical prophecy. Reading their own political and cultural desires into these Rorschach blots of messianic allegory, Rastafarians transformed the distant king into the Book of Daniel's bearded Ancient of Days, "the hair of whose head was like wool, whose feet were like unto burning brass."

As with Elijah Mohammed's Black Muslims, the early Rastafarians also racialized their theology. As the religious scholar Leonard Barrett explains, "the Whites' god is actually the devil, the instigator of all evils that have come upon the world, the god of hate, blood, oppression, and war; the Black god is the god of 'Peace and Love.'"[4] Though contemporary Rastafarians speak of One God more than a black god, it's important to note the loosely gnostic elements here. Along with the Manichaean tension between the two gods, we have the vision of a dark tyrant god who rules over souls in exile. According to Barrett, the early Rastafarians believed that slavery was initially a punishment for their sins, but that "they have long since been pardoned and should have returned to Ethiopia long ago."[5] Only the evil trickery of the slavemaster prevents them from returning to the heavenly home where their living King awaits.

Both the separatist practices and the emotional core of Rastafarian life can be traced to this deeply felt sense that the Rastaman is in Babylon, but not of it. As Silja Joanna Aller Talvi writes, "From the Rasta's perspective, the whole world is full of Babylon, and Babylon systems are constantly seeking to oppress (or 'downpress') and exploit the African."[6] Rejecting the authorities of this world, Rastafarians attempt to create a separate holy culture, in part by embracing the organic world of nature as a kind of anti-modern alternative to Babylon. Most Rastafarians are vegetarian, eat only *ital* (fresh and healthy) food, and reject commercial products and medicines; many also grow their hair in dreadlocks—the natural shape of long kinky hair that's washed but neither combed, cut, nor treated. Though Rastafari was spawned in the slums, many locksmen abandoned the urban hustle for lives as fisherman or simple farmers; those who remained were shunned by most respectable Jamaicans as Blackhearts or boogiemen.

Though the movement had a handful of charismatic leaders early on, and today includes organized sects like the Twelve Tribes of Israel and even members of the Ethiopian Orthodox Church, most Rastafarians abhor institutions, grounding their faith in their own direct participation in the divinity and holiness of Jah. As Ras Sam Brown said, "The Rastafarian movement is not a movement with a central focus."[7] Most Rastafarians also believe that the Bible is an intentionally mistranslated document whose scrambled signals must be read selectively and allegorically in the light of personal revelation.

One of the brightest guiding lights of Rastafari is the flame of the chalice, a great pipe stuffed with sticky marijuana buds that crackle during sacred inhalation. Addressing the sacramental use of marijuana among Rastafarians, Barrett argues that "the real center of the movement's religiosity is the revelatory dimensions brought about by the impact of the 'holy herb.'" Long a Jamaican folk medicine, marijuana was probably introduced to the island by indentured East Indian Hindus, who gave the plant its popular name *ganja* and may have inspired its religious use (many of India's wandering mendicant sadhus also wear dreadlocks, eat vegetarian food and smoke hashish in a spiritual context). For all their glassy, bloodshot stares, it's wrong to think of Rastafarians as stoners; hardcore adherents consume ganja as a sacrament and rarely use other drugs or alcohol. One Rasta explained the role of ganja in strongly gnostic terms, a vision of personal revelation shot through with Rastafari's powerful social consciousness:

> Man basically is God but this insight can come to man only with the use of the herb. When you use the herb, you experience yourself as God. With the use of the herb you can exist in this dismal state of reality that now exists in Jamaica . . . When you are a God you deal or relate to people like a God. In this way you let your light shine, and when each of us lets his light shine we are creating a God-like culture . . . [8]

Barrett explains that to the Rastafarian, "the average Jamaican is so brainwashed by colonialism that his entire system is programmed in the wrong way . . . To rid his mind of these psychic forces his head must be 'loosened up,' something done only through the use of the herb."[9] As one Montego Bay dread described the plant ally, "It gives I a good meditation; it is a door inside . . ."[10]

Music can also serve as a door inside. The chants and "churchical" beats of traditional Nyabhingi drumming played a vital role in Rastafarian Grounations, communal celebrations notable for their ital feasts, ganja smoking, and mystical theologizing. Though not directly influencing the reggae beat, Nyabhingi's meditative rhythms did infuse reggae with the sense that music can help loosen up the shackles of everyday consciousness, sparking the inner light of righteous contemplation.

Bob Marley was not the first musician to bring Rastafari into

Jamaican dance music, but with earthy hymns like "400 Years," "African Herbsman," and "Duppy Conqueror," he and Perry injected folkloric nectar into their spare and sinewy arrangements with divine panache. Even more than American soul, reggae became a commercial product that derived much of its power and appeal from a deeply religious set of images and desires. By no means was all reggae Rastafarian, but with message producers like Perry leading the way, Jamaica produced the juiciest spiritual protest music of the 1970s. By the time of his death at the end of the decade, Bob Marley would rear his lion-like mane over a global stage as the first Third World pop star, his plaintive redemption songs spreading the message of Rastafari across a shrinking planet desperate for spiritual heroes.

Though Marley's records were cleverly packaged by Island's Chris Blackwell for a white rock audience, much of their appeal derives from the unshakable authenticity of the man, the righteous integrity he shared with many of reggae's stars. In the '70s, the cries and beats of Jamaica's new roots music seemed to spring, not only from the hearts of suffering black folks, but from the island soil itself. You could hear these roots in the music's moist guitars and stoned pace, its vibrating air of nature mysticism, and its crunchy, spongy beats (Marley called it "earth-feeling music"). And you could feel the roots as well in the virtual Africa that hovered on the messianic horizon of the music, an ancient motherland and future kingdom built from the visionary longings of souls exiled in the brave New World of Babylon.

But dub music, reggae's great technological mutant, is a pure artifact of the machine, and has little to do with earth, flesh, or authenticity. To create dub, producers and engineers manipulate pre-existing tracks of music recorded on magnetic tape. Dubmasters saturate individual instruments with reverb, phase, and delay; abruptly drop voices, drums, and guitars in and out of the mix; strip the music down to the bare bones of rhythm and then build it up again through layers of inhuman echoes, electronic ectoplasm, cosmic rays. Good dub sounds like the recording studio itself has begun to hallucinate.

Dub arose from doubling—the common Jamaican practice of reconfiguring or "versioning" a prerecorded track into any number of new songs. Dub calls the apparent authenticity of roots reggae into question because dub destroys the holistic integrity of singer and song. It proclaims a primary postmodern law: there is no original, no first ground, no homeland. By mutating repetitions of previously used material, dub adds something new and distinctly uncanny, vaporizing its loops into doppelgänger. Despite the crisp attack of the drums and the heaviness of the bass, dub swoops through empty space, spectral and disembodied. Like ganja, dub opens the inner door. John Corbett even links the etymology of the word dub with *duppie* (Jamaican patois for ghost). Burning Spear entitled the dub version of his great *Marcus Garvey* album *Garvey's Ghost,* and Joe Gibbs responded to Lee Perry's production of Bob Marley's "Duppie Conqueror" with the cut "Ghost Capturer." Perry once described dub as "the ghost in me coming out."

Though he became one of its most surreal experimenters, Lee Perry did not invent dub reggae. That honor goes to Osbourne Ruddock, aka King Tubby, an electrical engineer who fixed radios and other appliances in Kingston in the 1950s and who built his own sound system amplifiers to get the big bass sound. A musical genius, Tubby was also a gearhead, a tinkerer, an experimentalist geek. After discovering that he could remix the backing track of a popular tune into a new piece of music, Tubby played these "dub plate specials" to enthusiastic crowds at his Home Town Hi-Fi dances, where Tubby would stand behind his customized mixing console, tweaking the beats on the fly while the DJ U Roy toasted over the rhythms.

Jamaican trends spread like wildfire, but Tubby stayed ahead of the dub game by working with top producers like Bunny Lee and Lee Perry while endlessly tinkering with what ska musician Prince Buster called the "implements of sound." Tubby constantly toyed with his four-track console, jury-rigging echo delay units and created sliding faders that allowed him to bring tracks smoothly in and out of the mix. He also just played tricks with the machine, generating his famous thunderclap sound by physically hitting the spring reverb unit, or using frequency test tones to send an ominous sonar through the depths of dub's watery domain.

Though Tubby gave his records names like *Dub from the Roots* and *The Roots of Dub,* he had genetically engineered those roots from wires.

However, dub did restore the roots of reggae's own "dread riddims" by conjuring the ghost of West African polyrhythms via the unlikely mediation of the machine. Though modern Jamaican dance music adheres to the same 4/4 beat that drives most popular music, reggae was already unusual in accenting the second and fourth beats of the measure and in dropping the initial beat, all of which produced the music's unmistakable pulse. By anchoring the beat with the bass guitar rather than the drum kit, reggae also freed up the drums to explore subtler and more complex percussive play. As Dick Hebdige points out, by the end of the '70s, drummers like Sly Dunbar were playing their kits like jazz musicians, improvising on cymbals, snares, and tom toms to "produce a multi-layered effect, rather like West African religious drumming."[11]

Dub launched these already tangled riddims into orbit, using technological effects to thicken the beats and to stretch and fold the passage of time. Besides stripping the music down to pure drums and bass and adding raw percussion, dubmasters introduced counter-rhythms by multiplying the beats through echo and reverb while splicing in what the producer Bunny Lee called "a whole heap a noise." And by abruptly dropping guitars, snares, hi-hats and bass in and out of the mix, they created a virtual analog of the tripping, constantly shifting effects of West African polymetric drumming. Though the hallucinogenic effects of dub are usually attributed to its spacy effects and the role of ganja in both its production and consumption, the almost psychic pleasures of the music also arise from its silly putty beats and their ability to yank the rug out from under your deeply ingrained sense of a central organizing rhythm.

By giving flight to the producer's technical imagination, dub sculpted a sort of science-fiction aesthetic alongside reggae's crunchy Afrocentric mythos. As Luke Ehrlich wrote, "If reggae is Africa in the New World, then dub music must be Africa on the moon."[12] Just look at the cover art: Mad Professor's *Science & the Witchdoctor* sets circuit boards and robot figures next to mushrooms and fetish dolls, while *Scientist Encounters Pac-Man at Channel One* shows Scientist manhandling the mixing console as if it were some madcap machine out of "Marvel Comics". It's important to note that in Jamaican patois, "science" refers to obeah, the African grab-bag of herbal, ritual, and occult lore popular on the island. And as author Robert Pelton points out, the figure of the scientist is not so distant from the spirit of the trickster that runs throughout this tale: "Both seek to befriend the strange, not so much striving to 'reduce' anomaly as to use it as a passage into larger order. ... like the scientist the trickster always yokes just *this* world to a suddenly larger world."[13]

And Lee Perry continued to serve as reggae's trickster king. Not only did he make some remarkably spare and intense forays into dub, but he applied dub's spectral aesthetics to the rest of his increasingly surreal, popular, and unorthodox productions. In 1974, the producer built the Black Ark, the studio that was destined to become the launching pad of reggae's most surreal and moving tunes. A year later, he acquired a demo version of a unique phaser from the States; using it alongside with a Roland Space Echo—an analog unit that uses magnetic tape loops to produce continuous delay—Perry whipped up multi-layered cakes of warbling noise, ghostly polyrhythmic percussion, and sounds lifted from other records. He took advantage of anomalies, especially those generated from his limited four-track mixer. As the producer Brian Foxworthy explains, Perry would fill up the four available tracks and then mix them onto a single track on another machine, freeing up three tracks to add more effects and percussion. Like photocopying a photocopy, each go-around degraded the signal, yet the literal decay of the sound source added a moist, organic depth to the music. It's a classic example of the trickster's mischievous relationship to disruption and chaos. As Foxworthy told *Grand Royal* magazine, "Tape saturation, distortion and feedback were all used to become part of the music, not just added to it."[14]

The Black Ark was more than Jamaica's most innovative studio; it was the visible vehicle of Perry's passionate otherworldly imagination. Its walls were covered with portraits of Selassie, magazine collages, lions, and Stars of David. Visitors would sometimes find Scratch planting records and tapes in the garden. As Bob Mack writes, "By the mid-70s, Perry's Black Ark had become the cultural/spiritual center of hip Kingston and birthplace of reggae's most conscious black pride anthems, all of which were either written or coaxed out of the artist by Perry (who at that point was beginning to infuse all his productions with the complex set of Christian, African, Arthurian, and Jamaican folk references that comprise his current cosmology.)"[15] Soon after Haile Selassie died in 1975, Perry and Marley helped reaffirm the faith for millions by cutting the ardent "Jah Lives." Even the name of Perry's studio was archetypal, resonating with any number of prophetic crafts: the Ark of the Covenant, Noah's craft, Garvey's Black Star Line—all messianic transvaluations of those vessels that shipped abducted and enslaved Africans to the New World. But the Black Star that Perry followed lay in the depths of space. In an interview with David Toop, Scratch discussed the Black Ark in such extraterrestrial terms:

> It was like a space craft. You could hear space in the tracks. Something there was like a holy vibration and a godly sensation. Modern studios, they have a different set up. They set up a business and a money-making concern. I set up like an ark . . . You have to be the Ark to save the animals and nature and music.[16]

Perry's unique fusion of premodern myth and postmodern machines not only shapes his lyrics—in one of his weirdest songs, Perry warns scavengers, vampires, and "sons of Lucifer" that "Jah Jah set a super trap / to capture you bionic rats"—but also his technological practice. Exploiting equipment that was archaic even for its day, Perry became a dub alchemist, weaving magnetic tape, wires, and circuit boards into the playful web of his magical thinking. Indeed, Perry spoke about his relationship to technology in explicitly animistic terms:

> The studio must be like a living thing. The machine must be live and intelligent. Then I put my mind into the machine by sending it through the controls and the knobs or into the jack panel. The jack panel is the brain itself, so you've got to patch up the brain

> and make the brain a living man, but the brain can take what you're sending into it and live.[17]

Improvising his cuts on the fly, Perry would whirl like a dervish behind his SoundCraft mixing board, blow ganja smoke directly onto the recording reels, even drink the alcohol used to clean the tape heads when he ran out of Dragon Stout. This erratic behavior came to a head in the late 1970s, when Perry started glimpsing UFOs, kicked anyone with dreadlocks out of the Black Ark, and covered its walls with deranged scatological prophecies. In 1979, during what could generously be called a bout of severely eccentric behavior, Perry trashed and burned his studio, and according to some reports wound up briefly in a mental institution.

The question of Perry's sanity opens up the tangled relationship between tricks, madness, art, and the prophetic imagination, but what is most important about Perry and his astounding musical legacy is how they highlight an often ignored strain of New World African culture: a techno-visionary tradition that looks as much toward science fiction futurism as toward sacred African roots. One finds this fusion in the experimental cosmological jazz of Sun Ra, who also pioneered the use of synthesizers and African percussion; in Jimi Hendrix's "electric church music," which psychedelicized the guitar with feedback and studio effects; in the juicy cosmic technofunk of Parliament-Funkadelic mastermind George Clinton, which, as author Cornel West writes, "both Africanizes and technologizes Afro-American popular music."[18] Hip hop music also began with a totally unexpected redeployment of turntable and mixing technology (introduced to the South Bronx by the Jamaican DJ Kool Herc), creating what Tricia Rose describes in her book *Black Noise* as "an experimental and collective space where contemporary issues and ancestral forces are worked through simultaneously."[19] Though predominantly secular, hip hop nonetheless hosts an intense subgenre of rappers who belong to the Five Percent Nation, a street-wise offshoot of the Nation of Islam. In contrast with the worldly concerns of gangsta rappers, acts like Brand Nubian, the Poor Righteous Teachers, Paris, and Lakim Shabazz fuse hard-hitting political prophecies, righteous moralizing, and bizarre numerology into a forceful amalgam of Black Pride and imaginative Afrocentric science.

This loosely gnostic strain of Afrodiasporic science-fiction emerges from the improvised confrontation between modern technology and the prophetic imagination, a confrontation rooted in the alienated conditions of black life in the New World. According to journalist Greg Tate, who sees science fiction as continuing a vein of philosophical inquiry and technological speculation that begins with Egyptian theories of the afterlife, "black people live the estrangement that science fiction writers imagine."[20] As Perry's own scathing protest music proves, the prophetic art that arises from this condition of perpetual exile does not simply escape from the pragmatic demands of politics. But neither does it deny the ark of the imagination that lies on the other side of the inner door—a trickster craft that navigates the shadowed valleys of this world, guided by a black star whose very invisibility renders its possibilities infinite.

1997

Notes

[1] John Corbett, *Extended Play: Sounding Off from John Cage to Dr. Funkenstein* (Duke, Durham, 1994), 128.

[2] *Grand Royal*, issue 2, 1995, 69.

[3] Ibid, 62.

[4] Leonard Barrett, *The Rastafarians: Sources of Cultural Dissonance* (Beacon, Boston, 1977), 108.

[5] Ibid, 111.

[6] Unpublished thesis.

[7] Barrett, 173.

[8] Ibid, 217.

[9] Ibid, 216.

[10] Ibid, 130.

[11] Dick Hebdige, *Cut 'n' Mix* (Comedia, London, 1987), 82.

[12] Luke Ehrlich, "X-Ray Music: The Volatile History of Dub," in *Reggae International*, ed. Stephen Davis and Peter Simon (New York: R&B, 1982), 106.

[13] Robert D. Pelton, *The Trickster in West Africa: A Study of Mythic Irony and Sacred Delight* (University of California Press, 1989), 267-8.

[14] *Grand Royal*, 64.

[15] Ibid, 62.

[16] David Toop, *Ocean of Sound: Aether Talk, Ambient Sound and Imaginary Worlds* (Serpent's Tail, London, 2001), 114

[17] Ibid, 113.

[18] Cornel West, "Out of Motown," *Semiotext(e), Oasis*, vol IV no 3, 93.

[19] Tricia Rose, *Black Noise: Rap Music and Black Culture in Contemporary America* (Wesleyan, Hanover, 1994), 59.

[20] Mark Dery, "Black to the Future," in *Flame Wars*, ed. Mark Dery (Duke, Durham, 1995), 208.

THE SOFT MACHINE

A glossy, violet glop is oozing through ten-year-old Magda Gross's fingers. "It feels like clams," Magda says, holding a pendulous glob over a nearby minirecorder. "It doesn't drip that easily." With the air of a fifth-grade science whiz, she pads the clammy goo together and holds it next to my Sony. "Let's see what it sounds like," she says, shoving her fingers into the synthetic sludge. "Here's the music!"

Ffflarrpptt.

The source of the emission was not Magda's intestinal tract but Gak, the latest pop virus to blaze through the pleasure circuits of America's prepubescents. What is Gak? On the one hand, it is the latest mutation in the phylogenic line of kidgoop (Silly Putty/Flubber/Play-Doh, etc.), whose last evolutionary leap was Slime, that '70s sticky green goo that came stuffed in plastic garbage cans. The first known Gak sighting occurred not in toy stores but on television—Nickelodeon's anarchic and messy *Double Dare* to be exact. There, Gak smothered folks and grossed-out kids competing for prizes. Like Tribbles or Transformers,

Gak is one of those odd things that are born and nurtured on TV before oozing through the tube into three-dimensional reality.

In fact, Gak may also be as virulent among adolescents as that fire-breathing, PBS-shilling purple doofus, Barney, is among tots. In 1992, the year it was introduced, Gak was Mattel's best-selling product; for 1993, the company estimated it would sell eight million "splats"—the air-tight plastic containers that package Gak. Teachers across the land, tipped off by the unusually animated expressions on their pupils' faces, have snatched away their charges' Gak, while some schools have simply banned the stuff. "That's a good sign," says John Handy, the head of the Mattel design team that spawned the glop. "If it's so prevalent that they actually have to form a rule that you're not allowed to bring it, then you know you've arrived."

But unlike other kid fads—action figures or water pistols or noise-makers—Gak is as difficult to classify as its globular, shifting shape—which is part of its appeal. Drooping the cool glop through your fingers, one cannot help but muse on its meanings. Toy? Compound? Food? Industrial by-product? Entity? Is it a solid or a liquid? Does it take a definite article? If you split your Gak in half are there two Gaks? Or is each splat a node in the great Gak Monad?

Magda has no interest in such questions. Like most kids, she's an imaginative pragmatist, focusing not on Gak's essence, but on its attributes. "Its squooshy and good to play with and you can throw it around and drip it." She also notes that it smells like tempera paints, shakes like Jell-O, and hardens into clay if you leave it outside of its splat for too long.

Magda's thirteen-year-old brother Tomek has been conducting research of his own. Employing experimental parameters appropriate to his age group, he threw Gak against the nearest vertical surface. "It doesn't stick very well. It kinda flops up against the wall and falls off. Cafeteria food sticks much better."

"Yeah," Magda chimes in. "You know the scrambled eggs that are actually made out of powder and you put water in them? If you touch those scrambled eggs it feels exactly like the Gak. I'm serious." She pauses. "Except you can't drip it as well."

While Magda covers her face with a Gak pancake, Tomek drops the stuff on the floor to see how well it bounces. Then he demonstrates how you can rip Gak apart to make it resemble chunks of chicken meat. Tomek acquired his first splat of Gak with two Rice Krispies proof-of-purchase seals, but he swears the stuff dissolved—a mysterious process the boy links to the tiny clear crystals he found buried in the substance. "They're kinda hard to find. I was taking them out because I thought they weren't supposed to be there. And the gak got smaller. It would, like, shrink." So in order to prove his hypothesis, Tomek starts picking out the crystals and putting Gak back in its splat and eyeing the change. "It's definitely getting smaller," he insists. "It's really annoying. This is a gyp."

Magda gets the experimental urge, and leans towards the cassette recorder to document her protocol. "I'm putting an ice cube in the middle of Gak. We're going to wrap it around. I'm holding it." She waits a minute and then unfurls the glop. "It melted a little and the water sorta sank into it." She probes the surface with her finger. "Ewwww!"

In *A Thousand Plateaus*, the French theorists Deleuze and Guattari's technical manual of conceptual mutation, the authors direct our attention towards the importance of "destratified, deterritorialized matter." This mode of matter "is not to be confused either with an intelligible, formal essentiality or a sensible, formed and perceived, thinghood." Destratified matter is always deforming, passing to a limit, changing state between solid and liquid. Such matter propagates itself through what D & G call "the machinic phylum," a nomadic space that is "matter in movement, in flux, in variation."

D & G were anticipating Gak. For Gak, too, is nothing less than a plastic machine through which matter probes its own fluid possibilities. While it vaguely resembles fake vomit, Gak cares nothing for simulacra or the easy metaphors of Slime, whose name and trash-can packaging gave the substance a specific identity. Gak is metamatter, a gooey question mark, an ontological murk. It is at once the primal ooze and the apocalyptic sci-fi blob. We can only impose ourselves on it so much, after which point we can only follow its flows (or its oozes).

Kids dig this because Gak, like Warner Bros. cartoons, suggests that the laws that govern physical reality are malleable. This accounts for the experimental dimension of so much Gak play, for Gak incites an exploratory urge that combines the joy of mud puddles with the scientist's clinical investigations. One of Gak's most popular features—the noises it makes when you cram your fingers into a full splat—was discovered by kids, not by Mattel. Now the most-asked question on the company's 800 number is how to make Gak fart.

Gak also conjures up weird science because the stuff looks like it crawled out of a Chernobyl swamp or a galactic meteorite. And, according to a *Scientific American* article, researchers are beginning to develop "intelligent gels"—polymer substances that shrink and expand in response to specific changes in their environment with the precision of machines, converting chemical energy into mechanical work. Gak, too, is a product of science, but of a very peculiar sort. Whereas goofy foods like Gummy Bears, Jell-O, bubblegum, and marshmallows share Gak's aesthetic, and Nickelodeon's original Gak was reportedly a kind of rancid pudding, Gak is not a food but a lab compound. Besides designer drugs, Gak is one of the few substances on earth invented by scientists driven neither by the joys of pure research or strict utilitarian goals (excluding the bottom line, that is). Mattel's chemists were driven by the search for fun.

Not surprisingly, the company is being very James Bond about Gak's chemical composition, and their in-house chemists are shrouded in secrecy. But independent research reveals that Gak is composed primarily of acrylic (a thickener which holds Gak's considerable moisture inside) and silicone (which accounts for the stuff's airtight stretchiness as well as, presumably, its jiggle). Mattel spokesmen will not confirm this information but did admit that Gak's chilly feel—especially noticeable when the stuff is stretched across the room—was due to evaporation. Though company officials claim that what they call "those amazing little crystals" are an inconsequential by-product of Gak's principle elements, the possibilities that Gak is powered by the resonant frequencies of those crystals cannot be dismissed out of hand.

The most significant thing about Gak's composition is that, like us, the stuff is made up mostly of water—about 80 percent. This sets up a powerful tactile empathy between our bodies and Gak. "It's one of the things that makes it feel so alive," says Mattel's John Handy. More importantly, it makes us feel a little like Gak. Not that we're violet (or green or orange) or smell like finger paints, but that our bodies, too, are in some mysterious way as malleable as a T2 morph. Perhaps this corporeal empathy explains an aspect of Gak that is almost unique among toys: boys and girls play with the stuff in identical fashion. It seems as if Gak catalyzes a body that eludes strict codes like gender. While this body is in some sense an infantile corpus of pure sensations, it is also the emergent body conjured up by yoga students, dancers, clever hedonists, and practitioners of certain alchemical arts.

For if Gak takes us back to our primal sensations, so too does Gak take the science of chemistry back to the primal metaphysical ooze of alchemy. Conventional history has it that the alchemists' most cherished goal, the Philosopher's Stone, allowed them to transmute lead into gold. But in more esoteric terms, the Stone was imagined as the mercurial soul of the Earth itself, as well as the alchemists' own magically transformed bodies. The Lapis Philosophorum was the original metamatter.

It's easy to make the analogy that Gak has become the TV-toy industry's Philosopher's Stone, turning goop into gold. But perhaps there's a deeper connection as well. In his play *The Alchemist*, Ben Johnson described the Lapis in strangely familiar terms:

> Tis a stone and not,
> A stone; a spirit, a soul, and a body,
> Which if you do dissolve it, it is dissolv'd,
> If you coagulate it, it is coagulated,
> If you make it fly, it flieth.

1993

ALIEN VIEWS

Joe Firmage, Silicon Valley UFOnaut

Late one night in October, 1997, just for the heck of it, Joe Firmage decided to go web surfing. As the CEO of a major Silicon Valley start-up, USWeb, Firmage didn't have a lot of leisure time. But he had studied physics as an undergrad at the University of Utah, and wanted to brush up on some of the latest findings. So he plugged in a few searches, and soon came across a report by a Lockheed Martin scientist asserting that inertia, the Newtonian force that makes your tennis balls sail, was an electromagnetic side effect of something called the zero point field. To the author, this suggested a new method of space propulsion—a way of conquering gravity without rockets—and Firmage, who was fascinated by all things extraterrestrial, was intrigued. Very intrigued.

But Firmage, then twenty-six years old, couldn't concentrate on the article with everything else pressing down on him. He had been in Silicon Valley for two years, and USWeb, which he founded with his partner Toby Corey, was hitting the big time. An Internet consulting firm that was launching monster companies like Harley-Davidson and Levi Strauss into cyberspace, USWeb had snatched up scores of Web development shops on its way to becoming a billion-dollar operation. That night, frazzled from preparing USWeb for its IPO, Firmage downloaded the article to read later and went to bed.

The next morning his alarm buzzed at 6:00. Instead of getting up to go to the gym, Firmage rolled over and hit the snooze button. As he lay there half-slumbering, an image appeared over his bed, a bearded gentleman with a dark brown head of hair.

"Why have you called me here?" the being asked, clearly irritated.

"I want to travel in space," answered the astonished Firmage, who spoke without a moment's deliberation, as if in a dream.

The fellow remained nonplussed. "Why should you be granted the opportunity?"

"Because I'm willing to die for it!"

Then, says Firmage, the man produced a sphere, an electric blue ball about the size of a cantaloupe, that entered Firmage's body, taking command of his muscles and producing unimaginable waves of über-orgasmic ecstasy.

As you might expect, Firmage greeted the day feeling rather light on his feet. Which was a good thing, because the Asian currency crisis was unfolding just as USWeb's pre-IPO road show was set to begin. But Firmage came through with flying colors—USWeb raised $50 million—all the while secretly nursing memories of his baffling encounter. "Anybody you'd talk to prior to this whole escapade would describe me as about the most rigorously logical, analytic type you could possible meet," he says. "So for me this was a particularly profound experience, because it was inexplicable."

Nonetheless, Firmage's visionary experience did not exactly appear out of thin air. A descendent of Brigham Young, Firmage was raised a Mormon, and grew up hearing tales of the otherworldly humans who led the young Joseph Smith to the golden plates he translated into the Book of Mormon. And though Firmage abandoned his faith at age fifteen, the precociously intelligent boy brought rather religious emotions to his new world view of science, feelings of cosmic awe that he traces to that defining moment of his generation: *Star Wars*. But sci-fi wasn't enough. What really sealed his galactic passions was Carl Sagan's *Cosmos* series. "It was beautiful and it was science, and therefore it was real, far more real than religion to me."

Driven by his enthusiasm for all things cosmic, Firmage continued to investigate zero-point energy following his otherworldly encounter. Zero-point energy, or ZPE, is the term some physicists use to describe the enormous store of quantum energy that fills even the smallest and most empty regions of space. Given its enormous potential energy and quasi-mystical character, ZPE has also become a flash point for all sorts of fringe scientists, free energy researchers, New Age physicists, and maverick inventors. As Firmage used the Internet to absorb findings and build contacts in the ZPE world, he came to believe that human civilization was on the verge of radical technological discoveries, breakthroughs that would enable us to replace fossil fuels and to fly to Alpha Centauri at the drop of a hat.

As he researched ZPE, Firmage also heard the siren song of the extraterrestrial. Having scarfed up flying saucer books as a teen, Firmage delved once again into the house of mirrors that surrounds the UFO, chasing whatever elusive truths snake through that labyrinth of vision and hoax, conspiracy and anomaly, science and psyche. Having already used the net to build connections with physicists and researchers exploring ZPE, Firmage wound up collecting a more esoteric range of contacts, including, he claims, top military and scientific leaders. These people proceeded to convince Firmage that UFOs were absolutely real, and that the government has kept the knowledge under wraps since the fabled Roswell crash of the 1940s.

Like many buffs, Firmage found himself longing for the day when this dense fog of official lies and obfuscations would finally dissolve in the light of alien truth. In a rather messianic twist of the tale, Firmage came to believe that he, Joe Firmage—brainiac whiz kid, triumphant CEO, digital darling—was the man to tip the scales. And so Firmage decided to write a book, or rather, he gathered fifteen anonymous "experts" to write a book along with him, nondisclosure agreements and all. With foolish and naive courage, Firmage went public with his beliefs late last November, promoting and Web-publishing, at considerable expense, a 600-page tome called, unbelievably, *The Truth* (www.the-word-is-truth.org). And once *The Truth* got out, Joe Firmage's silicon success story came tumbling down.

The shit hit the fan even before *The Truth* launched. The day after Firmage put his name on one of the pre-publication teaser pages for the book, a call came in to Mark Kvamme, the CEO of CKS, a slick Silicon Valley ad agency that USWeb had merged with just that fall. "Boy, I am going to enjoy competing with you now that your CEO is becoming the next L. Ron Hubbard," gloated the rival. Soon panicked investors started ringing up. Wryly, Firmage notes that these calls came in before anyone knew that his book concerned UFOs—it was simply the religious undertones of his teaser site that got folks riled up.

Within a week, Firmage voluntarily stepped down from his corporate position—though he admits that if hadn't gone willingly, he would have gotten the boot. He retained the title of head of strategic planning, but when his ET research hit the press, even that largely symbolic post became a thorn in the side of USWeb/CKS. Wall Street thought he was nuts, and the headlines didn't help: "From IPOs to UFOs," "The Ex-CEO Files," or "The Truth is Out There—And Joe Firmage is Paying For It." Nor could people keep a straight face when confronted with Firmage's suggestion in a Silicon Valley paper that some of the tech that put the Valley on the map was reverse-engineered from crashed Roswell saucers—a process Firmage compares to a bunch of chimps getting their hands on a Palm Pilot. It was all getting to be too much. In January, he simply resigned from the firm. For all the "visionaries" and "gurus" it claims to harbor, Silicon Valley still answers to the bottom line, and the bottom line these days does not include room for alien hieroglyphs—at least when you step outside of Hollywood.

Having helped turn the Internet into a major vehicle for corporate presence, Firmage became its victim as well. After all, Firmage made his silicon millions from the very same medium that sucked him into the UFO paradigm. "I can assure you of one thing," Firmage tells me. "We would not be having this conversation today if it weren't for the Internet. Without it I would not have been able to cross critical mass in my own knowledge." By its very nature, the net dissolves the formal distinction between truth and image, center and margin, rumor and news. The Web is a kind of conspiracy machine, a mechanism that encourages speculative leaps and dream-like links between tons of datafiles, linkages that in turn make whatever phenomenon you are investigating seem substantial. Just tap "zero-point energy" into your favorite search engine, and you too can slip into a strange world of tantalizing theories and amazing claims that would require years of your average layman's brain to properly assess.

For Firmage, the net is also a kind of harbinger of the technologies that he believes are just around the corner: revolutionary mechanisms that will fundamentally change the economy, culture, even consciousness itself. "In my opinion it is no accident that society develops an Internet before the types of things that I am talking about could ever become realized," he says. "From my perspective, the Internet is very literally the mind of humanity, in every way you would call something a mind."

Firmage still holds onto his USWeb office, which lies at the end of a long corridor near the desk his assistant is forced to rent from the company. The shades are drawn against the bleached Santa Clara light, and his desk is a jumble of NASA videotapes, financial grimoires, and copies of the *Journal of Religion and Psychical Research*. There are boxes piled on the floor, giving the room the unsettled feel of a house whose occupants are halfheartedly preparing for a move they don't really want to make.

The man himself is slight but handsome, with sharp blue eyes and a close-cropped reddish beard, and he seems wound as tight as a spring. The moment he begins to speak, it becomes instantly evident that Joe Firmage is not some brain-baked abductee, or straw-chewing hick mumbling about funny lights over the cornfield. He is an astonishingly bright and articulate man, who enunciates crisply and treats every conversation as if it were a debate between gentlemen. "I assert to you," he'll say, before his razor-sharp mind starts pursuing some curiously logical proof of alien contact.

Joe Firmage is hardly alone in his interest in things extraterrestrial. Ufology is full of kooks and hustlers, but it is also full of many men who are like him: geeky and deeply sincere left-brain mystics bent on nailing down truths which consistently elude the net of reason. But Ufology is only the tip of the extraterrestrial iceberg. Between alien rave logos, *X-Files* reruns, and *Men in Black* cartoons, aliens have achieved a pop presence not held since the days of 1950s B-movies or 1970s saucer cults. Alien abductees now run neck-and-neck with Satanic abuse victims in the race for the most outlandish psychological pathology, and even the Harvard Medical School psychiatrist John Mack is taking their claims seriously. Many hard-headed scientists who loathe UFO

buffs are also increasingly open to the notion that intelligent life exists elsewhere in the cosmos. UC Berkeley recently announced the establishment of the university's first chair for the Search for Extraterrestrial Intelligence, and the recent discovery of a planetary system surrounding Upsilon Andromedae, a nearby star similar to our sun, only bolsters the hunch that there are parallel earths out there.

This is an exciting idea for a lot of folks, especially folks in Silicon Valley. The massive signal processing effort known as SETI (the Search for Extraterrestrial Intelligence), which uses arrays of radio transmitters to scan the skies for intelligent bleeps, is headquartered in the Valley, and receives much of its dough from Intel co-founder Gordon Moore and Microsoft gazillionaire Paul Allen. Though Firmage went deeper into the heart of weirdness than most, his journey can hardly be considered anomalous in a place full of technological futurists, freethinking nerds, and hardcore science-fiction fans.

Nor is Firmage your average UFO buff. Unlike a lot of folks, whose idea of the big picture amounts to a 72-inch TV, Firmage thinks on a grand scale. As he makes clear in *The Truth*, which wends its way through a morass of theology, politics, physics, and natural history before it even gets to the Roswell goods, Firmage believes that the ETs only make sense when you see them against a larger backdrop, which Firmage calls the Kairos moment. "We are at a point of history where we are on the cusp of the grandest possible discoveries of human history," he says. "Five thousand years ago most of us were living in caves and huts, today our spacecraft are leaving the solar system. There is an undeniable trajectory there. Modern science seems to have its head in the sand believing, like every generation before it, that that trajectory somehow stops at the end of the second millennium."

Firmage's own trajectory blasts full speed ahead, into the potent vacuum of space. He believes we are on the cusp of learning how to tap the ZPE from the quantum vacuum, a cup of which has enough energy to boil the oceans of the earth. As you might expect, this opinion is not universally held among modern physicists. Even if you grant the possibility of exploiting zero-point energy—a notion that already sends the eyebrows of most physicists to the roof—you still have to build the damn thing. "There are plenty of physically possible mechanisms that are practically impossible," explains Andrew Jaffe, a Researcher at the Center for Particle Astrophysics at UC Berkeley. "And there are many more mechanisms that are impossible today but are still likely to be much simpler than dealing with vacuum energy!"

Such sentiments do not deter Joe Firmage, because he is the sort of man who can frankly utter statements like "modern physics is full of shit." According to *The Truth*, the ZPE breakthrough will happen soon, and will provide us with an essentially free source of energy that will eradicate our toxic addiction to fossil fuels. Firmage's book also argues that with ZPE in hand, we will be just a hop, skip, and a jump away from engineering gravity. In other words, warp drive, on demand.

In Firmage's mind, the feasibility of gravity propulsion devices destroys the only convincing scientific argument against UFOs (the lack of physical evidence doesn't seem to bother him). Moreover, our own imminent ZPE breakthrough also explains what all these alien tricksters are doing here in the first place. "If the child beings to climb out of the crib, parents get interested," Firmage says. "Its just like *Star Trek: First Contact*. You see a warp signature, and you know that the children have climbed out of the crib."

To his credit, Firmage does not claim to have a bead on the exact origins, identity, or purpose of the extraterrestrials, but he does know one thing: some of them wear white hats. At a time when many abductees report horrible little almond-eyed Dr. Mengeles armed with anal probes, Firmage has resurrected the Space Brothers optimism of the 1950s. Firmage believes that the aliens in our midst are teachers, here to help us strap on the psychological shoes that we'll need for our birth as galactic citizens. He even holds that the founding myths of world religions were created by these teachers in order to seed human culture with the ethical memes we'll need for our ultimate graduation into space. For proof, Firmage suggests rereading the New Testament, replacing the words *heaven* with *space*, and *angel* with *teacher*. "The book ceases to have the mythical quality and it begins to have anthropological sensibility. It begins to say to you, ah, this is how you take a chimpanzee and turn him into a space traveler."

By plugging spirituality into a galactic framework, Firmage hopes to keep the ethical and mystical core of religion alive in a world ruled by naturalism. It is his own fantastic attempt to heal the rift between science and religion, a rift that he believes must be sutured if we are to avert the environmental catastrophes that loom all about us. Indeed, the most moving and convincing passages of *The Truth* bristle with Firmage's informed passion for the physical world, and his perfectly reasonable pessimism about the present course of things. As Firmage puts it, "Y2K is a gnat compared to the seriousness of the damage we are inflicting on the biosphere."

Firmage's ultimate faith is not that the aliens will save us, but that the stone-cold truth about their existence will trigger a massive transformation of human culture. "It will indelibly mark in the consciousness of an entire species that the cosmos is coherent, that the majestic and sweeping history of human art and science, of war and peace, had a point, and the point was to build sufficient coherence that a birth was possible, the birth of a species into space." Firmage's ZPE hypothesis is thus a species of technological apocalypse, if we remember that apocalypse does not mean fire and brimstone but revelation. "People will instantly and viscerally understand that there is a far grander scheme, that they are part of a Star Wars script. Then they will start to behave in ways that naturally tend to self-organize a new type of vision."

If the flying saucers of the late 1940s and 1950s were manifestations of nuclear anxiety, our current crop may be tied to the more pervasive if ill-defined sense that we are making mincemeat of our lonely orb. In his book *Passport to the Cosmos,* Harvard Medical School psychiatrist John Mack writes that one of the central themes of the alien encounters he studies is the conviction that Gaia is on the brink. Mack has worked with over 200 abductees, whose experiences tend to be far more freaky than Firmage's bedside chat, and he is convinced that we cannot explain the phenomenon within our conventional categories of reality. "There is some kind of intelligence that we are connecting with," Mack told me. "It's not simply the imagination of people." This intelligence seems particularly obsessed with the ecological crisis, as if it were a cosmic feedback loop that kicks in as the world decays, breaking through our scientific materialism in the only way it knows how: waking dreams, persistent myth, and supernatural anomaly. ETs are the new elemental heralds, the elves and leprechauns of a dying global forest. And while encounters with these critters are often traumatic, Mack insists they can be transformative as well. "This experience shatters people's constricted world views, which can then connect them to a larger reality. It opens their pores to the divine, to home, to source, to what we once called God."

Firmage has certainly had his pores pried open, and is willing to weather the slings and arrows of outraged commentators because he thinks he'll get a ringside seat at the glorious eschaton ahead. But for the moment, the truth has yet to materialize outside his web site, and so Joe Firmage carries on. He is hunting down offices for his International Space Sciences Organization, which will quietly fund research efforts and his own proselytizing. A glossy, full-color print version of *The Truth* is in the works, and will hopefully lie under hundreds of thousands of Christmas trees. He's also finishing up an hour-long film that he plans to take on a twenty-city speaking tour, a spectacular "History of The World According to Joe," brought to life by the Bay Area's best, and most expensive, computer graphics artists. Firmage has also become something of a star in the UFO community, a martyr for the cause who has used his authority to chat up millions on the Art Bell show and to launch public attacks on Richard "Face on Mars" Hoagland, one of Ufology's reigning charlatans.

For all his messianic fervor, Firmage is too smart to ignore the possibility that he's backed the wrong horse. "Whether I am right or wrong, I think that this will serve a valuable function for society. If I am wrong, it will be the most clear case yet with which to tear down the fiction of this whole domain. If it has infected someone as promising as me, then it should be taken down." After all, *The Truth* did not catalyze any of the official announcements that Firmage expected, and he admits that if nothing happens he will be extremely disappointed. "I genuinely feel like I've leaped off the cliff, and I hope that there's a parachute when I pull the ripcord."

1999

MELANCHOLY MACHINES

Boards of Canada

Even since Luigi Russolo bent his avant-garde ear to trains and bombs and automobiles, declaring the arrival of a new "art of noises," the music of machines has been the site of future shock. As the British critic Kodwo Eshun argues in his book *More Brilliant Than the Sun*, today's samplers, synths, and drum machines breed "sonic science fictions," rippling portents of the technocultural tsunami to come: high-speed, recombinant, and thoroughly posthuman.

At the same time, a deep strain of nostalgia runs through electronic music, a wistful melancholy often bound up, in strange, indeterminate ways, with childhood and nature—in other words, with loss. Electronic music often makes melodies of these moods, brief haunting phrases that float above whatever beats happen to be percolating about. Eno was a light-handed master of such naive melodies, which he partly copped from the German electronic duo Cluster, and that eventually evaporated into the more diffuse and depersonalized moods of his ambient work. And though we now remember Kraftwerk as the white-smocked Doktors of proto-techno beats, the German act's records are suffused with a dorky sadness, as if they glimpsed the human world receding in their rearview mirrors as they hurtled down the autobahn, and could do nothing but muster forth a few android swan-songs.

Music Has The Right to Children, the debut album from the Scottish electronic duo Boards of Canada, is as sweet a work of electronic melancholia as you are likely to hear, proof positive, as if any were still necessary, that all those knobs and gadgets can indeed capture complex and contradictory emotional hues. Though its pensive, Moogy tunes often recall Aphex Twin's classic *Selected Ambient Works 85-92*, the album's sensibility, and particularly its beats, owes more to Autechre, who helps run the underground Skam label that released BoC's earliest vinyl. Like Autechre, BoC build upon the now standard strategy of layering lonesome phrases over repetitive rhythms by adding textured twists and turns to the beats. On cuts like "Telephasic Workshop" and "An Eagle in Your Mind," they chop up bits of human speech, most notably kids voices, to create rhythms that sound like stuttering memories. But the real strength of the album is its melodies, its warbling spaceflutes, polar plaints, and electronic wolf howls. Many of these cuts seem engineered to stir up a sense of loss—for one thing, they don't last long enough to satisfy, and many end with gorgeous new movements just beginning to develop.

The album opens with one of these haunting analog wobbles, a *Space 1999*-worthy drift called "Wildlife Analysis." The title is a clue: BoC take their name from the National Film Board of Canada, whose grainy nature documentaries and even grainier soundtracks influenced Michael Sandison and Marcus Eoin when they were tykes in the 1970s. There are lots of cryptic bits surrounding the band, but this nature doc fixation is worth a longer look. On the one hand, whatever washed-out TV memories haunt the duo's brains allow them to indulge the same nostalgia that underlies the Super-8 home movies they show during their occasional live gigs. You can catch this vibe from the photograph that graces the cover of *Music Has the Right to Children*: a group of literally faceless adults and kids, dressed in horizontally striped Ts and extremely flared jeans, posing for a snapshot now scratched and bathed in turquoise like the deep end of a pool.

BoC are also tuning into something specific about the 1970s, when the synthesized sounds that started to appear in popular media—educational films and public service announcements as well as prog rock and SF movies—became charged with some of decade's downbeat emotions. The '70s was the decade when space age longings collided with ecological gloom, and if you don't know what I am talking about, just dig up "After the Gold Rush" or pop *Silent Running* into your VCR. The '70s were sad the way vocoders are sad. Nature became an object of mourning, of a TV Indian's tear, and the canned soundtracks of the documentaries that little Mike and Marcus watched became unconscious sonic symbols of humanity's technological alienation from this, our only green world.

I don't know what their ecopolitics are like, but unlike the majority of electronica producers, Sandison and Eoin are not urban folks. They inhabit some vaguely communal set-up in the Scottish sticks, and from the occasional interview, it's clear that their idea of a good time is cavorting bemushroomed beneath a planting moon. I suspect BoC's rural imagination lends their music some of its visionary isolation, and also explains why so many of their tracks are covered with the grimy fingerprints of noise, warble, and hiss. In our high-tech world, signal degradation and analog fuzz express the organic because the organic always decays. It is how machines remember their roots.

1999

UNCANNY TV

So I sat there in front of the television Tuesday morning, with a whimpering woman by my side and the old tribal programs of vengeance and lament booting up in my breast, watching the '70s disaster flicks of my youth remade in hardcore, 21-C stylee. The now familiar scenes of the United jet slicing into the upper stories of the south tower, soon to collapse to its knees like a dispirited giant, were unnerving enough. More to the point, they were unbelievable and so, as many would say that day, "surreal"—our word for that reality we are programmed to disavow even as it swamps us like a dream tsunami.

That morning I also saw some genuinely uncanny media: a few short seconds of live broadcast that rank as some of the most disturbing moments of TV I've had the mixed blessings to see. A blond female reporter was standing on the trashed streets of southern Manhattan, narrating her horrifying and, for a journalist, exhilarating morning. (Forgive me if I recall neither the network nor the name of the journalist, but the TV became a babel-box that morning, a slice and dice machine of affect, image, and information.) The woman, who was only moderately in control of herself, was clutching a piece of paper in her hand. After finishing her brief tale she asked the cameraman if he could close in on the item, which, she said, resembled much of the debris about her.

The pink paper was some sort of invoice, and its entire edge was burned like an ancient map. As the camera zoomed in, nearly filling the screen with the document, the woman pointed at the address in the upper-left hand corner, which read: One World Trade Center. But as she read "One World Trade Center," some electromagnetic djinn decided to fuck with the feed, for what I then saw and heard was an eerie one-second loop of voice and image: "n world trade center . . . n world trade center . . . n world trade center," over and over a half dozen times, her staccato finger jabbing at the address like a robot on the fritz. For a moment the TV became a portal into the compulsive repetitions of the media unconscious. And then the invisible studio editors sweating over their live decks switched away from this abysmal mantra to another, more coherent feed.

For that brief passage, the news stream so many were feeding off of that day erupted with information's terror: noise. The transmission snafu reminded me that explosions do not just happen in the material universe of airplanes and stock brokers; info-bombs also rupture the noosphere, dividing, confusing, and destroying minds, our minds, even as the machines that network those minds—the telephones, the web servers, the satellites—groan under the weight of our sudden compulsive need to tune it, to talk, to witness. Our helpless but strangely reassuring envelopment in a frantic media storm was, of course, part of the spectacular plan, admirably orchestrated by these terrorist DeMilles and utterly unavoidable. With our eyeballs glued to the tube, our symbolic landscapes ruptured, we were got good. But for a few seconds, even that symbolic turbulence was disrupted by the tape loop, stinging my throat with the tang of the Real. The glitch was abstract, an artifact of data transmission, and yet it radiated like shrapnel through the Mobius strip of media. This is the trauma that changed everything, and us, in the blink of an eye.

2001

REMOTE CONTROL

A couple of months ago, after flying into Chicago on assignment, I rented a car. Since it was on someone else's dime, I got a Chevy Impala, a smooth ride with cool bubble curves and a dashboard that glowed like the console of a shuttle craft. Making my way from O'Hare to the Doubletree Inn in Skokie, I turned on the radio, stumbling across the city's peculiar "progressive rock" station KXRT ("like dungeons and dragons on your radio"). Styx's "Come Sail Away" soon forced me to abandon ship. Then I tuned into a Christian station, where I spent the next twenty minutes listening to one of the most awesome sermons I have ever heard. Between throaty bursts of songbird glossalalia worthy of Al Green, the preacherman filled the rent-a-car with a powerful blend of joy and dread. "My God, my God, I don't wanna die!" Indeed.

The next evening, I was returning from Evanston to my hotel. For some reason, the car's interior light wouldn't shut off, and I fumbled for the proper button. (Like many Americans, I challenge the interface designers of cars—not to mention software—by not bothering to figure out how anything works before I hit the road.) I noticed a cluster of buttons lining the bottom of the rearview mirror. Accordingly, I aimlessly swatted them until the light blinked out. However, I also seemed to have triggered the car phone I didn't know I had, as the familiar drone of a dial tone came across the "entertainment system." Not knowing how to turn off the phone, I simply turned the volume knob on the radio down, figuring that, in the absence of a dialed number, the phone would simply shut off after the "If you would like to make a call" lady had her say.

I was feeling restless. Though the drive was short and I try to avoid switching on the radio simply to manage nervous energy, I turned up the volume dial and discovered the radio already on. I heard a droning male voice, which I assumed was another Christian preacher, although this guy sounded moralistic, boring, and white. Feeling displeased with myself for my inability to drive fifteen minutes without sonic distraction, I turned the volume knob down, still unsure about how to shut off the radio itself. But after a few moments, my restlessness got the better of me and I yanked the knob back up, enabling me to hear the following:

"If you do not respond immediately, we will automatically dispatch a police vehicle to your location."

A spine-trembling beat. Hesitantly, though without logically processing the action, I said, "Are you talking to me?"

"Yes."

"Ak!" I shuddered. "What's going on?"

"This is the OnStar advisor. You have activated the emergency system. It's our policy to contact an emergency service if we don't hear a response. Is everything OK?"

"Yeah," I said. "I'm in a rent-a-car. I didn't know what I was doing. You freaked me out. Sorry."

"That's OK. If you have any further questions, just press the blue OnStar button on your rearview mirror. Good night."

The radio stayed off the rest of the way.

Now, you may pay more attention to car ads than I do, so you may already be hip to OnStar: an onboard, location-based information and safety service available for GM cars. OnStar pumps out a strong three-watt GPS signal which supposedly works even if your antenna gets ripped off. With this location info-streaming into their computers, OnStar advisors can give you real-time directions, tell you about nearby hotels and restaurants, or direct emergency services to your car if an airbag is deployed or if you happen to press that little button on the rearview mirror with a red cross on it (duh). Later this year, OnStar's "Virtual Advisor" will also enable you to personalize a speech-activated flow of sports, stock, news, and weather data from the Internet—you know, kind of like the radio used to do.

It was only later that I found out about OnStar's GPS technology, their one million customers, and their ridiculous marketing tie-in with DC's Batmobile (an ad campaign that forced them to include the following passage in their FAQ: "Q. Why can't I buy the Batmobile? A. Batman and the Batmobile are used solely for advertising purposes and are not available through OnStar."). But though this information explained what happened to me, it did not entirely eradicate the blast of the uncanny that my unwitting encounter with OnStar uncorked inside the confines of my rented Chevy. For a few seconds, I had entered Philip K. Dick land: my radio suddenly and pointedly spoke directly to me. Moreover, the voice knew exactly where I was—in Evanston, Illinois, heading east on Golf toward Skokie Boulevard. In a beat, reality seemed to fold inside out, the general became particular. This is what paranoid schizophrenics might feel like at the beginning of an episode.

I suspect that most of us have had similar encounters with technology, especially over the last decade—moments when our media, for whatever reason, momentarily deliver us into some uncanny zone that lingers on the edge of the Real. Usually we sweep these experiences—strange radio static, surreal computer shenanigans, the snafu synchronicities of the cell phone—under the rug. But I don't think we should so readily dismiss the feelings that accompany these experiences, because they have their own truths to tell. For as media increasingly colonize social reality, they scramble the space-time boundaries of the self. And this always feels a little weird.

For the most part, we quickly assimilate these mutations in subjectivity. The human mind seems to naturally adjust itself to perceive its current reality as normal and mundane (and usually at least vaguely dissatisfying to boot). Nowadays, we can hardly believe that our great-grandparents experienced Ford jalopies as demonic speed machines, or that the bodiless heads of the cinema screen triggered nausea. These perceptions become normal, even though, in some basic sense, they are not.

One reason that these uncanny experiences are important, then and now, is that they speak to the conflicted and ambivalent feelings that technology provokes—feelings we usually bury beneath the quotidian operations of getting and spending. In this sense, they are like the symptoms in a dream, except that they arise in the midst of the everyday. Even more importantly, though, they have the almost oracular ability to reveal the new and often rather disturbing social realities that are emerging beneath the veneer of business as usual. In this sense, the technological uncanny—in both fiction and paranormal "fact"—is a gateway to the new mutations of the Real.

Consider the oft-noted resemblance between businessmen barking into their cell phones and crazy homeless people talking to their invisible companions. Late-night comics have already milked this one dry, but what does it actually tell us? Wireless technology, by removing physical connections, erases one of the last signs that our communication technologies are material and not etheric. Though we "know" that electromagnetic modulations of the spectrum are no less material than waves of electrons cruising along a wire, wireless nonetheless amplifies the experiential sense that we live and move in a world of invisible intelligences, a magic world verging on telepathy. Simply put, the more the physical apparatus disappears, the more we are simply listening and responding to voices in our heads.

I am not saying that the mobile hordes of demon-haunted suits prove that our society has gone insane. The world is subtler (and crazier) than that. Instead, technology is colonizing zones of cultural perception previously occupied by madmen, drug fiends, and religious fanatics. Everyone knows that many schizos fear nefarious mind-control microwaves, or tune into visionary messages through their TVs and radios. But few of us recognize how old this phenomenon is and how fundamental it is to the social phenomenology of electronic media. Shortly after the telephone was introduced, for example, Thomas Watson—Bell's famous partner—met a man who claimed that two New Yorkers had connected his brain to a telephone circuit, and used this device to give him various diabolical orders.

Unlike madmen, cellular users are presumably speaking to other people. But even these legitimate signals have their own uncanny stories to tell. Bad connections on copper lines were often noisy or faint; satellite signals introduced delay. Now, because of cross-talk, bounced signals, and who knows what, millions of people routinely hear the voices of their friends and colleagues spliced and diced through hideous Lovecraftian Cuisinarts of sound. Our cell phones have become effects boxes worthy of the headiest dub or industrial music, and they render our intimate communications trippy. Once I heard the distant voice of my friend Christy multiply into scores of slightly off-beat sonic doppelgängers, so that the telephone call sounded like a thousand Christys were talking to me at once. It was one of the most psychedelic things I've ever heard. That is, until my radio talked to me.

As with so many technologies, the penetration of wireless into global society will be simultaneously convenient, weird, banal, and deeply disturbing. We already accept the little antisocial wormholes that cell phones open up in the midst of public space, a phenomenon that, while further cranking up the knob on individualism, at least adds another wrinkle to the boundaries that define our social interaction. But the growth of wireless access to data may have a very different effect, because it erodes the sense that the world we wander through has any real variation at all.

Here's why. Societies have increasingly come to define reality—or, less philosophically, "the action"—by media and information flows. The old days were very "lumpy" when it came to the density and availability of cultural information, because the city had more access than a cornfield. Nowadays, though, universal wireless access to the net makes our particular somewhere feel like anywhere—or even nowhere.

We are all familiar now with the non-linearity of the web, its simultaneously liberating and woozy sense that everything seems connected to everything else. Despite the best efforts of 3D-cyberspace builders, the "distance" between points online is entirely virtual. Once we can use our wireless PDAs, fancy cell phones, and other nomad computers to access this data-dense nonspace from anywhere in fleshland, that flattening all-at-onceness leaks into the world of trees and cafés and cathedrals. As the net becomes ubiquitous, the physical world becomes hollowed out in roughly the same way that collective social space is hollowed out by cell phones. It's like wandering into a heavily touristed medieval city in Europe: the exotic spaces that initially seem to transport you beyond the fields you know turn out to house variations on the same global consumer themes. If deep travel implies wandering and wondering, which I suspect it does, then travel becomes impossible, or at least utterly transformed, when you are outfitted with a yellow pages, map, and guidebook in your palm.

GPS and other location-based services add a new twist, offering at first what appears to be a return to specific locality: You are here. But the global reach and ubiquity of the network ultimately undermines that sense of specific location, supplanting "place" with "space"—the abstract space of information. When I accidentally contacted OnStar, I established a real-time connection between my body and the company's virtual map of the material world, a connection that, in some fundamental way, brings those two worlds closer together. I was on the grid, and the sudden recognition of my individual capture by a satellite-based system of virtual control partly accounted for my little *mise en abime*. Because I did not consciously initiate the link, I directly experienced the fact that the safety and control we are offered through new technology generally comes with our incorporation into what Foucault might call a "disciplinary order." The actual content of my uncanny moment was my own translation into a blinking red light in a system designed to, in some sense, remotely control my body.

In other words, the real spookiness of my experience did not come from my schizophrenic encounter with a talking radio but from my close brush with cops. I won't speculate about what would have happened had some of Skokie's finest actually pulled my scruffy, ignorant ass over, nor how friendly they might have been had that ass been black. Nor will I bother you with another rant about privacy, fast-track toll systems, and the latest mark of the beast. There is a lot of debate about privacy in the information age, but much less discussion about the profound psychic unease that most of us feel, in our dreams if not in our waking worries. There is a peculiar wooze beneath our willingness to sacrifice anonymity on the technological altar of safety and convenience, and the wooze tastes like an almost drug-induced fear. And fear rarely just sits there: It motivates us, if not to act, then to act out. The psychic dis-ease unleashed by the technological erosion of privacy will not only continue to feed paranoid narratives but will cloud the transparency we demand in both our technologies and our political systems, because whatever local clarity we gain depends on a hyperdimensional grid whose depth, extent, and uses extends utterly beyond our ken.

2001

MATRIXTER

The most curious feature of Warner Bros' official *Matrix* Web site is not the handful of jaw-dropping *Animatrix* clips, but the collection of high-quality philosophical essays by heavy hitters like Hubert Dreyfus,

Colin McGinn and the cognitive science superstar David Chalmers. These essays, which hash out Descartes, Mahayana Buddhism and the proverbial "brain in the vat" problem, are all the evidence you need that the Wachowski brothers' original 1999 film has vaulted into that curious category of Big Think mainstream sci-fi films—and that they want the "kickass" sequel to extend the beard-pulling.

No one is surprised when filmmakers like Andrei Tarkovsky or Chris Marker or Stanley Kubrick use future shtick for metaphysical purposes, but it's another thing for Hollywood action fare—designed to reap big bucks from the popcorn crowd—to create a space of inquiry into philosophical, political and spiritual questions, however "comic book" the frame. Movies like *Blade Runner, Robocop, They Live, Minority Report* and the *Alien* and *Terminator* flicks have managed, sometimes through no fault of their own, to edge toward the profound. But the Wachowski brothers made it to the top of this heap with the most lucrative sci-fi action empire to feed the questioning, and questing, mind.

Now, with demiurgic ambitions matched only by *Lord of the Rings* director Peter Jackson, the brothers have unveiled the next chapter of their live-action post-apocalyptic anime franchise. As a movie, *The Matrix Reloaded* has some serious flaws: Many sequences drag, the pacing is jangled and there are far too many dreadlocks. But I have no problems with the pretentious, concept-heavy dialogue. Some reviewers imply that this metaphysical kitsch detracts from the fun; for some of us, it is the fun. At one point in the new film Neo returns to the Matrix and wanders through a street market full of religious junk: chintzy Catholic saints, head-shop Shiva posters, and blinking Jesus plaques. This is the pop carnival of souls where the Matrix films rightly take their place—the flea market of genre movies and rumors of God that, for many these days, is the only portal left into the meaning of it all. In the words of Philip K. Dick, whose spirit (but not tone) hangs over the Matrix, "The symbols of the divine initially show up at the trash stratum."

The Wachowski brothers may be too self-conscious about their divine trash, but in the end that's what feels true, or at least contemporary, about the Matrix films: their excessive self-consciousness about selves and consciousness. The original *Matrix* hit home by digitally remastering a time-honored (because always timely) conundrum: How do I know that reality is not a total illusion? Though this question gives off a cheesy adolescent fizz, it's more than a stoned *gedankenexperiment*, like Pinto's speculation in *Animal House* that our entire universe might be an atom in some all-being's fingernail. The question lies at the heart, at least, of Western epistemology, with Descartes.

In order to escape medieval authority and embrace the proud autonomy of the rational "I," Descartes battled a "demon of doubt" that undermined everything it could, including the reality of the world before the philosopher's eyes. Descartes's skepticism, with its sci-fi scenarios of false worlds and automatons disguised as human beings, initiated a revolution in thinking that, in some sense, ultimately leads to the universal machines that sit on our particular desks. The Matrix, with its mathematized objects and Cartesian coordinates, is really Descartes's storyboard.

Descartes dreamed great dreams as well—like the angel who appeared to him one September night, proclaiming, "The conquest of nature is to be achieved through measure and number." Most of us have such veridical dreams on occasion, when visionary Technicolor truths burst through the usual REM murk. At the very least, the power of these dreams reminds us that the "false reality" problem strikes a far deeper note than skepticism alone can sound. Millennia ago, human beings had to face the fact that our minds regularly pass through realms very different from the seemingly solid world, however we choose to interpret them. In other words, the Matrix problem arises from our wetware's capacity, through dreams, drugs or trance, to boot up radically different worlds of consciousness. That's why Descartes's skepticism still resonates with cultural narratives as different as Hindu folklore or gnostic myth or the Taoist Chuang Tzu's famous quip (intended with more humor than I think we now hear): "How do I know I am a man dreaming he was a butterfly, and not a butterfly dreaming he is a man?"

The Matrix problem becomes particularly unavoidable in the age of virtual technologies, which constantly narrate their own totalizing dreams of "world-building" and "experience design." The history of media is littered with immersive spaces of fiction: Baroque cathedrals, nineteenth-century panoramas, even, perhaps, the Paleolithic caves of Lascaux or Altamira. Today, the accelerating perceptual technologies of media are on a collision course with cognitive science and its understanding of how the human nervous system produces the real-time matrix we take for ordinary space-time. So we should not be surprised at the massive popularity of a Hollywood slugfest where dream and reality and virtual technology enfold one another. Not only does the film mythologize the game-world aspirations of so much popular media, it stimulates the corresponding desire to crack through—and remake—the construct.

What was particularly savvy about the Wachowskis' comic-book movie was that its mirror-shade cool reflected any number of readings—Marxist, Lacanian, utterly stoned. Perhaps most surprising, and influential, was its use of religious symbols and viewpoints. Most viewers picked up on the Christian elements of the first film, which center on Neo's role as a savior figure, but the deep frame of both movies is a more esoteric pop stew of gnostic and Buddhist ideas. The gnostics of antiquity transformed the analogy of Plato's cave into a full-blown and harrowing cosmology: We are strangers trapped in a strange land, they argued, immortal sparks slumbering in a material cosmos fashioned by an evil or ignorant demiurge and his nefarious archons. The Buddhist analysis is less personalistic: We are stuck on the delusive merry-go-round of samsara, an almost mechanical system of causes and conditions that fools us into believing the self and the world are substantially real. In both cases, we step toward the light not through grace or the remission of sins, but through the direct awakening of insight into our condition. Neo must swallow his pill and take the ride himself.

Opening in theaters on Buddha's birthday, *The Matrix Reloaded* clearly places itself in a crypto-religious landscape. There's a ship called the Logos, characters like Seraph and Persephone and Neo's hushed worship by the multiculti masses of Zion. Neo's mystic powers are growing as well: His "second sight," which allows him to see into the underlying code inside the Matrix, lets him read energy bodies and, in a remarkable fusion of Christ myth and shamanism, resurrect Trinity by removing a bullet embedded in her body. But *The Matrix Reloaded* would have been lame if it had simply followed its gnostic bodhisattva superhero around as he kicked ass in Jesuit robes. Instead, to keep the cognitive sparkle, the Wachowskis altered the conceptual maps of the two worlds that Neo moves through: Zion and the Matrix.

In the first film, these two worlds had the virtue of simplicity: We slipped neatly between the world of the Matrix, with its single nefarious agenda, and the revolutionary messianic world of Morpheus's ship, the *Nebuchadnezzar*. But *The Matrix Reloaded* complicates these two worlds. Before the *Nebuchadnezzar* even arrives at Zion, we realize that Morpheus—previously the hierophantic voice of truth—may simply be crazy, an irrational demagogue, a renegade believer. Meanwhile, the Matrix grows far more complex. In the first film we sensed a unity of purpose and design behind the agents and their urban landscape, but now we confront a Babel of programs: rogue self-replicating agents, the power-mad Merovingian, the intuitive Oracle, all competing in an open-ended nest of potentially infinite regress. As the Oracle admits to Neo, it's a pickle: there's no way for him to know what's going on or whom to believe.

The Matrix comes to resemble the multifarious world of shamanism rather than the black-and-white world of the Christian afterlife. Neo, the otherworldly voyager, encounters a wide variety of beings, each with his or her own contradictory raps and agendas, and none entirely trustworthy. The architecture of the Matrix has also become pickled, an Escheresque Swiss cheese of transdimensional hallways and quantum portals. If *The Matrix* was all about screens and mirror shades, *The Matrix Reloaded* is all about keys and doors. The keys are codes of course, the language of encryption, but they are also the keys of magicians navigating through angel-space. And the portals we keep passing through remind us that the action lies between the worlds, as the conventional cartography of the Matrix melts into the metamorphic palaces of dream.

After all, however much you resonate with the kabbalistic or Marxist metaphors, the Matrix most resembles the shifting virtual worlds that our brain conjures nightly. The first glimpse that *The Matrix Reloaded* gives us of the Matrix—when Trinity falls to her apparent demise beneath a rain of bullets—turns out to be a recurrent dream in Neo's head. What makes this dream a nightmare is not just Trinity's death, but Neo's own inability to intervene in the scenario. We've all gotten caught in these hypnagogic snares, where you face some horror but cannot move—encased, as it were, in the amber of dream time. What we want in these moments is the secret wish whose fulfillment animates these films: the desire to awaken inside the phantom world and wrest control from the dream machine.

On this level of psychic control, both Matrix films can be read as Castaneda-esque instruction manuals for lucid dreamers. As the first film suggests, the simple knowledge that one is dreaming is not usually enough to exert control on the illusory world; instead, one achieves full creative action only after a lot of training in the dreaming dojo. The first thing that a lot of dreamers do when they first go lucid is also one of the first visual pleasures *The Matrix Reloaded* gives us: flight. Neo's bat-winged cruise through the moonstruck heavens is not just a Superman reference, but also a specific invocation of our own dream experience. This is what people don't understand about the Wachowskis' special effects, many of which revolve around virtual camera moves impossible to generate in the real world. Remember the subconscious equation of film: I am the camera. When the Wachowskis propel their camera faster than a speeding bullet, when it swoops and dives with angelic grace or whips through a frozen moment of space-time—these novel perceptions strike us at first as virtual experiences, familiar only through dream time or trance.

The novelty of these effects wears off fast, of course, and we soon assimilate the technique as mere technological rhetoric. "Bullet Time" sells beer now; we are not impressed. Our rapidly jaded eyes drive the arms race of special effects, a race that suggests that we will not be satisfied until we somehow break through and manipulate space itself—a pleasure now increasingly available through computer games, like the Wachowskis' own *Enter the Matrix*. As in lucid dreams, the question is all about control, a control that necessarily implies a certain technical disenchantment. We can control our dreams when we recognize they are merely dreams, just as we can create the "magic" of FX only with the total mathematization of space-time and the images of human bodies. The Matrix films are not neo-Luddite propaganda; the Wachowski brothers recognize that technology accompanies all our dreams. Early in the second film, an insomniac Neo wanders through the depths of Zion as Councilor Hamann draws his attention to an irony only implicit in the first film: The good guys also depend utterly on machines. In their stilted chat, Neo differentiates between the Matrix and Zion's technological infrastructure, a steam-punk space of Tesla-coil arc lights and corroded *Modern Times* gears that looks back to the organic textures of the last century. Neo implies that Zion is free because humans have control. But this nineteenth-century romance only raises the question Hamann asks him: "What is control?"

This question is not just the nut of the movie. It is the central koan of cybernetic civilization and our ever more intricate symbiosis with algorithms, control systems and the kind of self-replicating bots suggested by Agent Smith. All the representatives of the Matrix, even the Oracle, continually suggest that conscious human agency is not what it's cracked up to be. During his first balletic bash with Neo, Smith, though now apparently a "free agent" like Neo, insists that everything is determined by its purpose. He does not use the term as Morpheus later does, to suggest destiny or a higher calling. Instead, he means a techno-Darwinian logic, a programmed calculus of success. His is the voice of the evolutionary psychologist, who delights in deconstructing our most spirited social actions in terms of the base advantage they confer. This is also the perspective of the Merovingian, who comes off as a curious hybrid between Herod and Pilate from *Jesus Christ Superstar*. With the aphrodisiac piece of pie he feeds a future fuckbunny, the Merovingian raises the distinct glandular possibility that "decision" is simply the story the brain tells itself about the neural cascades of electrochemical reactions that underlie behavior. Code rules: Despite appearances, we are out of control.

As mythographers, the Wachowski brothers realize that the cybernetic problem of control reboots the hoary old struggle between freedom and fate. Morpheus, for example, is convinced that everything is proceeding according to cosmic plan, but his increasingly tedious speechifying about destiny and prophecy weirdly mirrors Agent Smith's grim talk of mechanical purpose. What, then, is the proper rejoinder to determinism? The Oracle tells Neo that "You are here to understand why you made the choice, not to make the choice." I take this to mean that, to an awakened one, events and decisions have always already occurred, but that understanding and compassion can still dissolve their karmic hold.

OK, enough already. It's silly to squeeze too many meanings from a cyber-chopsocky flick; as in the anime tradition the Wachowskis draw from, metaphysical puzzles are more for atmosphere than answers. I won't even get into Neo's final chat with the Architect, although I suspect that all the talk of anomalies and contingent affirmations won't really add up in the end. But adding up is not really the point (unless you are talking about adding up the merchandise sold to fans who want to spend as much time as possible in the Wachowskis' endlessly nested construct). Like the overly complex plots of film noir, which ultimately serve only to increase the vibe of claustrophobic paranoia, *The Matrix Reloaded*'s fractured chatter is in service of an old gnostic hunch: There is a crack in the cosmic machine, and we are the crack.

As I left the theater after watching the new film, I was handed a slick little flier. "Take the Red Pill," it said. "Join the Resistance." At first I thought it was a Christian tract, but it was Not in Our Name's clever attempt at a wake-up call for a very sleepy nation. Here are the truths the tract's authors offered: slaughtered Iraqis, Orwellian homeland security, deportations and military tribunals, endless war and repression. But they also saw a light at the end of the rabbit hole. "Another world is possible and we pledge to make it real," they said. "Join us." They listed some numbers, and I impulsively looked around for the nearest public phone, as if I were Clark Kent, or Neo trying to slip back out of the Matrix. I didn't see one. They're not easy to find these days.

2003

KALIFORNIKA

CALLING ALL GODS

Crash Worship

The Crash Worship acolytes packed into the cavernous hall in San Francisco's SoMa district are ready to roll. Pierced, tattooed, or perfectly unadorned, they look focused and expectant, like they're about to leap. Some are smeared with greasepaint, some wear animal horns, some have bared their breasts. Richard Kern nazi-chick softcore flutters on a screen, and the grrrl behind me is dropping urban myth: "I heard her brother forked his eyes out because he thought he saw the devil," she says. Her companion pauses not a second. "One fork or two?"

Then a creaky tape loop kicks in with insect castanets, Roadrunner *bleep bleep!*s and groaning chains from Davy Jones's locker. The sharp, woody smell of burning piñon hits my nostrils. Suddenly, smoke bombs erupt in the hall, and fireworks start rattling their fiery retorts. And then the beats begin, monstrous rolling thunderdrums that grip your gut like Japanese taiko or a marching band of evil clowns. There's so much smoke you can't see the band, and though there's "vocals" (think shards of sheet metal) and "guitars" (think warbling ghoul moans from a wired six-foot slab called a "megalyra"), it's the pounding polyrhythm that rivets me and my neighbors. These beats have nothing to do with rock, and everything to do with ritual.

Then "Fat" Jack Torino rears up from the nebulous gloom, a damaged cowboy in shades and sheep chaps, slinging what looks like a fire extinguisher. A Thick jet of clear liquid sprays over the gleeful crowd like a spout of ectoplasmic jizz, followed soon after by beef blood, wine, flour, and milk, much of which has been distributed by "crowd motivators" sliding through the dance floor. I too am anointed with Gallo. And no one need slap footnotes from *The Bacchae* on all these Dionysian fluids, because Crash Worship has no interest in Neopagan postures or primitivist shtick. They call the gods raw.

The first time I attended a Crash Worship show, I was blessed with no expectation, and what hit me was the most spontaneously libidinal and polymorphous group funkfest I've had the woodie to experience. Tonight, two years later, the crowd is overpacked and a lot more aggro, but I still feel the neck hairs rise when the diminutive Dreiky, CW's rhythmic heartbeat and the band's only female musician, leads a drum procession through the crowd. We press in as the diabolic crew forms a circle. Blazing torches whip past our ears, illuminating the drummers, their wet skin glinting in the firelight.

There is no order to the memories that follow: a skinhead bathed in blood, the smell of sulphur, the touch of damp fabric and damper skin (mine? his? hers?). A half nude female fire swallower toasting her nipples onstage, where the only constant is a single red bulb smoldering like ancient embers. The sudden thought: "Shit, is that something burning?" Like no one since the Butthole Surfers, Crash Worship bring fear and disorientation back to the concert hall. What are fire codes compared to the atavistic fete that has circled around this globe since the first hairy wizard beat time with a bone? What is danger in the face of surprise?

You might think that Crash Worship, who got their start in San Diego in 1987, would have a tough time translating their chthonic tantra into plastic, but *Triple Mania II* (Charnel Music)—the first all-studio long-player in the band's eight-year history—is a pretty fine slice of hyperspace. If you're lucky, you'll get an individually tweaked Independent Project Records-style cardboard folder graced with stunning screen-printed copper plates and art "blatantly inspired" by Henry Darger, an insane gutter-culture saint known for Dick and Jane-style drawings of skewered and exploding children. Though the band pin themselves with an obvious badge by covering a Manson Family tune, other songs like "Wild Mountain" and "Vitamin K" are fresh, serving up wah-wah incubi, beached whales, wheezing Moogs, Spanish poets, and mad clarinets. And through it all, from ambient pitter-patter to chunky protofunk, the drums, the drums, the DRUMS!

1995

THE ALCHEMY OF TRASH

West Coast Spiritual Collage

You have probably already heard the one about the yogi huddling in his mountain cave who believes he's finally cracked through the cosmic egg. Having reached enlightenment, he decides to clamber down to the village below and spread the love. As he wanders through the town's crowded market, some poor slob jostles him; without a thought, the holy man turns on the guy with anger. The point is that it's easy to get clear on a mountaintop, but much tougher to manifest the light in the messy world most of us actually live in. But the tale also makes an ecospiritual argument, of sorts: mountains are the sites of mystical transcendence, while the human towns below embody the ordinary grind of the world.

The art and spirituality of California in the twentieth century subtly undermine this polarity between mountains and towns, transcendence and immanence, high and low. In "Time Is the Mercy of Eternity", the San Francisco poet Kenneth Rexroth—anarcho-leftist, Buddhist, and proto-Beat—describes his own mystic moment in the Sierras. This opening in time does not put him in touch with God or cosmic forces, but with the simplicity of ordinary material life: "The pale new green leaves twinkle / In the rising air." What he sees is the "holiness of the real," an experience he contrasts with the faraway city, "burning with the fire of transcendence and commodities." In a key Californian insight, Rexroth recognizes that the urban market, rather than the Zen mountaintop, is the zone enflamed with transcendent desires—or rather, that the desire that enlivens the commodities of the urban milieu is, at its essence, a desire for transcendence. Arising from the core of human suffering and dissatisfaction, the essential energy of desire is not separate from the sacred, even through it gets funneled into the secular and frequently crass fantasies that drive city life: lust, entertainment, distraction, power.

By the same token, spirituality takes place in the midst of the market and its commodified fantasies. This feedback loop is especially true in California, where esoteric spirituality has long been a part of a feverish and mercantile popular culture rife with trash. What religious seeking and California culture share most essentially is an investment in fantasy—fantasy not simply as illusion, but as the forms that fuse imagination and desire. As both ironic and populist fans of low-brow culture can attest, the ferocity of fantasy can lend a delirious dreamlike power to corny things like UFO cults and commercial entertainments like B-movies or comic books.

This paradox gets us close to the heart of sacred Los Angeles, a city that dreamt (and sold) itself into existence through real estate hype, Hollywood, and the siren call of the perfect bod. The very architecture of Los Angeles suggests this material dreaming: in the teens and twenties, the town exploded with fantasy buildings like Babylonian ziggurats, pyramids, witchy cottages, castles, teepees, and restaurants shaped like derbies. This slapdash and often garish architectural raid on the collective unconscious looked ahead to Disneyland, fast-food signage, and the corporate "thematization" of contemporary urban space. The exotic imagination crudely stimulated by these buildings, which were often crudely built, also prepared the ground for the Orientalist moods and esoteric concepts that exerted enormous influence on LA's spiritual scene. In other words, the construction of trashy fantasy in the built environment created the cultural and psychic space for exotic, imaginative, and otherworldly faiths and experiences to grow.

Some fantasy architects were themselves active in California's spiritual fringe. The most notable was Robert Stacy-Judd, one of countless Brits who long ago transformed Los Angeles into a sort of London-on-Pacific. As a young architect in England, Stacy-Judd designed various Orientalist structures, but in California he discovered his deep and abiding love: the Maya. He built the amazing Aztec Hotel in Monrovia, which remains his signature building; he also used Mayan stylings for private homes, a Baptist church in Ventura, and a Masonic hall in the San Fernando Valley. A kooky self-promoter, Stacy-Judd styled himself a Mayan explorer-archeologist; he also hobnobbed with Theosophists and the Philosophical Research Society's Manly P. Hall. Stealing a few pages from febrile crypto-archeologists like Ignatius Donnelly and Lewis Spence, Stacy-Judd argued in his *Atlantis: Mother of Empires* that the Maya descended from the Atlanteans. Presumably, Stacy-Judd believed that by creating a regional architectural style rooted in Mayan culture, the West Coast would tap into that mighty spiritual source, though it's tough to say whether the history of the Aztec Hotel—a brothel and speakeasy during prohibition—bears this out.

In the first decades of the twentieth century, a restless hunger for exotic fantasy and escape helped make Los Angeles ground zero for California's paradoxically popular esoteric scene—what I call its pop occulture. "No other city in the United States possesses so large a number of metaphysical charlatans in proportion to its population," wrote local Willard Huntington Smith in 1913. "Whole buildings are devoted to occult and outlandish orders—Mazdaznan clubs, yogi sects, homes of truth, cults of cosmic fluidists, astral planers, Emmanuel movers, Rosicrucians and other boozy transcendentalists." These groups drew from the creative imagination and a common pool of psycho-spiritual motifs in order to sculpt a range of sects, fads, and mental-health regimens. Futuristic pseudo-sciences fused with the ancient lore introduced by Theosophists, astrologers, and encyclopedists like the aforementioned Hall, author of the classic omnibus folio *The Secret Teachings of All Ages* and collector of one of the world's greatest library of hermetic and alchemical texts (the best of which were eventually pawned off to the Getty Museum). Even Protestant fundamentalism was transformed into Hollywood spectacle by the evangelist Aimee Semple McPherson, who wore costumes, played jazz music, and hired Hollywood special effects guys for her "illustrated sermons."

Given all this activity, Los Angeles grew into a kind of theme park of the soul, a carnival of transcendence offering esoteric sources of entertainment, transport, and commodified wonder. Understandably, many of us react to this spectacle with mockery or befuddlement, sometimes leavened with pity for the poor dupes who get taken in. The metaphor of Oz lies heavy over California (L. Frank Baum wrote nearly all of the Oz books while living in the state), and its pop occulture is dense with humbug and hucksters in wizard capes. But cynicism about this scene is the easy road. Such mockery usually comes from secular people—in other words, from people who believe that religion is just a cultural invention. But if this is the case, why not appreciate and enjoy the creativity? By recognizing religion as at least partly a cultural creation, we can appreciate how, in a rootless place like Los Angeles, this creativity can and does run riot, generating novel and mutant forms for ever more deracinated souls. In its own plastic, Hollywood-backlot way, sacred LA came to resemble ancient Alexandria or modern India. Different times and places smashed into one another in a restless quest for the beyond. Syncretism reigned: esoteric notions and symbols mingled and mixed; forms of practice were nailed together as quickly as they imploded. By the time the counterculture arose, everything had become a potential source of mystic lore and spiritual intensity: surfing and comic books, sadomasochism and pharmacology, electric guitars and military research.

There is a gnawing absurdity at the heart of this mystic carnival, this tacky tinseltown of snake-oil simulacra. At its most extreme, LA's restless sacred imagination grows violent and apocalyptic; at its most banal it becomes the spiritual supermarket, a California condition of mix-and-match cafeteria religion that has now gone global. But even the spiritual supermarket, with its Sufi audio books, Tibetan trinkets, and pre-packaged ayahuasca vacations, has a truth to tell. The truth is that the universe is pluralistic, down to its very marrow. There are many ways to God, and some of them dodge the Big Guy altogether. My way is not your way, and my way will probably change as my perspective, and the self that holds that perspective, changes.

In contrast with the absolute claims of traditional monotheism, a creative spiritual life is fundamentally relativistic. This does not mean that it denies the Beyond, only that it distrusts the packaging we give it. Whatever essential truths it seeks, such a life demands that we shift artfully between different forms, adopting multiple perspectives on a reality that remains an essential mystery. One is called upon to shake up the usual binary distinctions, like sacred and profane, trash and treasure, commerce and consciousness. Perhaps the spiritual culture that emerges from such a shake-up is, in the open-source software guru Eric Raymond's terms, not a cathedral but a bazaar. In any case, by the middle of the century, California's pop occulture was a popular market dominated by fragments, fusions, exotica, invention, and juxtaposition—a bazaar of the bizarre. But this garish and sometimes exploitative scene also suggested a more subtle lesson: that a conscious spiritual affirmation of relativism gifts us with creative uncertainty and an openness to ordinary things that can become, in the right hands, simply extraordinary.

IMAGES JUXTAPOSED

California's heterodox market of "transcendent commodities" helps explain why the best postwar California art of the 1950s and '60s was so overtly concerned with spirituality. Here I want to dodge the well-trampled territory of Beat mysticism and ramble around the formal territory of juxtaposition, particularly as it was manifested in assemblage, collage, and other appropriation-based arts and practices. Though rooted in any number of popular and folk practices, assemblage and collage represent distinctly modern artistic strategies that reflect the twentieth-century experience of a cultural landscape densely cluttered with signs, commodities, and urban detritus. Juxtaposition was important to Surrealist Europeans like Max Ernst and New Yorkers like Joseph Cornell, but, for a variety of reasons, it also flourished in the postwar West. As Peter Plagens noted in his book *Sunshine Muse*, "Assemblage [with its essential logic of juxtaposition] is the first home-grown California modern art." Simon Rodia's cathedral-like Watts Towers, constructed out of broken pottery, chicken wire, and the fragmentary flotsam of consumer culture, prophetically foreshadow a number of postwar artists—like Jess Collins, Bruce Conner, Larry Jordan, George Herms, Wallace Berman, and Helen Adam—who appropriated and recombined images, styles, and materials in a variety of media.

If West Coast spiritual bricoleurs had a guru, that person would have to be Wallace Berman, a quiet but powerfully influential *mensch* whose work and life seemed to achieve the Beat blend of sacred and quotidian. Though he crafted some remarkable work, particularly a series of collages made with an old Verifax machine, Berman was less a formal trailblazer than a germinator of scenes and styles, a diffuse presence who influenced his peers with an underground Beat sensibility both hip and human. Berman was a disseminator. In a brief cameo appearance in his friend Dennis Hopper's film *Easy Rider*, he plays a sower of seeds.

Berman grew up a secular Jew in the Boyle Heights and Fairfax districts of Los Angeles. Hebrew letters were scattered throughout his environment, on newspapers and in butcher shop windows. Later this alphabet became his signature sign, especially the letter aleph, which he painted on his motorcycle helmet. In the 1950s, Berman created faux-Dead Sea Scrolls parchments using the alphabet, and placed the letters in assemblages; later he would paint them on rocks. But these letters never formed actual words; they remained conventionally meaningless, at once surface decorations and hieroglyphs too deep for common sense. If you want to, you can go Kabbalistic on all this, though Berman himself was typically uncommunicative about his intent. During one early show of his parchment paintings, Berman told the actor Dean Stockwell about the work's Kabbalistic dimensions; to the poet Philip Lamantia, who, unlike Stockwell, actually knew something about Jewish mysticism, he denied any connection.

In Kabbalah, language is not seen as a human filter that we overlay onto some more primordial reality; instead it is that reality. There are many visions of this original Torah, and a few of them anticipate Berman's linguistic assemblages. One eighteenth-century rabbi from Syria claims that, before creation, the original Torah was "a heap of unarranged primal letters." In response to Adam's actions, this original alphabet formed the particular words that made the world the way it is today. But it does not have to be this way; some Kabbalists suggest that the messianic world will come about through a renaming. Berman's "meaningless" combinations are in a sense a kind of sacred "cut-up." Though he ignored the divinatory and synchronistic potential of the cut-up that so compelled Brion Gysin and William Burroughs, Berman does gesture towards the redemptive potential of hermetic nonsense. His letters are playful but profound mysteries—an attempt to invoke the creative plenitude of language as if it were the jazz scat singing that Berman imbibed as a zoot suit-wearing hepcat in LA's 1940s jazz scene.

David Meltzer, the West Coast Beat poet and sometime Kabbalist, approaches Berman's mysticism in a less literalistic way. Meltzer explains that his friend was acutely "aware of an unarticulated imperative to sacralize and somehow repair the broken post-war world." He compares the operation to *tikkun,* the notion, drawn from Isaac Luria's messianic Kabbalism, that humans must put back the fragmented pieces of creation. For many twentieth-century mystics, this sort of labor is placed under the goals of unity and wholeness—noble goals that don't often make great art. More subtly, Meltzer compares the work of *tikkun* to the hipster trick of "digging" something, which he characterizes as "appropriating the most mundane object, the most vilified or rejected artifact, and restoring it to a primary glory." Meltzer describes in loving detail the marvelous bric-a-brac found at Berman's home; many of us have experienced "bohemian" spaces whose poverty is redeemed by strange and gentle shrines constructed from marvelous ground scores or thrift-store finds. Once these objects have reached the end of their life cycle as commodities, another kind of life is possible, the life of sacred appropriation. Explains Meltzer: "It was a hybrid kind of anti-materialism or counter-materialism, privileging the continuously-new beauty of a particular stone or a time-deformed mass-produced object found in the gutter in the same way it embraced Cocteau's *Orphée* or Vivaldi."

Berman actually made only a few assemblages during the 1950s, and many of those are sculptures or installations. However you pigeonhole them, his most important mixed media show took place at the Ferus Gallery in 1957. His religious concerns were palpable. *Temple* resembled a large wooden sentry box or confessional. Inside, a robed figure stood with a key hung from its neck, its head turned away from the audience. The floor beneath the figure was strewn with pages of *Semina*, a collage-like "magazine" of images and poems by friends and heroes that Berman sent for free to his circle of compatriots through the early 1970s. Though it came in different forms, *Semina* was essentially a folder of loose paper that had to be arranged, Tarot-like, by the reader; Michael McClure, whose "Peyote Poem" debuted in *Semina 3*, called it a "scrapbook of the spirit."

Panel was a much denser piece than *Temple*: a mysterious wooden cabinet that incorporated photos of his wife, hidden compartments, mirrors, letters, and a long narrow image of swimmers surfacing into the light. There was a hushed mystery to the piece, at once a wrestling and an opening. *Cross* featured a slender wooden cross; from its left arm dangled a small shadow box that included a mandala-like photo of a cock plunging into a cunt above the inscribed motto *factum fidei* (true facts). As Rebecca Solnit points out, in the hypermodernist American art world of the mid-1950s, such hieratic objects—which "pointed at something beyond themselves and drew their meaning from that beyond"—had the force of blasphemy.

Local law enforcement also found them blasphemous. Summoned to the gallery because of *Cross*'s photo, they ironically overlooked the graphic shot, but busted Berman for an sketch included in the *Semina* issue scattered on the floor: a lusty, almost Frazetta-esque fantasy of a demon taking a woman from behind. The item was drawn by Marjorie Cameron, Berman's most direct connection to LA's occult underground and a woman whose full story remains to be told. The red-headed artist, scenester, and occultist had been married to Jack Parsons, the

Jet Propulsion Labs rocketman who led the Pasadena Agape Lodge of Aleister Crowley's Ordo Templi Orientis and took the Beast's sex magick perhaps even more seriously than Crowley himself. Cameron served as Parsons's muse during the latter part of his apocalyptic "Babalon Working." Following Parsons's mysterious death in 1952 (he exploded in his garage lab), Cameron became LA's pre-eminent bohemian witch, making talismanic art pieces, upstaging Anaïs Nin as the Whore of Babylon in Kenneth Anger's 1954 film *Inauguration of the Pleasure Dome,* and even frightening Dennis Hopper. She also clued Berman's scene into the power of magick (which, as Anger's film suggests, is itself all about acute psychic montage). George Herms, whose assemblages would outpace Berman's tiny output in both formal power and enigmatic fire, said that Cameron "molded and formed me."

Berman's Ferus installation was a pretty hermetic deal; you get the sense that you kinda had to be there, maybe be part of the scene to really get it. But in the early 1960s Berman began to work on his most accessible and compelling works, a series of collages that seemed to tune directly into the collective mind. Using an obsolete Verifax photocopier, which used negatives and treated paper, Berman made a series of pieces that channeled the overwhelming spew of images, ads, and information that came to define the '60s mediascape. Each image contains single or multiple repetitions of the same visual placeholder: a hand holding a small AM/FM transistor radio. Within the "frame" of the radio, Berman placed an enormous range of images, including magic mushrooms, cheetahs, astronauts, hermetic glyphs, naked ladies, pot leaves, Buddhas, airplanes, Indian chiefs, popes, starbursts, movie stars, dolls, and clocks. Originally Berman used a TV set for the frame, but the transistor radio fused speech and image into a deeper alchemy that Christopher Knight called a visual chant. The resulting collages suggested that the emerging global mind, for all its image storms, had the magical intimacy that McLuhan dubbed acoustic space.

Berman's Verifax collages had a modest influence on the art world, earning Berman a spot in the gallery of oddballs that Peter Blake created for the cover of *Sgt. Pepper's Lonely Hearts Club Band.* Berman's repeating figure and appropriated images also clearly anticipate Pop Art's later obsession with mechanical reproduction and commodity images. But as with other California artists, Berman's relationship to the signs on the street carries a more esoteric intensity and fragile sense of yearning than the self-conscious impersonality of Warhol, Lichtenstein, or Rauschenberg. Part of this difference is environmental; New York was at the heart of the secular world of media, whereas California's strong media culture, however dominated by the culture industry, has always radiated an air of fantasy and transcendence, however garish. But much more important is the lived context within which Berman and his fellow friends and artists worked: a life authentically rooted in the noncommercial margins of bohemia, a magic circle of art and fellowship and esoteric romanticism that transmuted the objects and images it embraced.

TRANSLATIONS

Berman was by no means the only spiritual bricoleur on the West Coast. The godfather of California collage was Jess Collins, who went by the artist name Jess. Abandoning his career in atomic chemistry in the late '40s, Jess pursued abstract expressionist painting at the California School of Fine Arts until he gave himself over to making "Paste-Ups" out of pop ephemera. 1954's *Goddess Because Is Is Falling Asleep*—whose regal central figure sprouts a huge foot beside a lobster bouquet surrounded by text like "Of Nature and Art and a Puppy Pilgrimage"—is halfway between Max Ernst and Terry Gilliam. At the time Jess also made seven Dick Tracy comic-strip collages called *Tricky Cad*; by placing odd text in the dialogue balloons and mocking the authoritarian slant of a comic he had loved as a kid, Jess anticipated not only the Situationist *detournement* of comic strips but the vital postwar strategy of scrambling high and low art.

By the 1960s, Jess's earlier, more satiric and disjointed Paste-Ups had evolved into fantastic landscapes assembled from hundreds of puzzle-like fragments. Dense and fluid, and with an architectural sensibility lacking in many later pothead collages of this type, these worlds are chock full of visual puns, curious correspondences, and shining denizens of the archetypal otherworld. Even in reproductions, which make large-scale collages look flat and busy, Jess's work still radiates an intense, hallucinogenic suggestibility. Many, like his incomplete Tarot series, directly engage esoteric themes; others pursue a hermetic homoeroticism that reaches its apex in his late work *Narkissos*. In light of later hippie excesses, such esoteric subjects may seem banal, but in the late 1950s the material had not yet gone the way of mystical kitsch. Jess engaged the mysteries with a romantic intelligence both modern and anti-modern. On the one hand, he was an appropriation artist celebrating the possibilities that arise when art world hierarchies are inverted and fragments torn from the passing surfaces of modern life are slammed together. At the same time, these possibilities also suggest the old romantic heresies of magick and transcendence: faced with a jumble of resonant and juxtaposed images, our minds inevitably start playing the game of analogies and correspondences. As we connect fragments into hidden networks, the logic of those connections becomes dreamlike, even erotic. Such subconscious montage, which is what authentic magick entails, was well known to the Surrealists, but by using appropriated materials, Jess moves even closer to a direct enchantment of the ordinary fragmentary world.

For all their immersive intensity, many of Jess's collages are marred by the giddiness inherent in such dense and richly colored overlays, and they largely lack the clarity and power of his Translations. This series of oil paintings, which he began in 1959, are based directly on images Jess would lift from old yearbooks, alchemical tomes, bubblegum cards, or moldy stacks of *Scientific American*. Strictly adhering to the outlines (though not the colors) of the original images, the Translations gesture towards Warhol's later by-the-numbers paintings. Though they are tinged with a similarly tart sense of belated irony, the Translations more closely resemble the internal theater of creative memory, which remakes—or translates—random but resonant snapshots of the world into internal phantasmagoria. When Jess reproduced the Translations in books, he paired them with texts from sources as wide-ranging as Plotinus, the Popul Vuh, and the American John Uri Lloyd's 1895 proto-psychedelic fantasy *Etidorpha*. Oftentimes these parings juxtapose modern and mythic, as when a somewhat bilious image of a nineteenth-century grinding machine is paired with a scene from Celtic lore where the hero Fionn mac Cumhal asks the druid Finnegas for the craft of poetry. These pairings deepen the question of what, exactly, is being translated: is it the images, the words, or some more ineffable spirit behind such markers and correspondences? What fuses fragments when they remain, for all intents and purposes, fragments?

Like the Paste-Ups and his later Salvages (thrift-store canvases reworked on the easel), Jess's work relies on his own resonance with largely marginalized pre-existing images. "I salvage loved images that for some reason have been discarded and I come across them. I've, at times, found wonderful things on the street, just thrown away. If you find something that you really respond to that someone else has thrown away, it's a kind of mini-salvation." This is the alchemy of trash. Though recognizing his high-art predecessors (the Translations quote Kandinsky and Gertrude Stein, and Surrealism looms large), Jess also tipped his hat to the popular and folklorish dimension of the art of appropriation—an affirmation of premodern sources that set the West Coast apart from Europe and New York. When discussing influences, Jess would place San Francisco's Playland-by-the-Beach and John Neill's Oz illustrations alongside Ernst and Gaudí. Today this kind of hip populism is tediously de rigueur ("Margaret Keane and Esquivel are geniuses!"); in the 1950s, before the self-conscious ironies of Pop, it was scandalous, visionary, romantic, and, perhaps most importantly, rooted in the ordinary truth of modern experience. Jess, who grew up in LA, talked about visiting old mining towns in the Mojave Desert with his dad. The fabled prospector Old Sourdough was still alive, and Jess remembers the slapdash collage of calendars, posters, and ads that graced one of his ramshackle cabins: "a little palace assembled from scrap wood, pieces of aluminum, junk, tins, almost any type of found object you can imagine."

Jess was no gutter artist, though, and his most profound work of mythopoetic collage achieves a high tone of lyrical and philosophical intensity. *Narkissos* is an immense Paste-Up assembled from hand-drawn copies that Jess made, in pencil, of bits and pieces he had cataloged over the decades. Based on a sketch first made in 1959, *Narkissos* stands almost six feet tall and took Jess over twenty years of obsessive work to complete (and then only after he gave up the plan to execute a mirror image of the work in oils). *Narkissos* is a masterpiece, perhaps the single greatest work of collage by an American, and, for my money, the high peak of spiritual plastic art in California. It is a dark and playful palimpsest of fairy tales, homo-eroticism, and heavy gnostic truths, a hall of hieroglyphic mirrors that reflects on the myth of Narcissus until the reflections—and the desires that motivate them—melt into the empyrean. *Narkissos* drips with allusions, inside jokes, puns, and echoes (including Echo). The figure of Pan, for example, is a composite figure drawn from a Panamanian flute player. Similar, if less corny, gotchas await those who contemplate the woman on the tricycle, or the ergot of rye that lies near the pool, or the figure of Eros himself, which Jess assembled from a Hellenist bronze, a hunk from *The Young Physique*, and a trippy design from the Post-Impressionist painter Charles Filiger.

Behind all this archetypal ping-pong lies the mystical real deal: an elusive and many-layered invocation of the romantic imagination based on Jess's deep study of the hermetic, Neoplatonic and Romantic transformation of Ovid's classic telling of the Narcissus myth. Of course, Jess doesn't hand you such meanings on a platter, and not just because he wants you to do your own conceptual and spiritual work to make the meanings real. In Jess's romantic conception, meaning itself is infinite, not in the endlessly deferred sense of the deconstructionists, but in the excessive, almost carnivalesque sense of dream's endless labyrinth. But even as Jess's esoteric reading resonates in the primal Platonic cave of myth-making and desire, its echoes can also be heard in the clamorous din of commercial culture. *Metropolis* and a Maurice Sendak frog both make an appearance in the work, and the figure of Narcissus prominently clutches a strip of *Krazy Kat* panels (whose creator, the brilliant George Herriman, lived and worked in Los Angeles). Myth-time is always ready to burst through modern time, or even the personal mythology of the individual, countercultural artist. In other words, if Jess's romance is true, then the forces he evokes are much larger than the individual artist:

the imagination we discover working in this hermetic cartoon does not, as he once said, "stop where my imagination leaves off."

As with Berman, Jess wove together his work and his life. And that life in turn was thoroughly intertwined with the life of poet Robert Duncan, whom he first met in 1951. A Bay Area denizen whose poetic voice matured in the 1950s and '60s, Duncan's standing among popular readers of poetry has suffered unfairly from the fact that, while he wrote some of the most spiritually intriguing poetry in postwar America, he was not a Beat. It also can be difficult stuff. As a poet, Duncan was more an heir of H.D. and Mallarmé than of Whitman or William Carlos Williams, and, though he shared the romanticism of figures like Ginsberg and Snyder, his tastes and sensibility were almost anachronistic. The mountain-man populism and loud-mouthed, self-promoting sass of so much Beat poetry, which for all its marvels is largely to blame for horrors like the 1990s poetry slam scene, was alien to Duncan, who was deeply versed in hermeticism, mythology, and gnostic literature. Like Yeats, he was beholden to a high and esoteric romanticism, but a romanticism whose spectral beams he redirected through a postwar filter of Freudian self-consciousness, social fragmentation, and an acute awareness of the violent contradictions of eros and the mercurial inconsistency of the psyche.

RISKING HEIGHT

Commentators often explain the Beat celebration of drugs, mysticism, and Zen as merely a bohemian resistance to the mundane values forced upon them by their upbringing. This pat reading, which tends to reduce transcendence to rebellion and the spiritual to "culture," does not work with Duncan, whose adoptive parents were bourgeois occultists—members of a small Bay Area hermetic brotherhood that had spun off from Britain's proto-Theosophical Hermetic Brotherhood of Luxor. Duncan's parents picked their baby based on his astrological chart, which suggested to them that his last incarnation occurred during the fading days of Atlantis. As a boy, Duncan had a recurrent apocalyptic dream that he came to believe was a memory of Atlantis; this dream later formed the psychic seed of one of his most famous poems, "Often I Am Permitted To Return to a Meadow."

Though a lifelong acolyte of the romantic imagination, Duncan was never a true believer, nor did he become a public mystic like Ginsberg or Gary Snyder. But though his appreciation for the occult was in a large part aesthetic—one senses that he loved Hermes Trismegistus the way he loved *Tic Toc of Oz*—he intimately understood that esoterica was, in essence, a spiritual assemblage. Syncretism was the name of the game. Duncan was fascinated, for example, by the core Theosophical texts of Madame Blavatsky, *Isis Unveiled* and *The Secret Doctrine*, both of which are frothing stews of astrology, alchemy, numerology, neo-Platonism, Buddhism, Kabbalah, and Vedic systems. Duncan called them "midden heaps where, beyond the dictates of reason, as in the collagist's art, from what has been disregarded or fallen into disregard, genres are mixed, exchanges are made, mutations begun from scraps and excerpts from different pictures . . . to form the figures of a new composition." While he did not believe Blavatsky's mystic claims, he still bought her basic line. As Duncan put it in his amazing unpublished *H.D. Book*: "until man lives once more in these awes and consecrations, these obediences to what he does not know but feels, until he takes new thought in what he has discarded, he will not understand what he is."

Duncan tried to live and write his life in obedience to these "awes and consecrations," those transpersonal forces that surround and in some sense compose the self. Rather than "express himself," like the heroic Beat soul, Duncan took the passive part, opening his soul to influences incoming from literature, dream, painting, the newspaper, the gods, and the spontaneity of language itself. Poetry was the "opening of a field" where such forces would meet, combine, and clash; as the poet, he was as interested as anyone to see how it all came out. Of course, there is an oracular dimension to all this. Duncan did not revise his poetry much, and his great "Medieval Scenes" were essentially channeled in a Surrealist fashion later greatly elaborated by Duncan's friend and rival Jack Spicer.

On a more intimate level, this field is a frame of spiritual collage.

Duncan's relationship to the forces of the psyche was essentially that of an appropriation artist who, as Jess once described it, allows found images to find him. On a broader level, Duncan believed his writing was part of a "grand collage" of aesthetic and imaginative life, a belief reflected not only in the numerous citations he weaves into his verse, but also in his poetry's almost Borgesian ambiance of allusion, reference, and bibliomania. His long series of "Passages" poems cite Emperor Julian and Ezra Pound, and occasionally simply list cool books like *The Aurora, The Secret Book of the Egyptian Gnostics,* and *The Princess and the Goblin.* "Apprehensions," perhaps his single most haunting and convulsive work, weaves quotations from Marcilio Ficino and Bruno of Nola into a poem that reads like the tendrils of a fast-fading revelation tickling you from the far sides of dream.

Duncan's citations and allusions are hardly bubblegum cards found at the side of the road, but his work is still an extension of the Californian alchemy of trash—the "midden heaps" of its pop occulture, the ugly bric-a-brac of a mercantile frontier awaiting transformation. In "Nel Mezzo Del Cammin Di Nostra Vita," written in 1959, Duncan reflects on this alchemy in his praise of the Watts Towers, built in the flats southeast of downtown Los Angeles by the untrained Italian tilesetter Simon Rodia:

scavenged
from the city dump, from sea-wrack,
taller than the Holy Roman Catholic church
steeples, and, moreover,
inspired; built up from bits of beauty
sorted out—thirty-three years of it—
the great mitred structure rising
out of squalid suburbs where the
mind is beaten back to the traffic, ground
down to the drugstore, the mean regular houses
straggling out of downtown sections
of imagination defeated.

Nothing shocking here: these are good old twentieth-century bohemian values. Duncan praises the outsider artist, who goes against the grain, risks height, ignores dogma. This is all part of our alternative myth these days, but it remains to be seen whether the margins still exist—culturally, economically, spiritually—that could allow such creative feats to flourish. Juxtaposition has become an advertiser's art. Trash is not the same thing today, in our belated self-conscious world of thrift-store savvy, mediated hipster rebellion, and omnivorous collector mania. Before you know it, it's on eBay. Many of us still hear the spiritual call of redemptive refuse, of glimmers, junk, and "bits of beauty." But it remains to be seen whether we can join the ranks of those who, in Ginsberg's howling words, "dreamt and made incarnate gaps in Time & Space through images juxtaposed . . ."

2005

JACK SPICER'S GHOSTS

In the summer of 1965, the poet Robin Blaser discovered his friend Jack Spicer lying comatose in the poverty ward at San Francisco General. The forty-year-old Spicer had passed out drunk in the elevator of his North Beach flat a few days before and was wheeled in, without ID, in a torn and befouled suit. When an attending doctor suggested to Blaser that Spicer was just your typical middle-aged alcoholic, Blaser grabbed the fellow's shirt: "You're talking about a major poet!" This was as true then as it is now. But in that moment, Spicer was also a dying poet. After days of fever and mumbling, he managed to shape what would be, more or less, his last coherent sentence: "My vocabulary did this to me."

These final words serve as an apt title for Peter Gizzi and Kevin Killian's 2008 Spicer collection, *my vocabulary did this to me*, the first thorough gathering of the poet's extraordinary and challenging writing to appear since the '70s. The phrase itself could be a line from one of his mature poems: matter-of-fact and bleakly funny, like the recoil from some inconclusive blow in a verbal joust. A similar voice closes one of Spicer's best-known poems, an invocation of the ocean that crowns the late sequence "Thing Language":

Aimlessly
It pounds the shore. White and aimless signals. No
One listens to poetry.

Spicer wrote from that pounded shore, a site as geographic as it was Orphic. Born in Los Angeles to midwestern stock, Spicer was a fiercely regional writer, a proud habitué of Berkeley and North Beach who hated New York and loved loved loved the San Francisco Giants. With Blaser and Robert Duncan, two other homosexual poets he met at UC Berkeley in the late '40s, Spicer helped establish one of the most thriving communities within the motley fabric of the San Francisco Renaissance. In bars and in his beloved Aquatic Park, Spicer actively (and fractiously) cultivated a highly social circle of poets and artists and influenced writers like Jack Gilbert and Richard Brautigan, who dedicated *Trout Fishing in America* to him. Spicer was so committed to the local that he insisted on limiting the distribution of his publications to the Bay Area, as if poetry were a kind of community-supported agriculture. (He also, presciently, refused copyright.) But though he cofounded the "6" Gallery, the site of Allen Ginsberg's legendary howl, Spicer was no Beat—he disliked pot, thought Zen was stupid, and made fun of Lawrence Ferlinghetti. "Be bop de beep / They are asleep," he wrote in 1960.

The young Spicer proclaimed that he wanted to write a poem "as long as California," but the state he rendered into verse was more than a place of fogs and cliffs or even "The sea- / Coast of Bohemia." California's geography also staged a liminal poetics, what Robinson Jeffers—the brooding and misanthropic poet of isolated Carmel, whom Spicer very much admired—called "the verge extreme." Spicer stalked that verge, loosing the discourses that bind the self. Though his early lyrics are well wrought and often disarmingly beautiful, his mature writing is a vexed threshold of sense and nonsense, a jagged, pun-strewn, and sometimes harrowing crossroads of romance and straight talk, machines and the voices of the dead. "Fifteen False Propositions Against God," written in 1958, contains a striking example of Spicer's skittering play of interruptions and arresting images:

> Beauty is so rare a th—
> Sing a new song
> Real
> Music
> A busted flush. A pain in the eyebrows. A
> Visiting card.

Poetry with such cross talk asks a lot of the reader, of course, and Spicer—who dismissed poems that easily please their audience as "whorish"—is a notoriously tough nut to crack. Much of this difficulty is both explained and illuminated by his peculiar poetics. Unlike his Beat peers, Spicer did not believe that poetry should be the expression of an inspired and uncorked self. Instead, he reduced the poet's work to an almost mechanical act of listening to and receiving what Spicer called *the Outside*—an almost Lovecraftian field of forces that invade rather than inspire, and before which the poet is little more than a secretary taking dictation. In a fascinating series of lectures that he gave in Vancouver shortly before his death, Spicer explains that the poet's task is to get himself—his loves, his plots, his beloved meanings—out of the picture, so that what he only half-humorously calls "spooks" or "Martians" can enter. The content of the poet's mind, his memories, lore, and language, is just "furniture" that the Outside arranges into a poem, a process that Spicer compares to a Martian arranging a kid's alphabet blocks to form a message.

Spicer's concept of poetic dictation, not to mention the word puzzles it catalyzed, owes a great deal to the poet's formal training and occasional research in pre-Chomskyan linguistics. At the same time, the Vancouver lectures make clear that Spicer approached poetry as an effectively spiritual practice, one that demanded both an ascetic erasure of the personal and a practical engagement with the tradition of spiritualist poetics. Spicer begins his first lecture with a description of the spirits that, in addition to inspiring W. B. Yeats's *A Vision*, brought the aging Yeats "metaphors for [his] poetry." Tellingly, Spicer places Yeats and his wife, George Hyde-Lees, on a train from San Bernardino to Los Angeles when she first establishes contact with the spirits through automatic writing. Spicer is probably bullshitting here—there is no evidence for the claim—but his desire to establish a West Coast tradition of oracular aesthetics is palpable.

Spicer's own initiation into occult poetics occurred when he met Duncan at Berkeley in 1946, a year Spicer once proclaimed as that of his real birth. A native Californian whose adoptive parents belonged to a Theosophical order, the older Duncan introduced Spicer to a nuanced but overtly magical approach to poetry—a literate and deeply aesthetic hermeticism that also cast a glamorous light on the gay demimonde that surrounded Duncan and drew the awkward Spicer out of his shell. Along with Blaser and others, the young men experimented with parlor games, spiritual dictation, and bibliomancy, and began developing the sort of esoteric poetics that Charles Olson later attacked, in his essay "Against Wisdom as Such," as an "école des Sages ou Mages as ominous as Ojai." But though Spicer later taught a workshop at San Francisco State called "Poetry as Magic," he never confidently embodied the magus the way Duncan did. Linguistically sophisticated, a lover of puzzles, Spicer was content to treat the occult as another game, a contest of signs playing hide-and-seek with meaning. What seemed most important for Spicer was the practice of dictation itself, a practice that demanded a dismantling of what he called "the big lie of the personal." In his Vancouver lectures, Spicer describes taking hour after agonizing hour to clear out his mind enough for a handful of truly dictated lines to appear.

Does Spicer's spectral poetics represent a last-gasp Romanticism or postmodernism's last-ditch turn towards "the abject" and the materiality of language? This fluctuation is fundamental to his poetry and accounts for much of its relevance and power. On the one hand, the muse of Tradition has been body-snatched by one of William Burroughs's alien viruses, whose codes and messages, Spicer insists, are not necessarily right or wise or beautiful. But behind this science-fictional frame—rooted in part in Spicer's love of *Astounding Stories* and pulp writers like Alfred Bester—is a more traditionally Orphic stance, which finds the poet cocking his ear to the ocean beyond and transmitting its white noise and ghostly signals into the tangles of our fixed tongue. One of Spicer's favorite images for this process is, in fact, the car radio in Cocteau's film *Orpheus*, which broadcasts verses from a deceased poet—verses that the handsome Orpheus transcribes obsessively.

This circuit of parasitic haunting also forms the framework for Spicer's 1957 breakthrough, *After Lorca*, a collection of purported translations of the Spanish poet. The book opens with an introduction from the dead Lorca, who complains, justifiably, that Spicer has taken undue liberties with the translations that follow, and that some poems are not his—Lorca's—at all. Not only do Spicer's translations interrogate originality, they recast the poem as a kind of time machine, or what he elsewhere calls a "machine to catch ghosts." Most of these ghosts are other poets throughout time, "patiently telling the same story, writing the same poem." But one of these captured specters, it begins to dawn on the reader, is none other than you yourself—you and the voice now in your head, dictating a poem like "Alba":

If your hand had been meaningless
Not a single blade of grass
Would spring from the earth's surface.
Easy to write, to kiss—
No, I said, read your paper.
Be there

Like the earth
When shadow covers the wet grass.

After Lorca was Spicer's first realization of the serial poem, a form he shared with Duncan. Dismissing his earlier, stand-alone writings as "one night stands," Spicer wrote nearly all his mature poems in series. Though he did continue to write and submit single poems for publication until his death, his serial poems were often published, independently, as small books. *The Holy Grail* (1962), which includes seven "books" with seven untitled poems each, is the most balanced and structurally harmonious of these works, even as the clash of its voices, images, and beats creates, as Spicer himself acknowledged, an "uncomfortable music." The sprawling lack of closure inspired by the serial poem also invites us to read *my vocabulary* itself as a serial "book of Jack." For though it is too much to say that there is unity in its diversity, there is, beyond the repeated images and tropes that reward tracking throughout his career (lemons, rope), an essential condition to this work—even if that condition is nothing more than "a simple hole running from one thing to another."

Any attempt to read that hole holistically, however, runs against the heterogeneity of its materials—not just poems but prose fragments, commentaries, a "textbook," and personal letters Spicer presented at readings that blurred public and private. And the poems themselves are patched together from all manner of language: ordinary speech, myth, epistle, foreign language, folk song, list, in-joke, street sign, homily, personal address, journal. Spicer wanted to make poetry a "collage of the real," an ambition that linked him to West Coast visual artists like Bruce Conner, Wallace Berman, and George Herms, bohemian bricoleurs who created their assemblages from junk, pop culture, and oracular fragments. Rather than practicing some version of the cut-up, Spicer achieves a sense of poetic collage through the intense and sometimes claustrophobic material collisions of his language. Blaser noted that while Duncan sits comfortably within an almost regal sense of language as support, Spicer's language is piled up in front of him, like a "cubist painting where you can't get through the fucking frame." Spicer's copious use of puns and syntactic ambiguity returns us to this consternating surface, where slips of the tongue turn poems into Möbius strips of meaning, figure-ground fluctuations over an essential groundlessness. This self-deconstructing passage through sound and sign marks Spicer as a prophetic postmodern and a crucial influence on the Language poets.

At the same time, Spicer never abandoned himself to the linguistic turn that marks postmodernity. On this, the poet is unambiguous: the Outside uses language but is not identified with it. In his 1960 masterpiece, *The Heads of the Town up to the Aether*, Spicer proclaims, "From the top to bottom there is a universe. Extended past what the words mean and below, God damn it, what the words are." Like Wallace Stevens, whose metaphysical telegrams he sometimes echoes, Spicer remains a poet of the real, or at least of the mantic, tricksy zone where poetry touches the real. By staying open to this zone in all its undecidability, Spicer subjected himself to the Outside—an almost penitent supplication that helps explain his sometimes startling "God language." There is, in the poet, a Puritan or even Calvinist strain of deeply American dread:

> Mechanicly we move
> In God's Universe, Unable to do
> Without the grace or hatred of Him.

As the ambiguity of this last line shows—is "of Him" possessive?—Spicer's Christianity is no less riddled than his other language games; his Logos is always condensing into what he called the Lowghost. For all the problems with the term *gnostic*, it remains the best characterization of Spicer's spirituality. He named *The Heads of the Town* after a lost Gnostic text, and the title perfectly suits this tripartite book's etheric fluctuations, its battles between divine and human love, and between the warring poetic agendas of personal gain and impersonal transmission—what Spicer elsewhere distinguished as the difference between "pawnshops and postoffices." The book's third section, "A Textbook of Poetry," is a prose work of immense noetic power, an oblique catechism that bears uncanny fruit under sustained meditation. Spicer considered it one of his greatest feats of dictation.

That said, "No / Gnostrum will cure the ills that are on the face of it." And Spicer saw a vast conspiracy of ills, within poetry and within the world. By 1962's "Golem," he was offering a harrowing view of the economic, political, and linguistic "fix" we're in—a claustrophobic scam, not unlike Burroughs's concept of Control, that insures that transcendence in Spicer is always wily and furtive. In a marvelous letter to James Alexander, a young Hoosier poet who became one of Spicer's most powerful romantic muses, Spicer speaks of the "random places" where "they" will deliver their missives: "A box of shredded wheat, a drunken comment, a big piece of paper, a shadow meaningless except as a threat or a communication, a throat." This is not Ginsberg spotting Whitman in a California supermarket. This is Oedipa Maas wandering San Francisco in Pynchon's *The Crying of Lot 49*, looking for muted post horns.

There is an even stranger synchronicity lurking in Spicer's California mysterium. In 1948, back in Berkeley, he and Duncan roomed briefly with a peculiar young man named Philip K. Dick, who once supplied an LP-recording device for their parlor games of poetic performance. As Killian and Lewis Ellingham point out in their definitive Spicer biography, *Poet Be Like God*, the books of Dick and of Spicer later became mirror images of each other, in theme as well as in imagery—grasshoppers, Martians, radios, salesmen, cities. Like Dick, Spicer was an impoverished and alienated artist for whom writing was, as Darko Suvin famously described the genre of science fiction, a motor of "cognitive estrangement." Both are cult artists who wrote, it can seem, as much for our time as for theirs. Spicer, who worked with computers in the course of his linguistics research, wrote about silicon and punched IBM cards; he cannily foresaw, in 1962, an America ruled by networked computers. This is the America that "drowns itself with machines and weeping," where "Death is not final. Only parking lots." We can still hear Spicer through all his uncomfortable music because he channeled something of our condition: all those angry spirits, this aimless noise.

2009

BEYOND BELIEF

The Cults of Burning Man

> For without corruption, there can no Generation consist.
>
> —*Corpus Hermeticum*
>
> I tell you: one must still have chaos in one, to give birth to a dancing star! —Nietzsche, *Thus Spake Zarathustra*

Black Rock City cliché has it that you can't say anything very penetrating about Burning Man because its diversity and contradictions undermine whatever generalizations you might be tempted to make. This truism is solid enough, and should be mulled over by any Burner foolish enough, like me, to venture into a written analysis of the festival, which takes place every summer in northern Nevada. Yet behind this notion lurks a higher and more important injunction: to keep the event free from the prison of interpretation and explanation, from the insidious net of Meaning. This refusal is prophylactic. By setting their bullshit detectors on high alert, Burners ward off pretension, self-consciousness, and all of the pre-packaged "experiences" that have come to define late-capitalist subjectivity. This tactic also helps sustain the event's tribal vibe. On the playa, we are united in our evasion of significance.

Thus it is with some trepidation that I turn to one of the more vexing questions that you might ask about Burning Man: can or should we speak of the event as a sacred gathering? Even if we acknowledge the vagueness of terms like *sacred*, *spiritual*, and *religious*, it is still safe to say that, from the outside at least, Burning Man comes off as exceptionally profane. Ironic and blasphemous, intoxicated and lewd, Burning Man's ADD theater of the absurd could be said to embody the slap-happy nihilism of postmodern culture itself. Moreover, many Burners would agree with this characterization. According to my own anecdotal inquiries and observations, a good portion of committed attendees would deny that spirituality or sacred emotions have any bearing on their rollicking good times.

In matters of the spirit, however, you cannot always believe what people say. Sometimes you have to look at what they do, and what they do at Burning Man features clear parallels to some mystic fetes of yore. Take the Eleusinian Mysteries, the greatest public cult of ancient Greece. The mysteries took place at harvest time on the outskirts of Athens and continued annually for almost two thousand years. Initiates came from all walks of life, and made their way to Eleusis only after preparing in the city for weeks. The days leading up to the core rite featured torchbearers, pig roasts, and Dionysian pageants. The peak of the festival took place in the secret *telesterion*, where initiates witnessed a "great light."[1] Though we know next to nothing about it, the experience, which some believe was mediated by psychoactive drugs, seemed to provide direct insight into matters of life and death. The similarities between the mysteries and Burning Man are notable, and are certainly not lost on the festival's founder, Larry Harvey. Writing under the pseudonym Darryl Van Rhey in a 1995 issue of *Gnosis* magazine, Harvey noted that, like Burning Man, the mysteries attracted a largely urban and sophisticated crowd. "Intense, ecstatic, and immediate, the rites did not stress doctrinal belief, but valued outward show and inward feeling."[2] Though this historical resonance might sound like wishful thinking on Harvey's part, no less august a figure than Aristotle basically concurred: "that the initiated learned nothing precisely, but that they received impressions and were put into a certain frame of mind."[3]

Even more immediate than such classical resonances, though, are the religious frameworks and sacred symbols that Burners regularly make use of. Whatever their degree of implied irony or seriousness, participants regularly cannibalize Christianity, Satanism, Buddhism, shamanism, Western occultism, Tantra, Judaism, Wicca, and other theme parks of the spirit for their costumes, camps, sculptures, and performances. Since 1994, I have participated in or observed vodoun invocations, Balinese monkey chants, shabbat prayers, Santeria drum circles, sunrise yoga, spiral dances, and group zazen. A friend and I once got shushed for our play-by-play commentary of a ponderous Ordo Templi Orientis Gnostic mass. While some of these appropriations are sarcastic or even blasphemous (especially in the case of Christianity), many are serious attempts to squeeze the juice from more or less traditional rites and images.

But how far does the distinction between serious and sarcastic get us? It's much too literalistic to investigate the spirituality of Burning Man by cataloging its samples of religious traditions or by isolating instances of "authentic" practice. Authenticity, in context, may well be a trap. At its best, Burning Man twists authenticity and irony into a Möbius strip that never lets you know what side you're on but always keeps you going. This productive ambivalence is fundamental to the event's sacred power, a power that derives, paradoxically, from a circular *coniunctio* of sacred and profane. The specifically religious elements of the Burn are important not in themselves, but in relation to one another and to the less ethereal aspects of the festival: the carnality, the trash, the desert dust. This wider field of relations is not holistic but multiple: a promiscuous carnival of souls, a metaphysical flea-market, a demolition derby of reality constructs colliding in a parched void.

So can we say anything meaningful about Burning Man's spirituality? My approach here is to tease out some cultural patterns within the festival—patterns I am calling "cults"—and to hold them up against the history of countercultural spirituality on the West Coast. The essential cult is the Cult of Experience, a cult to which all Burners in some sense belong. I will also talk about the Cult of Intoxicants, the Cult of Juxtapose, the Cult of Flicker, and the Cult of Meaningless Chaos. My list is not at all definitive. Important Black Rock cults, such as the Cult of Flesh and the Cult of Sleeplessness, will have to be treated elsewhere.

Though my comments are rooted in cultural history, I will also draw, inevitably, from my personal experience of the Black Rock gatherings I have attended, not quite continuously, since 1994. By *experience* I don't simply mean my firsthand observations and reflections, but also the moments of cosmic wonder and insight that have occasionally flared up in my nervous system, at times with a disarming incandescence. One particularly vivid moment occurred during the 2002 *Floating World* incarnation of the event. Given the year's aquatic theme, I finally got around to performing a solo shtick I had been planning to do for years, but somehow could never pull off in the face of sloth and distraction. I donned a bathing suit, snorkel, mask and flippers, and plopped down on a touristy Brazilian beach towel at the edge of the playa, near the Esplanade's main drag. I twisted my legs into lotus position and settled down to meditate for forty-five minutes or so.

As a statement, I guess you could say I was performing my response to Freud's dismissal of the mystic's "oceanic" consciousness as an infantile resubmersion into the womb.[4] Whatever. What *really* made the act work were the flippers: huge, yellow duck feet that I picked up at a second-hand sporting-goods store in San Francisco's West Portal neighborhood. Enhancing my already somewhat freakish meditation posture with these Donald Duck jobbies was, simply stated, a hoot—amusing enough, in any case, to wind up featured on a Burning Man web site for a spell. As a bonus, the gag also allowed an internal experiment: what happens when you juxtapose such absurdity with serious meditation?

My snorkel-sit began auspiciously. As soon as I settled into the posture and relaxed my gaze, I inhaled a distant whiff of sage, which grew in strength until I sensed that some unseen person was smudging me with the Native American/New Age power plant. Gradually I opened my mind to the wide space of sounds encircling me. I was not so much listening as generating a diffuse awareness of ambient events knitted together gently into a single acoustic space. Though I was trying to avoid identifying the source of sounds or focusing on particular noises, I soon became aware of a moving cluster of guttural barks and impassioned "Arrgghs." I could not resist categorical identification: *Pirates*. Given the year's theme, I had expected to see many such crews: loud, obnoxious young men walking a dangerous line between honoring the anarchist sodomites of yore and using a tired Hollywood cartoon to float stupid frat-boy antics. But this was my first encounter.

Within moments I heard, or rather sensed, a large animal hurtling my way. In an instant, I was tackled by a pirate. He slapped and rolled me around, slobbered curses down my snorkel, and mimed my decapitation by pressing a red plastic sword against my neck, none too gently sliding it across my Adam's apple. I remained perfectly still throughout this commotion, registering but not reacting to it, and because padmasana is an extremely stable posture, I kept my shape even as I was rolled around in the dust like a human pretzel. After capering around for a minute or so, the pirate politely set me back on my haunches and ran off to enjoy further escapades. I immediately recommitted to the posture and my breath, and sat for another half hour or so.

For all of Burning Man's rhetoric of participation, such spontaneous interminglings of theme are relatively infrequent. One commonly enters into another's "trip," but two trips don't often collide with such intensity, and rarely pass into physical contact without consent. To this day, I blaze with admiration for my pirate's aggressive lack of restraint, his perfectly Zen instinct for the performative possibilities of the moment—possibilities that were not only comic, but cosmic as well. I flashed on the Tibetan practice of *chöd*, wherein the yogi offers his body to bloodthirsty, blade-wielding demons in order to separate himself from self-clinging.

I suspect my pirate had no idea of chöd, nor of the *mahavidya* Chinnamasta, a Tantric goddess pictured with her own decapitated head in her hand, as blood spurts from her neck into her own mouth. But no matter: the fellow had split me open. I was facing the hot sun, and the glow behind my eyelids began to intensify, slowly swallowing me into a sad ecstasy. Inhaling and exhaling the light, I felt my heart open to the massive, glorious pain of all the beings in this world. There I sat, with a serene broken heart, the bands of my Donald Duck flippers cutting into my ankles and my magenta Toys-R-Us face mask slowly filling with tears. Gradually the trance passed. I could hear people stopping to take snapshots, and felt the stirrings of pride. But these feelings and sensations just melted into the red ball of yearning absurdity that the moment had become.

THE CULT OF EXPERIENCE

At the core of Burning Man's spiritual wager is the commanding claim of personal experience. "Beyond belief, beyond the dogmas, creeds, and metaphysical ideas of religion, there is immediate experience," wrote Larry Harvey.[5] Newbies quickly learn that status and fun are not to be gained through familiar modes of consumption or spectatorship. Instead, participation, spontaneity, and immediacy are prized, even (or especially) at the sizable risk of delirium, discomfort, or the sort of excess that your parents might call "making a fool of yourself."

At its most basic level, the cult of experience makes itself known through a continual parade of intense and not-altogether-pleasant physical sensations: the brain-numbing heat and Porta-potty stink, the crusty snot and the dry, cracked feet. These offer continual reminders to you and your body that something is definitely going on here. The cult also manifests itself in the pervasive mode of seduction: the blinky light or exotic body or hilarious performance that seeks to distract you from whatever goal or concept you were riding in order to draw you ever more deeply into the wildfire of energetic activity blazing in the Here and Now. Burning Man represents the ultimate attention economy: what participants exchange are the willingness, and the opportunities, to submit to new experiences. These experiences in turn create stories, which become the coin of the realm, fetishes traded over the fire, always pointing back to the *mysterium tremendum* of consciousness itself.

The cult of experience demands a Sisyphean struggle. Human beings are habit-breeding machines, and no more so than in our patterns of thought, sensation, and perception. Though the Dalai Lama might taste something like "pure experience" on his meditation pillow now and then, humans sink and swim along a rather mindless stream of consciousness choked with slogans, beliefs, recurrent memories, contradictory plans, and perceptual maps. Burning Man stirs all this stuff up. Moreover, as Burning Man ages, its own "immediacy" becomes routinized and codified—an inevitable process, perhaps, though one that has encouraged many old-school Burners to stop attending the festival. Theme camps and spectacles grow familiar, alternative styles of communication and consumption are established, and participants and planners develop systems—psychological and technical—to manage chaos and fear. Even the injunction to "Participate!" becomes rote, and part of the experiential ethos of the festival now includes the active and creative resistance to this creeping process of calcification.

What's important to recognize here is that Burning Man's rhetoric of experience is itself historical, and draws, in particular, from a deep well of American spirituality. The trope of experience already permeated Yankee Christianity by the mid-nineteenth century, when revivalist passions drew whole crowds into powerful fits and faints, visions and revelations. But it was William James who made this subjective turn fundamental to American religious understanding. In his famous tome *The Varieties of Religious Experience*, James argued that experience, rather than belief, was the ground bed of religious life, if not the cornerstone. "The plain truth is that to interpret religion one must in the end look at the immediate content of the religious consciousness."[6] This emphasis on consciousness anticipated the individualistic and subjective turn religion would soon take, a move that implicitly generated interest in mysticism and what have come to be called "altered states of consciousness." James argued that these states had to be taken into account if we were to develop an adequate picture of the universe in its entirety. Forever endearing himself to later psychonauts, James put his own neurons on the line by experimenting with ether, nitrous oxide, and peyote.

By and large, James couched the experiences he described in Christian terms, although he discussed movements, like mind cure and New Thought, that we would now recognize as progenitors of the New Age. But the "cultures of consciousness" that came to define the West Coast's spiritual avant-garde significantly detached altered states from well-defined religious forms. At Beat cafés and Acid Tests, and more formally at retreat centers like Esalen and the Ojai Institute, a variety of "post-religious" experiences began to be explored. Bohemianism has always placed a romantic premium on personal experience, and this romanticism flourished in the counterculture's embrace of primitive exotica and psychedelic Orientalism. But California's scene also reflected the West's pragmatic culture of sensation and know-how, an essentially empirical approach to matters of the spirit that made tools more important than beliefs. Consciousness-altering techniques like meditation, biofeedback, yoga, ritual, isolation tanks, tantric sex, breathwork, martial arts, group dynamics, and drugs were privileged over the claustrophobic structures of authority and belief that seemed to define conventional religion. "Spirituality" emerged as something distinct from religion proper. Even when established traditions like Zen or Sufism were creatively engaged, they were embraced more as practical means for changing consciousness than as arid cosmologies or rules to live by. Experience became the teacher. It's a tricky teacher, of course, and the ephemeral insights and ecstasies of consciousness can easily leave one in deep despair or confusion, high and dry without the raft of creed or belief. Nonetheless, given the sense that an imminent change was coming, either political or spiritual (or both), experience became the central countercultural path toward transformation.

Curiously, this attitude reflected contemporary anthropological concerns with liminality and rites of passage; as cultural anthropologist Victor Turner explained in *The Ritual Process*, the intense, novel, and destabilizing experiences associated with tribal initiations heralded a new mode of social being. Yet because this new context lacked a homogenous cultural matrix in the 1960s and '70s, the field of possibly transformative or meaningful experience was wide open—and certainly not limited to "spirituality." Everything was in potential service to the Happening. Every intense situation or wondrous rush was a potential launching pad of the new—or unraveled—self. This lack of distinction helps explain one of the more curious features of the era's subcultures: the commingling of overt hedonism and spiritual ascesis. Many people would routinely move between these modes—meditating and fasting one week, gobbling drugs and partying the next. Even more potent and characteristic were the "Dionysian" fusions of these two modes into a powerful *spiritual hedonism* that encompassed sacred sex, psychedelic magic, and dizzyingly imaginative gatherings.

Burning Man aggressively extends this tradition of hedonic ecstasy, especially emphasizing its technical or practical underpinnings. Op-

Art visuals, disorienting sonics, and a self-conscious excess of sensory stimulation and conceptual reference all help undermine the stabilized frames of reference that, so the story goes, frustrate our capacity for a fresher taste of the Here and Now. Indeed, the festival can often seem like a single, distributed, full-sensorium brain machine, designed to bring us in tune with our mind's ongoing construction of real-time on the fly.

Burning Man's bawdy blasphemy and hyperactive pace also insulate the festival from the sectarian excesses of California's consciousness culture, which led some spiritual experimentalists into the arms of repressive situations conventionally labeled "cults." It would be silly to insist that there is nothing at all cult-like about Burning Man, either in its organizational structure, its architectonics, or its transformative effects on participants. But it remains an open and rather slapdash cult, one that offers no particularly coherent message or any coercive demands. By multiplying the opportunities for novel perceptions and altered states, but undermining the coherence of individual trips with bacchanalian excess and a strong distaste for sacred cant, Burning Man represents, in comparison with the '60s and '70s spiritual counterculture, a "late" form of the cult of experience, at once an advance and a decline. The event is deeply skeptical about overt claims of power or meaning, but is also optimistic about the regenerative capacities of creative, full-intensity living. Though visibly ridiculous and profane, Burning Man's faith in sensation and the carnival of consciousness is, in the end, almost innocent, even pure.

THE CULT OF INTOXICANTS

One cannot overestimate the role that psychedelics have played over the last fifty years in giving modern spiritual seekers a real kick in the pants. Although avant-garde spirituality has marked the West Coast since the turn of the century, it remained a small and esoteric path until LSD and other drugs offered people a dependable and immediate access to powerful and compulsively intriguing expanded states of consciousness. Burning Man's most relevant psychedelic ancestors remain Ken Kesey and his Merry Pranksters. Profoundly influential throughout the West Coast, the Pranksters' Acid Tests were memorable expressions of the multimedia philosophy of party-as-drug. These improvisatory fetes deployed low-tech media, a ragged burlesque of thrift-store fashions, and the fusion of performance, participation, and prank. Kesey's famous bus, Furthur, is about as Burning Man as the '60s ever got: a gas-guzzling art car driven by a macho meth-head, hurtling down mountainsides with festooned crazies shooting film and barking bull-horn commentary through squealing roof-top speakers.

On the surface, the Pranksters distanced themselves from the explicitly esoteric maps that other psychonauts were using in order to make some sense of psychedelic experience. At Millbrook, the upstate New York mansion that served as the intellectual Mecca of psychedelia in the mid-1960s, Timothy Leary, Richard Alpert (later known as Ram Dass), and others were raiding the vaults of tantra, Vedanta and Tibetan Buddhism in their quest to maximize and comprehend their journeys. The Pranksters avoided such pretense, and their brief visit to Millbrook, as related in Tom Wolfe's classic *The Electric Kool-Aid Acid Test*, was a culture clash. Kesey told Wolfe that, as far as the religious use of LSD goes, "It can be worse to take it as a sacrament."[7] But Wolfe also noticed something deeply religious in the Prankster manner, a religion of unmarked experience that would go, occasionally, by the name of "Now." The Prankster's tomfoolery and systematic evasion of deep meanings were productive attempts to keep the Now fresh, to keep the scene close to the source.

Giving voice to the same hunch that Larry Harvey expressed above, Wolfe speculates that all the great religions begin, not with some conceptual or philosophical breakthrough, but with "an overwhelming *new experience*."[8] This gnostic flash radiates through the concrete lives of a small circle of folks, generally hanging around a charismatic leader who seems to have plugged into the hidden sources of life. To his credit, Kesey more or less dodged such a messianic role. As the "non-navigator," he interacted with his crew obliquely or through cryptic slogans: "See with your ears and hear with your eyes," "You're either on the bus or off the bus." In his role as Mr. Burning Man, Larry Harvey has played an even more humble hand, at least in terms of his quietly intelligent public persona. Though the "inner circle" of Burning Man has its own sectarian qualities, Harvey and crew are betting on an even more democratic model of participation than the Acid Tests: if you get anywhere *near* the bus, if you even see the damn thing glittering in the distance, then you're going to hop on.

One of the reasons so many have hopped on is that, before Burning Man is an art festival or a ritual of radical self-expression, it is a party—an uncorked hoodoo bash. Burning Man organizers ask participants to abide by the same laws that apply in the "real world," yet many disregard this directive. Indeed, indulgence in intoxicants is seen by many to be fundamental to the event's celebratory, neo-anarchist ethics. Though serious overdoses and sociopathic levels of drunkenness are relatively rare, the feral aspect of such voluptuary behavior should not be denied—I vividly recall one snarling female teen who thrust a grubby hand in my face, demanding that I sell her whatever Ecstasy she presumed, without cause, that I was packing. Nonetheless, despite the idiocy and thuggery they can inspire, intoxicants cannot be separated from the sacred potential of consciousness itself. In other words, once one acknowledges the transformative effects of cognitive ecstasy, then drugs are not far behind. Bacchus is a god of wine, Shiva the lord of *bhang*, and Siberian shamans aficionados of *Amanita muscaria*. In its most primary form, religious transcendence may be indistinguishable from psychoactive release.

Fundamentally, Burning Man's cult of intoxicants is a cult of pleasure, with MDMA rivaling alcohol as one of the most popular substances on the playa. Nonetheless, the more turbulent and mind-bending psychedelics remain a supreme sacrament in this particular cult, and they are pleasurable only in a qualified sense of the term. Psychedelics, or entheogens (as they are called when emphasizing their spiritual potential), amplify and transform perceptual processes, jacking consciousness out of its usual ruts and increasing the capacity for wonder and the weird. At higher doses, they seem to catalyze awesome experiences of cosmic fusion, revelation, synchronicity, and demonic paranoia that often seem impossible to process without invoking sacred frameworks, however provisionally.

Today, the question of psychoactive spirituality remains tied up with the problem of authenticity (see "The Paisley Gate" for more discussion of this theme). Shamanic societies the world over grew out of and maintain relationships with "plant teachers" in the context of deeply nuanced and relatively homogeneous world views. Modern consumers, on the other hand, are basically flying blind, whatever their self-styled shamanic beliefs. Despite the mystic insights and magical paradigms they may unveil, entheogens are also, for us, secular and modern: commodity molecules that rather dependably tune the nervous system to particular channels in the spectrum of consciousness. From this perspective, we might say that entheogens can produce *something like* spiritual or visionary experience. We can look at them as reality-modelers with powerful special effects but weak claims on truth. By thereby bracketing the "truth" of the experience, entheogens may paradoxically move spirit beyond the bugaboo of authenticity.

Such strange loops proliferate at the Burn, which few will be shocked to hear represents the bleeding edge of contemporary American psychedelic culture. Though detailed figures are impossible to come by, it seems that a moderately sized but passionate chunk of Burners amplify their playa escapades with compounds such as LSD, DOB, N2O, DXM4-hydroxy-DMT, or 2C-B. But the psychedelic intensity of the Man does not depend on the morphology or even presence of the "alphabetamines" saturating the cranial fluid of its more sophisticated drug users. It lies instead in the qualities of playa experience itself, especially at night, when lights and spaces take on the character of portals that shuttle your nervous system into a spin cycle of possible worlds. Even those hewing the straight edge launch into their evenings like trippers, packing supplies and opening their psychic gates to a diverse but strangely coherent stream of synchronicities, fractured archetypes, visual phantasmagoria, and unsettling transhistorical implications—the bulk of which will not be recalled the next morning. Wandering the playa in any state, one is simply no longer lord of one's house.

In contrast to the self-consciously "spiritual" frameworks that surround, say, the contemporary use of *ayahuasca*, Burning Man's psychedelia is raw, lusty, and chaotic. Its cult of intoxicants does not isolate "good" visionary compounds from party drugs. This resistance to explicitly sacred meta-narratives could well be criticized as a dangerous refusal to inculcate the higher, more integral potential of the entheogens. But I suspect that, as with the cult of experience, this refusal simply reflects Burning Man's spirit of cognitive diversity, one that takes psychedelics not so much seriously as aesthetically. As such, its psychotropic landscape disenchants as much as it enchants, and offers playful tricks and weird science as antidotes to the cosmic revelations that inevitably come. Even here we are reminded that, as Aristotle suggested, there is nothing to *learn* from the mysteries. For though Burning Man celebrates visionary capacity, it does not deny the peculiar and even garish emptiness of drugs. This void may offer the deepest teaching of all: you can't really see the patterns until you embrace the nothingness that they etch.

THE CULT OF FLICKER

In his 1970 media-freak classic, *Expanded Cinema*, the Los Angeles writer Gene Youngblood defined his era as the "Paleocybernetic Age." Pumped up on Marshall McLuhan and the cult of experience, Youngblood sensed a new phase of humanity emerging, one that unleashed the liberating power of archaic consciousness into a technological society whose growing understanding of systems—cognitive, technological, anthropological—was laying the groundwork for radical change. Youngblood saw his Paleocybernetic Age reflected in the media experiments he describes in his book, a catalog of underground cinema breakthroughs leading up to and including light shows, installations, and performances. For Youngblood, expanded cinema meant nothing more or less than expanded consciousness, the drive—spiritual as well as technological—to manifest the spectral machinery of mind in the world before our eyes. This is the cult of flicker.

However you dub the vibe—paleocybernetic, future primitive, or technopagan—West Coast artists have long deployed new visual technologies in the service of trance states far outside (and antecedent to) the official boundaries of modern consciousness. Well before the Prankster Acid Tests and Avalon Ballroom light shows of the '60s, San Francisco was home to a nuanced and esoteric tradition of expanded cinema that included Harry Smith's Bop City jazz projections and the profoundly immersive Vortex Concerts staged by Henry Jacobs and Jordan Belson at the San Francisco Morrison Planetarium in the late 1950s. During these concerts, Belson, who went on to make sublimely cosmic experimental films like *Samadhi* and *Re-entry*, projected largely abstract images through hundreds of projectors, some of which rotated or flickered or zoomed, against the sixty-foot dome of the planetarium. Belson described his Vortex work as "a pure theater appealing directly to the senses."[9]

Less visible (but nonetheless present) during the punk era, this Paleocybernetic vibe again rose to prominence in the early 1990s, when the incoming futurism of global rave culture fused with and rekindled California's penchant for psychedelia. Expanded cinema found its way into the photon jams of local club VJs, especially in the subculture surrounding trance music. (This explicitly psychedelic dance music, characterized by invariant beats and squiggly, heavily flanged melodies, has only recently begun to lose ground as the dominant party genre of Black Rock sound systems.) Although the digital mixtures of abstract graphics and mystic iconography associated with the trance scene rarely rose above candyflipping kitsch, a smaller group of sound-and-video artists continued to push the experimental edge, exploring modular programming tools and complex algorithms to massage and plumb new patterns of hypnotic abstraction.

But the screen only gets you so far. Given the ubiquity of LCDs and cathode ray monitors in our everyday lives, and the impossibly high production values that go into mass consumer simulations like Hollywood movies or Middle Eastern wars, a truly viable cult of flicker must reclaim the visual space outside the box. This is perhaps Burning Man's greatest aesthetic triumph: the creation of an immersive and chaotically collaborative arena of expanded cinema that marries a wide range of visual media, both fancy and crude, with the most powerfully archaic flicker tech of all: fire.

From the burning bush to Viking funerals to the iconography of hell, fire carries an intense symbolic load. But the true greatness of fire lies in the fact that such symbolism is nothing more than cardboard and Kleenex in the face of the blazing thing itself. We are all metaphysical children before arc lights or bonfires or propane explosions, fascinated by fire's all-consuming alchemy of beauty and threat. This fire-lust burns at the core of consciousness itself. Twenty thousand years ago, when the Black Rock Desert was bathing beneath tons of Pleistocene sea, our ancestors had already spent untold generations with fire. Its shadow dance must have formed the visual track to oral tales and goddess knows what manner of ancillary rites. We often hear that modern consumer culture has replaced the hearth with television, but we seldom draw the full implications out of this received notion, which is that *fire was the old ones' TV*. Some of that hypnotic power continues to animate the fire-twirling that remains (despite its formal limitations) Burning Man's signature performance art. For spectators, these highly ritualized performances function as a syncretistic cult of flicker and flesh; for twirlers, they offer an elemental encounter—a dance of power and risk, a mutual seduction, an erotic opportunity to lick and swallow an incorporeal flux that feeds on matter itself.

As the festival's early madness gave way, perhaps inevitably, to the demands of safety, the destructive potential of Big Fire was significantly curtailed. Burning Man's central event has now become a controlled fireworks display far less immersive than the fearsome and toxic rites of earlier years. In the Debordian sense, fire has become increasingly *spectacular* in these latter days of the Burn. For Debord, the spectacle—the totalizing pseudo-world of technical mediations that support the capitalist system—profoundly alienates us from actual life through its endlessly circulating images. Though Burning Man works against this alienation and scrambles its relationship to capital through a gregarious potlatch, the central event of the Burn, whose neon conflagration mingles with a myriad of camera flashes, reminds us that the festival is also shaped by postindustrial circuits of technical mediation. But perhaps Debord's situationist critique cannot really touch Burning Man's Big Fire, because the spectacle of fire itself is so deep and ferocious and old that for a spell its excesses consume all frameworks.

Although Burning Man has gentrified fire, the festival has also intensified the technology of flicker. Though screens are relatively rare in Black Rock City, the nighttime playa-scape has itself evolved into a vast, three-dimensional display of artificial *lumière*. At night we find ourselves navigating through the after-images of a friendly arms race of lighting designers, who continue to push the envelope on relatively new (and increasingly cheap) technology like lasers, electroluminescent wire, LEDs, glow sticks, and computer-controlled strobe lights. Myriad lines, dots, and blinky lights dance before your eyes, many forming specific icons like hearts or Mayan pyramids or mobile jellyfish. Burning Man's lightscape also serves as an open museum of classic visual phantasmagoria, like Brion Gysin's Dreamachine, or the moiré patterns and perceptual tricks of '60s Op Art, or the gothic lightning bolts of the almighty Tesla coil. Even the high beams and sirens of law enforcement vehicles weave themselves into the virtual scene, especially on Sunday night, when a bit of the old-school fire chaos returns. It's bardo time: the street signs are stolen, familiar structures are gone, and you are forced to navigate by nothing more than a hazy constellation of confusing lights, slowly shutting down.

THE CULT OF JUXTAPOSE

Like the institutionalized postmodern art it both imitates and mocks, the aesthetic language of Black Rock City is a language of juxtaposition. A potential effect of all collage and assemblage, the energy of juxtaposition is released especially where heterogeneous elements are yoked together without the intent to smooth out their differences. Juxtaposition is the fundamental strategy of surrealism and its postmodern descendents, which most certainly include Burning Man.

One often hears Burning Man dismissed as a theme park, but what's more important is that it contains thousands of theme parks—a host of pocket universes butting heads. Space-time itself seems to morph into a flea market, a masquerade of memes, or the Mos Eisley spaceport from *Star Wars*. Even though many of Burning Man's camps and costumes are, in themselves, devoted to a particular theme—the bayou, Bedouins, octopi—these elements inevitably crisscross in the turbulent, constantly flowing serendipity of playa life. Here juxtaposition is revealed as the formal playing field of synchronicity, as two apparently unrelated events or elements suddenly form a secret link that strikes, in the mind of the perceiver, an evanescent lightning bolt of meaning. Even lame or boring costumes or vehicles can be redeemed through the chance collaborations that define Black Rock City's densely layered polyurbanism, where synchronicity becomes a basic operation of social and cognitive reality, a kind of "grace" that emerges through clashing fragments.

Juxtaposition is also the chief strategy employed by many art installations, costumes, art cars, and theme camps. As in the case of Arcimboldo's Mannerist paintings, which depict human heads made out of fruits and twigs, many art objects derive their power through the juxtaposition of image and material: Dana Albany's recurrent *Bone Tree*, say, or her 2001 *Body of Knowledge*, a cross-legged man, built from old hardcover books, who bore more than a passing resemblance to Arcimboldo's *Il Bibliotecario*. Other surreal contrasts arise through the placement of objects—huge red fuzzy dice, a bed, a lone piano—against the stark minimalism of the playa itself. Theme camps like Elvis Yoga stitch together elements associated with divergent classes or cultures; costumes are often thrift store patchworks featuring bold clashes of color, material, and evocations of forgotten subcultures.

These different modes of juxtaposition generate many of the well-loved effects of the festival: absurdity, instability, irony. But they particularly inform the festival's treatment of spiritual and religious forces. In this context, juxtaposition allows people to invoke sacred forces while sidestepping issues of belief, or seriousness, or responsibility. I can think of four recent examples here. For his recurrent center camp piece *Twinkie Henge*, Dennis Hinkamp used the perennial Hostess treats to construct a small-scale version of the famous megalithic monument. In 2002, the esplanade was blessed with a huge seated Ronald McDonald, a golden inflatable who sported a Nepalese third eye and smiled beatifically onto the crowds. And since 1998, Finley Fryer has occasionally presented an incandescent chapel built of nothing but recycled plastic. And in 2000, David Best began a series of enchanting and celebrated Temples that came to demarcate the most authentically reverent spaces on the playa; with the exception of 2003's paper mosaic Mughal confection, he conjured the exotic filigree of these structures from the pressed-wood scraps left over from the manufacture of kids' dinosaur puzzles.

The apparent irony of these gestures is actually a doorway into a deeper and subtler movement of spirit. Modernity has bequeathed to many of us a profound disenchantment with both the cultural and institutional forms of religion as well as the beliefs that sustain them. At the same time, many feel the sneaking suspicion that such forms may be necessary as temporary vehicles or containers for the visionary insights and sacred energies they continue to crave. Though these forms can successfully channel the spirit for a time, inevitably they fail: they become consumer idols, or safety blankets, or cheesy parodies of themselves. By affirming an ironic relationship to such forms, we draw attention to their incompleteness, to their inability to satisfy our yearning or sustain the disenchanting movement of spirit. This sort of irony is more than a cynical operation in cahoots with the secular disavowal or mockery of spirituality. It is, rather, a sacred irony, one which itself marks the margins, and sometimes the core, of historical religions. When Ramakrishna donned ladies' clothes, or Yunmen proclaimed that the Buddha is a shit-stick, the point was to shatter form through contrast. Ironic juxtaposition, in this context, is revelatory. For minimalists of the spirit, such irony may clear the air for the formless beyond; but the maximalists at Burning Man heap together the broken shards of forms into a fallen Humpty Dumpty bonfire of apocalyptic collage.

West Coast spiritual culture has long shown an affinity for juxtaposition. Part of this is rooted in California's syncretistic religious supermarket, especially in Los Angeles, where Hindu onion domes and Mayan Masonic halls fit in just fine alongside eateries shaped like oranges or hats. But this sensibility also emerged from the plastic arts of the place, particularly the love of appropriation, collage, and assemblage (or structural collage). (See "The Alchemy of Trash" in this volume.) During the late 1950s, Beat artists such as Bruce Conner, George Herms, and Wallace Berman constructed objects and made collages that strongly engaged images of sex, fetishism, and spirit. Hearst Castle showed that even the wealthiest Californians yearned to sample and slam together times and places. But the iconic grass-roots example remains Simon Rodia's Watts Towers, three famous free-form spires built, without plans, from pop bottles, tiles, and teacup handles.

The bohemian economics of making art far from New York partly drove this bricolage—artists started playing around with bits and pieces for the same reason the Merry Pranksters were driven to scavenge thrift stores—and hence history—for clothes. An alchemy of trash emerged, one that not only made a virtue of necessity but also suggested a new kind of aesthetic pleasure. Today we enjoy some Burning Man artworks simply because of the low cost and crappiness of their materials. But such regenerative work has deeper implications. According to the San Francisco poet Robert Duncan, who used collage techniques in his gnostic modernist verse, "The trivial is as deep as the profound because there is nothing in creation that does not go to the profound."[10] If Burning Man needed a slogan for its spiritual esthetics, Duncan's alchemical insight will more than suffice.

THE CULT OF MEANINGLESS CHAOS

Perhaps you are wandering aimlessly across the playa at night, and, lo and behold, some distracting marvel captures your attention. In the ambiguous distance, you glimpse a filigree of luminosity and shadow, a surreal oasis, a portal to some possible pleasure. You head towards the dusty fairy lights as if they were a sci-fi tractor beam, the amazement increasing until you finally arrive and discover a rag-tag structure consisting of a few two-by-fours, some rebar and wire, and a nest of duct-taped Christmas lights feeding off a grumbling generator. Ingenious! Against the glimmering canvas of the night, this jury-rigged contraption produced just the right visual cues to conjure an empty thing of beauty and wonder right out of your own nervous system. You are simultaneously satisfied and disappointed; you admire the creative gift but sense a strange, smirking con in the works. The cosmic carnie barker leans forward and whispers in your ear: "Just a show, my friend, you pays your quarter and you takes your ride. Up for another turn on the wheel? Just watch out for those smoky lights . . ."

Burning Man's backdrop is more than the blank playa or the desert nightscape: it is the void. The barbarous, post-punk, devil-may-care panache of so many Black Rock citizens is only the most obvious sign of the nihilistic underpinnings of the event—especially resonant these days, when the cybernetic meltdown of civilization only magnifies the old familiar zero at the heart of the human condition. Burning Man's apocalyptic undertow—mocked, ignored, and indulged in with equal abandon—rescues the festival, at least some of the time, from frivolity and cliché. By opening its arms to the void, without fear or hope, Burning Man thickens the event's official discourse of celebration and community, lending these optimistic cultural narratives a darker urgency. Burning Man's void is not, however, a meaningless blank—it is a creative chaos, an intense invocation of novelty, humor, and weirdness on the lip of the abyss. This hyperactivity represents Burning Man's debt to the expressive mania shared by the Dadaists, the Pranksters, and every other group of void-gazing *artistes* who made kinky love among the ruins. But whereas the Dadaists unleashed their gibberish in small clubs in Berlin and Zurich, Burning Man turns the city form itself into a theater of the absurd—not just Marx Brothers absurd, or Kierkegaard absurd, but downtown-Hong-Kong-on-a-Saturday-night absurd.[11]

Burning Man's manic and generous creativity also suggests a deeper teaching. Buddhism, Taoism, and Hindu tantra all suggest that the reality that lies on the far side of form, the reality of emptiness or the unstructured Tao, is *full of potential*. Like the quantum vacuum pictured by free-energy enthusiasts, the void flings phenomena out of itself. Some Taoists considered meditation and ritual as means to return to the original unformed chaos that would connect them with the sources of life before returning them to the world of our senses five. At its over-saturated best, Burning Man rides the formless edge of form, generating shapes and signals that constantly slip back into noise and confusion. The festival beckons us, in Lex Hixon's poetic paraphrase of a line from the *Prajnaparamita Sutra,* "to abide without abode, to dwell where no objective or subjective structures can dwell, without any underlying physical or metaphysical foundation, totally isolated from conventional conceptions, perceptions and descriptions."[12] This is the realm of sacred chaos.

The classic Eastern notion of the pregnant void also happens to mirror one of the core intuitions of Western anarchism, which is that things get along just fine without order being imposed from without. Anarchism and Taoism's "chaos spirituality" thus share a faith in the spontaneous and fecund powers of the creative process, and a sense that this productive flux diverges from the overt organization of social forms. As the philosopher Gilles Deleuze would put it, the Tao *deterritorializes.* This process remains in a precarious and sometimes agonistic relationship with civilization, which not only demands order from without, but order from above. As N.J. Girardot wrote:

> The Taoist accepts the fact of being born into a civilizational order but does not accept the possibility that civilizational values define what it means to be fully alive and human. The acceptance of phenomenal existence requires a more profound recognition of the fact that fulfillment and renewal of human life depends on a periodic return to a chaotic or primitive condition.[13]

Civilization is not what it used to be; today's destratified empire of global capitalism has learned to absorb, exploit, and deploy chaos in sophisticated ways. Nonetheless, the archetypal conflict between chaos and civilization remains one of our deepest binary structuring myths, right up there with good and evil or male and female. In one of the primary versions of this tale, the Mesopotamian hero Marduk, the god-king of the founding city-state of Babylon, kills Tiamat, the old goddess of primal chaos. From her corpse he makes the heavens, with its fixed stars and ordered constellations. This myth suggests the way in which the urban state, with its investment in complex organization, would come to demonize the ancient seething matrix from which it emerged, and that always threatens to engulf it again in waves of destruction and social anarchy. Although traditions like Taoism retained organic connections to the pregnant void, and carnivals allowed little bits of chaos into Christian culture in the West, most avatars of chaos were shunted into the shadows of increasingly patriarchal religious forms.

The antiauthoritarian tendencies of bohemian culture have long given it a taste for Dionysian chaos, and its spiritual regimens have often mobilized a Rimbaud-like derangement of the senses. Consider Aleister Crowley, for example. In addition to his prophetic enthusiasm for sex and psychoactive drugs, Crowley reimagined the demonic dimensions of Western occultism as an atavistic and Nietzschean force field capable of creatively destabilizing patriarchal civilization. But the explicit countercultural worship of chaos proper did not emerge until 1958, when the beatniks Kerry Thornley and Gregory Hill, known eventually as Omar Ravenhurst and Malaclypse the Younger, had a vision of the goddess Eris (or Disorder) in an all-night bowling alley in California. Whether or not this origin story is true (and why not believe it?), Malaclypse the Younger put together the *Principia Discordia: or How I Found Goddess and What I Did to Her When I Found Her*. The pamphlet is a visionary assemblage of nondual wisdom, hotdog jokes, and appropriated collage art—a core sutra of the cult of juxtapose. An underground hit in the late 1960s and early '70s, the *Principia Discordia* communicates an eclectic, goofy, and skeptical anti-doctrine of spiritual chaos or "Zenarchy." "If you can master nonsense as well as you have already learned to master sense, then each will expose the other for what it is: absurdity."[14] This "magnum opiate," with its corny profundities and free-fall praise of the sacred Chao, would go on to influence *The Illuminatus! Trilogy* by Robert Shea and Robert Anton Wilson, the Church of the Subgenius, and, eventually, Burning Man.

Whether interpreted creatively or destructively, chaos proclaims the impermanence of all forms. That is why it is both funny and terrifying. In the case of Burning Man, one form that has notably fluctuated is the relation to chaos itself. The festival has witnessed some dramatic changes in structure and character over the years, and has passed through at least two major bifurcations. In 1990, the Cacophony Society's John Law led the gathering to the Black Rock Desert from San Francisco. Seven years later, after Law departed from the organization in a disagreement about how to manage the growing crowds, Burning Man moved off the main playa to a smaller, privately owned site known as Hualapai Playa. Although fortunately temporary, this move was accompanied by a permanent ban on automobiles and firearms, along with the imposition of the semicircular concentric grid of streets (and street-signs) that continues through today. The 1990 event was still a loose gathering of friends, whereas Burning Man has now shifted into a well-established and specifically *urban* phenomenon. In other words, like some freak show remix of *SimCity*, this festival of chaos came to replicate the core framework of civilization itself.

There were many reasons for this later, more "developed" phase: population pressure, the demands of various bodies of the state, and the inevitable desire to creatively improve public works. As such, this transformation by and large occurred with an air of organic inevitability. Burners with strong anarchist principles griped that such urban controls compromised the festival's incarnation of what Hakim Bey famously dubbed a "temporary autonomous zone." After all, the sacred Chao would have us interrogate all linear narratives of inevitable development—particularly when those developments concern the sacred Chao itself. Though not necessarily cooler or more engaging, Burning Man was a significantly more disordered (and less civilized) event before 1997. The presence of assault rifles, the lack of safety controls and street signs, the dizzying distance from mountains and roads, the more feral demographic—all these elements brought participants into a closer proximity to chaos, emotional and perceptual as much as physical and infrastructural. In contrast, the chaos of today's festival often feels contained, more semiotic than systemic, a perversion of the already surreal attention economy one finds in Las Vegas or Times Square. And much of this derives from the crystallized architectonics of the festival: the invariant city layout, the establishment of dance clubs along the Esplanade, the neon "advertising" of the nightscape, and the centralized logo-like presence of the Man.

No one should be surprised by this calcification; certainly not students of spiritual chaos. As Tom Wolfe showed in his study of the Merry Pranksters, the spontaneous immediacy of a weird scene's early "Now" is tough to maintain as the gospel spreads and the masses turn on. Sociologist of religion Max Weber described this process as "routinization." In Weber's view, religious movements begin with the otherworldly charisma of an extraordinary, even "supernatural" leader who punctures the everyday grind. Over time, in a quest to guarantee that believers have dependable access to this charisma, it becomes institutionalized in schools, positions of authority, and dogmas. As Weber notes in his book *Economy and Society*, charisma "cannot remain stable, but becomes either traditionalized or rationalized, or a combination of both."[15] Thankfully, Burning Man's charisma does not lie in a singular individual, but in the nonhierarchical social field of the collective. Still, though Burning Man's routinization has not created a particularly visible hierarchy of authority, the problem of routinization remains. In a sense, this problem is manifested as the urban form itself—a form that maintains a febrile and polyvocal diversity even as it constrains the more unsustainable excesses of chaos.

We should not conclude from this that Burning Man has at all lost its sacred spark. As the vampiric tendrils of consumer media and the surveillance society wrap themselves ever more tightly around the heart of human experience, the festival continues to successfully ride the paradox of regulating a temporary autonomous zone. The cults I have outlined all speak to the power of this paradox, since they reflect a cultural continuity that remains fresh and unstructured partly by erasing their own historical traces. Moreover, a powerful assemblage of social and creative energies has emerged from Burning Man's turn towards urban organization. The festival's later phase has also been marked, unquestionably, by its greatest art—art that absorbs and permeates social space and personal interactions. Utopia, we should not forget, is a city. For a week or more, Black Rock City is a polis largely without cash, where citizens walk and ride bikes more than they drive, and where the definition of civic duty is perhaps best expressed by that annoying Berkeley bumper sticker: "Practice Random Acts of Kindness and Senseless Acts of Beauty."

Northrop Frye reminds us that William Blake identified Eden with the realized human imagination, and that he saw this paradise not as a peaceful garden, but as a fiery city. Not a Rainbow Gathering, in other words, but a Black Rock town, going wild. Like the human imagination, the city is an absurd excess: it flickers, it intoxicates, it energizes forms that its own energies consume. At the same time, we can sense terrible forebodings in this incandescence, pulsing like warning lights on the near horizon of space-time. Burning Man stages the city as Utopia and as inevitable catastrophe simultaneously. But this city is also imaginal, remember, as much inside us as out. Rome burns as we burn, amazed adults in a Pleistocene playground, belting out the old refrain:

ashes, ashes, we all fall down.

2003

Notes

[1] Marvin Meyer, *The Ancient Mysteries* (Philadelphia: University of Pennsylvania Press, 1999), 38.

[2] Darryl Van Rey, "The Burning Man: A Modern Mystery," *Gnosis* 36 (1995): 6.

[3] See George Mylanos, *Eleusis and the Eleusinian Mysteries* (Princeton: Princeton University Press, 1961), 262.

[4] Available from http://www.anonsalon.com/bman02/bm02stills6.html (accessed April 1, 2009).

[5] Available from http://www.burningman.com/themecamps_installations/bm03_theme.html (accessed April 1, 2009).

[6] William James, *The Varieties of Religious Experience* (New York: Longmans, Green, and Co, 1902), 12.

[7] Tom Wolfe, *The Electric Kool-Aid Acid Test* (New York: Bantam, 1968), 112.

[8] Ibid., 164.

[9] David Curtis, *Experimental Cinema* (New York: Universe Books, 1971), 75.

[10] Peter O'Leary, *Gnostic Contagion: Robert Duncan and the Poetry of Illness* (Middletown: Wesleyan University Press, 2002), 112.

[11] Personal communication with Speed Levitch, San Francisco, November 23, 2003.

[12] Lex Hixon, *The Mother of All Buddhas* (Wheaton, Il.: Quest, 1993), 186.

[13] N.J. Girardot, *Myth and Meaning in Early Taoism* (Berkeley: University of California, 1983), 95.

[14] Malaclypse the Younger, *Principia Discordia* (Port Townsend, Wash.: Loompanics Unlimited, n.d.), 74.

[15] Max Weber, *Economy and Society*, eds. G. Roth and C Wittich (Berkeley: University of California, 1978), 246.

AU REVOIR *LA CONTESSA*

One Friday night in 2007, with a full moon glowering waxy from above, a feline and freaky crowd gathered on a toxic finger of San Francisco's bayside no-man's-land to bid adieu to one of the most powerful works of art that the Burning Man arts festival has ever seen: the great dame *La Contessa*. A massive Spanish galleon encased around a bus, with crow's nests and rigging and a scuttlebutt for all I know, *La Contessa* was, on the playa anyway, a manifest dream, a fully realized mobile archetype that featured such fetishistic and finely grained detail that it became a vessel in more than a literal sense. Standing on the bow at night, with the Dutchman sails flying above, a bardo-shaking brass band drowning out sense, and some unseen meth-head driving too fast or erratically for your own cowardly comfort, one did not need drugs to achieve the escape velocity of full imaginative transport. And last December, this great vessel of the wayward spirit, its forty feet parked on a ranch in Washoe County, Nevada, was torched to ruin by a local landowner who never hid his hatred of the event.

The creation of Simon Cheffins, Greg Jones, and the bulk of the Extra Action Marching Band, *La Contessa* made her first appearance at the festival in 2002. It was the year of the "Floating World," which is hands down my favorite Burning Man theme. Unlike so many themes, which are frustratingly abstract, and almost preachy, the obvious nautical misreading of the "Floating World" transformed the playa itself into an easy-access creative space, where some bonehead's blow-up octopus toy helped contribute to the collective hallucination as much as a marvel like *La Contessa* or those striking jellyfish. Moreover, the playa at night already is a sort of sea: the ocean of the unconscious, of drifting, fragmentary dreams within which one alternately sinks or swims. Or sails, in the case of this gorgeous, slutty galleon, which cut across the open lake bed like the *Pequod* in pursuit of a white leviathan—a scenario that, blessed be, actually manifested itself that ageless weekend in 2002, when *La Contessa* played nautical chicken with a monstrous glowing whale whose innards—another bus—were driven by the notorious Flash. The insane and patently unsafe jousting of these two behemoths, glimpsed by me and my pals from a few hundred yards away, was a vision of such fantastic hilarity that it seems incredible to report that the scenario was raised to an even higher pitch of glory by the spectacle, an hour or so later, of the white whale being ticketed by distinctly unamused BLM rangers.

All gratuitous acts of strong art are magickal invocations, but there is something particularly spellbinding about truly obsessive and basically useless degrees of detail. This is one of the strengths of Peter Jackson's *Lord of the Rings* films: the visionary reality of his Middle-Earth was partly a creation of the artisans who designed the props and costumes, and more often than not, added far more detail than the camera would ever pick up. Such excess marked *La Contessa*'s making as well, a work of manic devotion. Discussing the immense logistical challenges and passionate volunteer work that created the ship, Cheffins told the *San Francisco Bay Guardian* that "The idea of the ship is it was a lady that you end up serving, and she took on a life of her own. We all came to feel like servants at some point." Appropriately, the lady's most gorgeous feature was her female figurehead (which had already been stolen from the galleon before the ship burned and is presumably still at large). This gorgeous corseted wench, the work of the sculptor Monica Maduro, hung from the prow clutching a lamp, both eyes shut, as if she was leading the ship by feel into some nameless alien landscape that unrolled across the screens of her inner eyelids.

Many theme camps and art cars at Burning Man are all façade, like store fronts on a western set, concealing the usual mess of rebar and wires. And many more are themed in only the loosest sense, settling instead for the goofy juxtapositions and slapdash irony that form the basic—and often lazy and incoherent—foundation of playa art. But once you boarded *La Contessa* —after suffering the glowering gaze of some haughty Barbary bouncer—you passed through an appealingly soiled interior bordello before reaching the deck, all without glimpsing anything that resembled a modern vehicle. On deck you marveled at the rigging and sails and the weathered balustrade. Then some grizzled and likely sodomite demanded that you *please turn off your fucking blinky lights*, a demand considered fussy and elitist by some but that merely affirmed the crew's commitment to the visionary craft.

By hewing so closely to historical detail, *La Contessa* was much more "straight" than your average playa work. I was surely not the only passenger for whom *La Contessa* instantly resurrected a childhood love of Disneyland's Pirates of the Caribbean—a ride, by the way, that only fools mock. Like Burning Man, Pirates is a bardo run-through, a sometimes cavernous and claustrophobic cruise through the spectral realms of desire and anarchy and destructive imaginal machines. Think about it: in its original form, the ride ends with a burning city overrun with madmen high on intoxicants, explosives, and lust. Even more inspiring is the character known in fan lore as the "red-headed woman." We see her first as a portrait in the drunken skeleton's lair, a spicy pirate queen equipped with a cutlass, and then later as a woman abducted from the burning town, at which point we realize that the whole ride is a tale told in reverse, like a black mass, and that, once captured, the crimson-topped lass exuberantly embraced her sordid new life of high-seas crime, all before winding up as an image to delight the drunken dead. All very *La Contessa*, would not you say?

For Friday's wake, a crew of countess lovers built a small-scale replica of the galleon, a simulacrum of a simulacrum, and all the better for it. The crowd warmed itself with a few hours of whisky and reminiscences and banjo renditions of sea shanties and *La Contessa*'s two theme songs. A few speeches were made—Moms were thanked, Rimbaud's "Drunken Boat" was read—and then the Extra Action Marching Band, led by flag girls bearing silvery standards, struck up a dirge punctuated by bullhorn lamentations *en français*, and then led the crowd and the drunken boat to the damp sands by waterline. Dr. Hal Robbins intoned Tennyson's "Crossing the Bar," and the boat was committed to the sea, where it soon ballooned into flame like the Viking burials of yore. The ladies took up another round of "The Countess," which bounced and echoed off the metal walls of nearby industrial buildings like a spectral dub track:

They toiled for a thousand white nights to build the ship that
  they sail'd,
Bound together with salt & spunk, buckets of bloody nails.
They thought that their task would be easy; they learned their
  lesson well.
So No! Let it never be foolishly be said
That the countess is easily wooed into bed!

2007

CODA

BARDO FLIGHT

I just got back from a couple weeks in Costa Rica, where I spoke at the semi-annual Mind States conference and tooled around with some pals. I had hoped to herein recount some of the highlights of the trip, perhaps in an attempt to make up for my unmitigated writing sloth during the last fortnight, a laziness that was no doubt partly inspired by the actual sloths I saw blissfully konked out in the jungle foliage. But about the only thing on my mind right now is the hell-flight we endured on the return home.

At the conference I gave a talk on Philip K. Dick and led a vigorous group discussion about the filmmaker Richard Linklater's essayistic dream-film *Waking Life*, which is kinda like *Sans Soleil* for stoners. One of my major themes in these discussions was what Tibetans call the bardo: the insubstantial in-between state said to confront the soul after death, when the contents of mind return to seduce and terrify the ego's disoriented after-image as it reverberates into rebirth. A Dante-esque funhouse of ravenous demons, smoky lights, and copulating parents-to-be, the bardo is no doubt one of the most evocative sacred accounts of the afterlife. It may also be one of the most useful. Early in *Waking Life*, Ethan Hawke quotes Timothy Leary to the effect that, even if nothing of us survives death, the last few minutes of the brain's electrical activity may be experienced by the dying person as an entire life racing in time-lapse—or, as the film itself suggests, a nearly infinite labyrinth of dreams. From this perspective, the traditional teachings of bardo navigation may come in handy despite the basic reality of brain-death: even if we are only riding that last wave to flatline, it pays to know how to surf.

My other major point was that there are bardos everywhere—not just in death, but in dreams, in the transitions between waking and sleep, in sneezing and orgasm and the collapsing realities of Philip K. Dick novels. Death is simply the starkest transition; we are always undergoing the dissolution of the world (especially these days, when epochal change is assured).

Traveling, in its many guises, can be another bardo rehearsal, offering up hints and foreshadows, perhaps even a few tricks. And I am not just talking about the trials and delights of shoestring journeying through exotic and challenging backwaters where sacred images still hold sway. I am also talking about the grueling, mind-altering reality of twenty-first-century commercial air travel.

Say you are me, and you conclude your Costa Rican trip at the airport in San Jose. You step out of the world of place, of birdcalls and smog and wet air, and enter an air-conditioned terminal, formally identical to thousands of other spaces across the globe. The terminal is the gateway to an interzone of nowheres, a network of liminality, of thresholds and passageways and vehicles designed by the principalities of the air to move and distribute large populations of souls to their destinies—or at least their destinations. *Terminal.* What other journey, you might ask, begins at the end?

Moving through this system is, despite all the hubbub, a remarkably passive process—a submission that begins with the loss of your body, or at least with its relative autonomy and comfort. Lined up and forcibly unshod and radiated and patted down, your body is no longer your own, even before it reaches its final in-flight resting place, a seat that demands medieval metaphors—monk's cell, Iron Maiden, rack. Even before you strap yourself in to the mercy seat, a subtler torture of the spirit is provided by your journey through the first class cabin. This brief march through the Elysian fields of leg room and free booze goads the envious into remorse as it restores the otherwise forgotten theological category of the *elect*.

This is where my recent bardo trip really began. I was sitting in my coach seat on American flight 2614, waiting for the doors to close, when a young woman wearing some vaguely official garb walked up the aisle, asked if I was Erik Davis, then beckoned me to follow her off the plane. In the gangway I met two young Costa Rican men in plain clothes, with ordinary airport security badges dangling around their necks. One asked if I spoke Spanish ("un poquito"), and the other mumbled something about my "madre." My bafflement now mutating into fear, I flashed on the worst case scenario: my mother is dead, and these functionaries are here to break the news.

Seeing my concern, the young woman clarified that the gentlemen were after my mother's maiden name, which I gave them, along with the demand that they explain why they cared to know. Her English was not much better than my Spanish, but she explained that my name was on a Costa Rican no-fly list. I asked for clarification from one of the men, but he just smiled nervously as his partner got on the phone to, apparently, pass on the proverbial name. I wrote down my own given name, underlining the "k"—the sole mark of distinction in an otherwise generic name—but he just smiled and scribbled a "c" alongside the k. The other guy got off the phone, and I started to get mad. Then the first fellow grinned again, shook his head and said "Okay, okay, no problem." They ushered me back on the plane, leaving me and my buddies to ponder the imponderables. Whose "no-fly" list? Did they actually have a record of my mother's maiden name? Why would they think I wouldn't just lie? All of which really boiled down to one question:

What the fuh . . . ?

It seemed as if all those Philip K. Dick novels were coming home to roost, and if the rest of the journey was more of your typical commercial airline hell, it remained permeated with the woozy disorientation caused by mistaken identity and the arbitrariness of the archons who rule these transit zones.

My nausea was hardly alleviated by the greasy nuts and the Diet Coke and the Barney songs that cackled from some tyke's portable DVD player in the next row. Meanwhile, terrible and unusual storms—you know, the kind that are now business as usual—forced us to circle over Dallas awhile before we landed and sat on the tarmac for almost an hour, first to allow the gate to clear, and second to allow the lightning strikes that froze ground service to make their way elsewhere.

We made it through customs and immigration quite quickly, despite the general chaos the storm had brought to American's hub. We soon discovered that our flight to San Francisco had been cancelled, and lined up to talk to one of the two—count 'em—two service agents who had been dealing with this shit all day. As our fellow searched for an alternate route—finally setting us on a flight to Reno and a U.S. Airways hop to S.F. the next morning, which he nonetheless screwed up in ways I will not bother to recount—the line behind us grew and grew. Soon scores of frantic, fatigued, and harried customers stood and fidgeted, frustrated and angry, a line of refugees that grew into an anxious mob. I had not thought a single storm could have undone so many.

I will not continue to detail the slings and arrows that still lay in store for us, though it's important to mention that they included panicked dashes, confiscated shaving cream, lost luggage, telephone hold lines that switched impishly into dial tones, booked hotels, room 666, and a host of largely lame encounters with service agents and other dwellers of the threshold, most of whom were incompetent and frazzled, and a few of whom were so kind and helpful that they seemed almost angelic.

Suffice it to say that the only redemption lay in seeing it all as the bardo, whose deepest teaching seems to be that our uncontrolled fears, desires, and hatreds boomerang back tenfold. And I am sad to report that, unless my temper shapes up, I am probably doomed to flit about some angry little maze of hell whose labyrinthine torments resemble the endless branchings and recursions of the most fiendish and robotic phone trees. "If you would like to hear your options again . . ."

Romantics complain that we moderns have lost all rites of passage,

t Airli

but commercial air travel remains a fact of life that is both a rite and a passage, although it is a rite whose duress no longer offers transformation. The rewards are always later; in the meantime, we simply throw ourselves on the altar of an anxious, discombobulating drift.

Through the windows on the flight to Reno, J and I watched magnificent explosions of electricity in the thunderclouds, Dr. Frankenstein displays that almost made up for all the horrors. In flight, we sometimes glimpse the awesomeness of heaven and earth through the portholes, visions of clouds and lightning and deep blue black. But when we turn forward to look where we are going, all we face is another cell, another idiot screen, another prisoner chained to the galley. In the words of the English poet Henry Vaughn, much beloved by Dick:

> Man is the shuttle, to whose winding quest
> And passage through these looms
> God ordered motion, but ordained no rest.

2007